VOYAG

UTOPIAS

Also by Tony Fitzpatrick

Freedom and Security (Palgrave)

Welfare Theory: An Introduction (Palgrave)

Environmental Issues and Social Welfare (Blackwell)
(co-edited with Michael Cahill)

Environment and Welfare (Palgrave)
(co-edited with Michael Cahill)

After the New Social Democracy (Manchester University Press)

New Theories of Welfare (Palgrave)

International Encyclopaedia of Social Policy (Routledge)
(co-edited with Nick Manning, Gill Pascall, Huck-ju Kwon
and James Midgley)

Applied Ethics and Social Problems (The Policy Press)

VOYAGE TO UTOPIAS

A fictional guide through social philosophy

Tony Fitzpatrick

This edition published in Great Britain in 2010 by

The Policy Press
University of Bristol
Fourth Floor
Beacon House
Queen's Road
Bristol BS8 1QU
UK

t: +44 (0)117 331 4054
f: +44 (0)117 331 4093
tpp-info@bristol.ac.uk
www.policypress.co.uk

North American office:
The Policy Press
c/o International Specialized Books Services
920 NE 58th Avenue, Suite 300
Portland, OR 97213-3786, USA
t: +1 503 287 3093
f: +1 503 280 8832
info@isbs.com

British Library Cataloguing in Publication Data
A catalogue record for this book is available from the British Library.

Library of Congress Cataloging-in-Publication Data
A catalog record for this book has been requested.

ISBN 978 1 84742 089 3 paperback
ISBN 978 1 84742 098 5 hardcover

Cover design by The Policy Press
Front cover: illustration kindly supplied by Nick Mott
Printed and bound in Great Britain by TJ International, Padstow

FSC
Mixed Sources
Product group from well-managed
forests and other controlled sources
Cert no. SGS-COC-2482
www.fsc.org
© 1996 Forest Stewardship Council

Menippus: ...of such a discord is the life of men composed. Not only do they sing out of harmony, but they dress differently, move in opposite directions, and have no common purpose, until the producer drives them off the stage, saying he has no more need of them. Then they all alike become quiet....But in the theatre itself, with its diverse and changing scenes, everything that happened was really and truly ludicrous.

Lucian, *Icaromenippus*

Miranda: O wonder!
How many goodly creatures are there here!
How beauteous mankind is!   O brave new world
That has such people in't.

Prospero: 'Tis new to thee.

Shakespeare, *The Tempest*

Robby the Robot: Sorry, miss! I was giving myself an oil job.

Forbidden Planet (1956)

Acknowledgements

I am grateful to each and every one of various people who read earlier drafts of this book. They each peered into the pram, pretended not to react with horror and said 'Aaaahh, it'll be prettier when it's older.' If the kid is still an ugly sprog then it's my fault.

Particular thanks go to my student readers: Wendwossen Wole, Stephanie Hearne, Ed Brooks and Frances Pearson. To my colleagues: Tracey Warren and Sue Parker. To the anonymous referees. And my appreciation to all others who helped the project on its way.

My gratitude to all at The Policy Press for taking a risk in an academic climate which is, all too often, over-cautious. Special thanks to Laura Greaves and Alison Shaw.

Preface

A child raises her hand in class and asks the teacher why they are being given so many tests and exams. A victim of crime writes to her local politician complaining that too much public money is spent on locking people up rather than on support services for people like herself. An asylum seeker chains himself to a railing in protest at his treatment by a country within which he sought refuge from persecution. A benefit claimant in a job centre demands to know why he has to jump through so many hoops to receive so little money.

It might be that the pupil, the crime victim, the asylum-seeker and the claimant are seeking clarification of how, respectively, education, criminal justice, refugee support and benefit systems work. But they are also asking for reasoned and reasonable justifications of why they have been designed to work as they do. What principles, values and aims do they serve? Why do they work in this way? What explains how they treat the individuals relying upon them?

Just possibly, it is the pupil who is best placed to put the most interesting queries. Young children are endearingly naive about how the world works but can often ask the most fundamental questions about why. 'Because it just does', will often form the exasperated adult's response and, having smashed repeatedly into this wall, many children will eventually give up asking. The adult's impatience is understandable. Public debates in most countries are lamentably thin, often dominated by powerful political, economic and media interests, and habitually framed in such a way that the (official) outcome is already presupposed. Newspapers and TV will provide useful overviews of the arts and sciences, but normative discussions about recent developments in social science, philosophy and political theories occupy little space by comparison. (The internet compensates to some extent for those prepared to search for reputable sources of information and debate.) Adults can be startlingly incurious about *why* the world works as it does.

Exploring this gap between day-to-day social realities and philosophical foundations is an activity I have been engaged in for several years. This book is another bridge between the two. It attempts to summarise the essentials of the most influential political philosophies of the last forty or fifty years. In this, it is indebted to a long tradition of fiction that has incorporated an educational intent.

In the ancient world, Homer's *Odyssey* wasn't just a cracking story; it also represented an oral tradition by which a cultural community nurtured and sustained its mythological foundations. In *The Pilgrim's Progress*, Bunyan takes us on a spiritual, allegorical journey. As western society became more secular other fantastical journeys, such as Swift's *Gulliver's Travels* or Voltaire's *Candide*, dealt with the uncertainty experienced by people in a rapidly changing world. More recently, science fiction (or what Margaret Atwood and others prefer to call 'speculative fiction') has engaged with similar themes.

This book owes much to two recent examples of such 'fantastic journey' literature: Steven Lukes's *The Curious Enlightenment of Professor Caritat* and Jostein Gaardner's *Sophie's World*. There is some overlap here with the themes of Lukes' novel but also significant differences in the schools of thought surveyed. In addition, I have been particularly concerned to illustrate how and why those political ideas translate into more practical questions of distributive justice (questions of what should get distributed, who should receive those distributions, and why) especially as these pertain to welfare institutions and systems, broadly defined. All of this within the context of a hopefully entertaining satire. Which means I have tried to be unfair to everyone.

Thus, the book is designed to supplement, but certainly not replace, standard introductions to political ideas, ideologies and their relevance to social issues. But it also has two, somewhat deeper, purposes. Unfortunately, the first of these would be blunted were I to spell it out explicitly. But let me say this. The use of fiction to depict political philosophical ideas may appear incongruous, risky, conceited even, yet it taps into one of the oldest conventions of human thought, dating to the ancient world, which we have sometimes been in danger of forgetting.

In 'The Dinner Party', Xenophon uses comedy and drunkenness as an ironic counterpoint to the lesson of the story: the importance of moral goodness. For instance, the character of Socrates argues that he is more physically attractive than Critobulus. He argues this because, having bulbous eyes and a stubby nose, Socrates can see more and smell more than Critobulus. Thus his eyes and nose are superior! What Xenophon is doing is satirising those who confuse beauty with virtue.

And if philosophers wrote literature, so dramatists commented on the philosophical ideas of their day. Forty years before 'The Dinner Party' Socrates had also made an appearance in *The Clouds*. Here, Aristophanes caricatures him as a pretentious, must-win-the-argument-at-all-costs, know-it-all intellectual. (Fortunately, modern academics are immune to such *mauvais goût*.) Aristophanes is poking fun at philosophers who challenged received wisdom without having anything constructive with which to replace it. Not much room for moral goodness there.

The extent to which these fictional characters offered accurate portrayals of the actual Socrates is something we can only speculate about. What we have in both cases is a representation which serves the ideas of the writer. And it is from Socrates' appearances in the dialogues of Plato that we have inherited our understanding of the 'Socratic method': the idea that the teacher does not tell the student what to think but, through patient questioning and encouragement, guides the student and allows her to lead herself to wherever she needs to be. Yet we are basing this not upon the once living and breathing Socrates but upon a series of fictional characters. *The* method of education and philosophical instruction is based upon narratives and stories whose grounding in historical reality is uncertain.

Thus, philosophy and literature were originally intertwined. Sometimes plot, character and setting were woven into and indistinguishable from the philosophical content. Sometimes, literary form and intellectual content were only loosely related. This tradition has by no means faded. Rousseau wrote fiction, Hume used the dialogue form, while Kierkegaard and Nietzsche produced literary work that is impossible to categorise. And Sartre became one big bore once he stopped writing novels and plays. Conversely, history's greatest writer, Shakespeare, is increasingly treated as possessing a serious philosophical mind.

But there is a second and even better reason to attempt a novel of ideas. If philosophy is to wield more influence on public debate it needs to be rigorous and systematic. But it should also be fun!

Those who want additional guidance as they read should consult the notes and further reading suggestions at the back of the book. However, stop yourself from skipping ahead in the notes. Allow the ideas to reveal themselves gradually! And reflect back on earlier chapters as you proceed. The ideas with which the book deals and the chapters in which they are introduced are as follows:

Free Market Liberalism	Chapters Three–Four
Marxist Socialism and Communism	Chapters Five–Six
Conservatism	Chapters Seven–Ten
Egalitarianism	Chapter Eleven
Culturalism and Identity Politics	Chapters Fourteen–Fifteen
Environmentalism	Chapters Sixteen–Seventeen
Republicanism, Communitarianism and Deliberative Politics	Chapters Eighteen–Nineteen

Don't forget the companion website

Publishing books would be great, were it not for the indignity of having other people read them. Why, then, invite even more impertinent comments by adding supplementary material to a dedicated webpage? Because, as the book you are holding tries to argue, the conversation goes on. Visit The Policy Press website at www.policy-press.co.uk/resources/fitzpatrick

CHAPTER ONE

'And your brother's name?'

'Jake.'

'Same address and everything?'

'Yes.'

'Thanks. Mrs Gregbury's aide will be down in a few minutes. Bit of a walk. Would you like anything in the meantime?'

Zadie wasn't sure what this small office could provide but smiled at the receptionist anyway, shook her head and took a seat next to her brother.

He was staring into his phone again. The menu screen shuffled by at a speed Zadie couldn't keep up with. She'd asked Jake not to become distracted by his precious mobile on the underground, fearing that if he became as mesmerised as usual he wouldn't resurface in time for their appointment. He'd ignored her, naturally. The Christmas present was as much as three months old. 'So I have to enjoy it before it becomes obsolete,' he'd whined. Zadie had never been one for new technology. She got by on word processing and Google. 'Sure,' was her younger brother's favourite tease, 'why buy a phone when you don't have any friends?'

'We told Mum we'd be back for 12,' he abruptly reminded her. Never before had Jake deliberately been on time for anything but now, in this imposing, high-rise maze of corridors and plastic fluorescence, being anywhere else seemed suddenly important.

'You don't need to keep showering me with endless gratitude for setting this up, you know. A friendly hug from time to time would be enough.'

Jake snorted into his phone and tried to think of a riposte, but by the time it came they were already on their way, following a surly young man with permanently raised eyebrows, barely older than

Zadie herself, whose welcome had been a grimaced mumble,and who was hurrying them into the labyrinthine building. Jake waved a foot at her. 'Here, hug this.'

'Hmm?' Preoccupied, Zadie barely heard him. They were being rushed along, twisting and turning through endless passages. She scanned their rapidly changing surroundings, increasingly nervous, wondering whether they could make their way back without assistance. 'If only we'd brought some breadcrumbs,' she whispered to Jake. 'Do you have a satnav thingy on that phone?' The aide would also escort them out, wouldn't he? Zadie was hypnotised by the dark suits and gleaming black shoes hurrying past them. Don't bother me, the dour expressions said. Government business. Very important. No time for people like you. There was a self-satisfied confidence about the place.

She hadn't expected to feel this nervous. 'You look spruce, dear.' Spruce? That had been her mother's quaint reassurance. Now she worried whether all that nagging at her brother had distracted her from making the correct mental preparations. Before she left for university her grandfather had taught Zadie to visualise anxious situations away. Have to make a seminar presentation? Imagine rapturous applause. Then imagine uncomfortable silence. Then accept that the actual response will be somewhere in between. But here, now, Zadie felt like an alien being lost on a dark and distant planet.

Irritatingly, Jake did not appear fazed by their surroundings, though she knew that his constant texting could also be a sign of nerves, a desire to hibernate. Zadie's hopes had slumped when she'd spotted his half-ironed shirt and baggies. Why hadn't Mum made sure he dressed properly? But Mum had been less focused these past few months. Not for the last two years, really. Zadie reflected for a moment on this and, for the millionth time, on the reason why.

So it had been too late to reverse course sartorially and on the train Zadie had fought a losing wrestling match in getting Jake to smarten up. The shirt would be tucked into his trousers and then, mysteriously, manage to liberate itself from captivity a few minutes later. Little pot belly, she thought, almost affectionately. That's why he untucks everything. To hide his little pot belly! At least the sober 'interview jacket' their mother had bought for him months earlier looked smart and covered some of the worst fashion crimes. And the trousers had been waved in the direction of an iron. She prayed they weren't headed towards a Huge Family Embarrassment that she would dwell upon and pick at for months.

Now, though, they both seemed out of place as the corridors became more stately. Zadie noted solemn green wall-lights, expensive paintings and regal plants. The walls cloaked themselves in power and authority, expecting you to take them as seriously as they obviously took themselves. This was what she had expected, she reflected. Something more 'parliamentary'. Almost on cue the assistant slowed his pace to show appropriate reverence.

The assistant rapped sharply on a sluggish oak door and, without pausing, opened it and squeezed his head through the narrowest of gaps. Zadie quickly handed Jake the folder she'd been carrying and pointed at his phone. Reluctantly, he slipped it into a trouser pocket. A murmur from within and they were ushered into a large, neatly chaotic room. Zadie had a brief impression of shelves crammed with folders, of framed news clippings, of unwashed cups and half-open filing cabinets engorged with paper. She could see lots of photos of Mrs Gregsbury with family, Mrs Gregsbury with fellow politicians, Mrs Gregsbury with celebs, Mrs Gregsbury with... There was the faintest glimpse of a desk onto which the debris of a politician's life had repeatedly crashed.

You couldn't conduct affairs of state from here, could you? A beaming figure, familiar from television, was rising from an opulent chair to greet them. The junior minister's handshake was swift and sharp. A clipped, practised voice urged them further inside as a middle-ranking, middle-aged, middle-everything shape blurred around them. 'Morning! How are you? Come in. Sorry about having had to reschedule. Come in. Tea? Coffee? Soft drink?' Mrs Gregsbury exuded busyness; smiles and words launching out and whirling round in a tight orbit, not daring to venture too far from their point of origin. She waved them at chairs over which unreturned calls hovered. With a confidence she did not really feel Zadie replied that no, they were fine, and no coffee either as they didn't want to take up, and no, no soft drinks either, but thank you, and we don't want to take up too much of your time and are just grateful for any...

'Not at all. Of course. Happy to help.' The tidal force of this greeting swept Zadie and Jake into the two large chairs in front of a desk, slumping somewhere beneath towerblocks of papers and files. Mrs Gregsbury had to shift her chair so that she could see both of them.

It was only once she was settled that Zadie noticed a fourth person in the room, a young woman fiddling with one of those slim, gunmetal grey digital recorders. Zadie had absent-mindedly picked one up in class a few weeks earlier. It had bleeped and burped at her, much to the disgust of her neighbour who had quickly snatched it back. She'd spent the rest of the lesson red-faced and buried in her notebook.

She sometimes wondered whether she was too quick to dismiss her brother's intuitive intelligence because he wove it in and out of computer screens, playing some games that were just loud and horrendously violent and some she failed even to understand. Zadie still remembered with shame the day she'd walked into the university library and asked for directions to the card catalogue! 'It's all computers now, sweet. Don't worry, I'll show you.' 'This is Morela,' Mrs Gregsbury said, as the younger woman beamed at them, 'she's a journalist with the *Post*. They're doing another feature on me. Such is the life!'

A journalist? That explained it, Zadie realised.

'You'll have to forgive me for asking you to talk me through your project. Professor Yates did tell me...but...you know.... Many more young people take an interest in politics than the cynics would have us believe. Happy to help.' Mrs Gregsbury discreetly checked mailboxes, trays, documents, hairline. Yet the junior minister's presence also encircled the youngsters, reassuring them that *they* were the *real* centre of her attention.

Zadie had been prepared for this. Professor Yates had coached her and, besides, she'd anticipated that Jake wouldn't pipe up without being nudged. He was clutching his folder while smoothing the outline of his pocketed phone as a reassurance that contact with the outside world was still possible. Zadie hoped he'd had the good sense to turn it off.

'Well, let me just thank you again for your time. I'm Zadie Hale and this is my brother, Jake. We understand how busy you must be.' Mrs Gregsbury confirmed this by waving it away as a compliment. 'The project is actually my brother's. He's in his final year at school and I'm coming to the end of my first year at university and I'm just here to help out really. Just an observer.'

Mrs Gregsbury now directed her gaze specifically at Jake, offering some mumsy coos about exams. Zadie prayed that she didn't ask whether Jake would be following his big sister to university. That had been a back-and-forth argument for months now. The problem was that her brother was smart; he certainly had a better memory for facts than his sister. So Jake believed he didn't need anything else, complaining that he didn't really want to go back to a glorified school for another three precious years. But then he refused to be drawn on alternatives. He'd take a gap year to decide. For some adventurous teenagers this might imply trekking the hills of Bolivia, shark fishing off the coast of Australia or at least volunteering to nurse sick, blind orphan puppies. In Jake's case, as both his sister and mother knew, it would involve twelve months in his bedroom, trying to master the upper levels of DoomWar.

Eighteen years of age, peering down imperiously on her seventeen-year-old brother, Zadie should have been regaling him with tales of wild parties, nightclubbing and traffic-cone stealing. The problem was that, studious and largely invisible, she had no tales. Zadie had hooked up with the only two flatmates in the university as bookish and mousy as she was. They'd gone to a pub last month for all of fifteen minutes, fleeing when the toothy DJ waved a karaoke microphone at them.

So Jake's obstinacy had prevailed. It was late March and he hadn't made any applications. 'It's too late now anyway, isn't it?' he'd started to crow.

And for reasons Zadie couldn't guess her mother had refused to solicit the support of Zadie's grandfather, a retired physics professor, in trying to strong-arm Jake. Her mother was tight-lipped, snapping at Zadie whenever she suggested asking for his help.

So, this visit had been Zadie's last-ditch plan. Jake had an important project to complete about contemporary politics. Who better to approach, then, than a contemporary politician? Since Professor Yates had boasted that Mrs Gregsbury was an ex-student who still consulted him, Zadie had timorously made an approach. She had found this incredibly difficult. Zadie was someone who usually only spoke when spoken to and could never think of the first line needed to start a conversation. She avoided parties. Verbal sparring with her surly but often quick-witted brother was something she could just about manage, but even that had taken her years to develop.

Thus Zadie had tapped so weakly on the Professor's door that she'd had to try again, more forcefully, eight times before he'd answered. Professor Yates had been surprised first by her approach and then by the question she'd posed. He'd developed a panic-stricken that's-not-how-the-world-works look on his face. She'd wondered whether he'd been exaggerating his influence in the corridors of power as he'd shuffled her out of his office with a polite, 'I'll try but don't expect miracles.'

A week later the Professor had been even more astonished than her when he reported victory! They'd pondered, without success, the mystery of why a first-year undergraduate should be granted a meeting with a junior minister. She'd then endured two long and repetitive monologues in which it was stressed that she would be an ambassador for the university, ho-hum-blah. Now it was clear. They were helping to make Mrs Gregsbury look good in front of a reporter. They wouldn't have to have their pictures taken, would they? Zadie began to silently fret at the possibility, even more so when she realised her brother would be in the photo too!

'Jake,' Zadie leaned towards him encouragingly, 'do you want to fill us in?'

Silence. Zadie winked conspiratorially at Mrs Gregsbury.

'You'll have to forgive my brother. By the time he's fought off his early morning lethargy he's too exhausted to do anything else for the rest of the day.' Mrs Gregsbury chuckled on cue. Zadie was proud of that line. She'd been working on it for days.

'Future of politics in the twenty-first century,' Jake managed finally. 'The environment and that. Its impact on society. And politics, I mean.'

'Yes, I see. Well, there's hardly a subject more important for your generation. People connect the dots on the doorstep. And on television. Panels, you see.'

'Well, yeah, we're being asked to produce a report on what politics and society might like...look like in the twenty-first century. Within my lifetime, suppose. Zadie suggested I come to you since most others are interviewing their friends and relatives.'

Already, Zadie prayed for a ceasefire. She didn't know whether to duck as the verbal shrapnel exploded overhead or hazard onto the battlefield to tend the wounded.

Mrs Gregsbury, though, was nodding and staring off into the middle distance. Through the same window Zadie could see the tops of a few greystone buildings, huddling into one another against the March wind. What had been a foul winter still wasn't quite ready to ease its grip on the country.

'Now, Jake, it is Jake isn't it? Well, Jake, I don't know whether I can do justice to such a vast topic. The environment in particular... well, we all know this is one of the key issues of our time. One that we, the government, are very concerned about, as I'm sure you know, and are working to address. With our colleagues in other countries obviously. For this is a global problem requiring global solutions. We have to address not only the dilemmas we face now – flooding, famine, migration, terrorism – but also the longer-term challenges that require some very tough decision-making. We will be judged on our legacy and we don't want our legacy to be one of missed opportunities. For that's what we'd be doing. Betraying the obligations we owe to future generations. It's true that we have much to be grateful for. Without wealth we could hardly afford to address all of the many problems we face, including global warming. That is the challenge. How to combine affluence with environmental responsibility. How to make growth sustainable. How to harness nature's riches without spoiling them. It won't be easy but we have made great strides already, strides that I am certain we can build upon in years to come.'

Jake's pen had barely brushed the paper in the folder he had barely managed to open.

'Was that the kind of overview you had in mind?'

'Yes, erm. Exactly.' The folder snapped shut. 'Thanks for your time.'

Luckily, Zadie managed to haul her brother back down before he could really stand up. 'Aaahh, what Jake means is that you were obviously the right person to come to and perhaps you could answer some specific questions he had prepared.'

Something bleeped. Zadie paused as the others checked the electronic devices they seemed to be clothed in. It was Mrs Gregsbury who won the look-how-popular-I-am prize on this occasion. 'Oh, for me. Good news. Not to worry. Yes, Jake, questions. Love to. Fire away.'

''K, thanks.' Jake opened his folder and concentrated, reverentially, on his notes. 'So, Mr Slattery mentioned that perhaps you, I mean the government, were relying too much on Technological Fixes for Social Problems needing Social Solutions.' Though this didn't exactly constitute a question Jake looked up with a sense of accomplishment, his pen poised.

Mrs Gregsbury gulped quietly. 'I see. Sounds impressive but could you say more about actually what that might mean, Jake?'

Jake would normally have been more than willing but it was at this point that Mr Slattery had chosen to mine the dark recesses behind his left ear and by the time Jake had regained his concentration the lesson had moved on. 'Ahh...'

'I think,' Zadie offered, 'the teacher wanted people to question a business-as-usual approach. You know, where we imagine we can shop our way out of trouble or that science and technological innovation alone will solve the problems we face.'

'Oh, I don't think anyone is really that complacent. Technology is a tool, though surely a vital tool when it comes to combating global terrorism and achieving a sustainable economy. Think about targets to cut carbon emissions. It's important to have the public, especially businesses, on board instead of making Green issues seem, well, pessimistic and nay-saying.'

Zadie glanced over to Jake, hoping to hand the conversation back but diagnosed the quick onset of my-brain-doesn't-work syndrome, a dreadful condition that had been known to strike her otherwise bright sibling every day before noon and after 3 p.m., as well as during family visits, shopping trips and tv/games/internet/sofa time. Still, he was taking notes now, so at least today the disease wasn't completely debilitating.

Zadie decided to try out some of the ideas she'd come across in that – what was it? – social politics module from semester one.

'That's great, I'm sure. But aren't there those who think we ought to be making deeper changes to society? For instance, ah, if a billion Chinese people get a car each, and fridges and the like, wouldn't that put too much pressure on the environment? And so shouldn't we all be consuming less as a result?'

Zadie couldn't be sure but a faint rumble of disapproval appeared over Mrs Gregsbury's eyebrows.

'Oh, we've all heard this, of course, but why should we deny people in the developing world the comforts we take for granted? Politics is about making the tough decisions. I suppose, obviously, we need to find ways of using less energy in our consumables and so forth but we are doing that. The human race, species, has proved a remarkable capacity to adapt in the past to new challenges and why should things be any different now? We won't defeat global warming through pessimism, will we?'

'I'm not sure it's about pessimism or optimism,' Zadie persisted, after a respectful pause. 'More about whether governments have the vision needed. I mean, politicians need to win elections, don't they? But what about those problems which have a longer timescale, problems which are bigger than the cycle of elections? Isn't there a risk that these get ignored?'

'Mmm, I don't know, Zadie, sounds like pessimism to me. We can agree about what needs to be done and reach agreement about how to do it.'

Both women were startled by Jake chirping up. 'What about when agreement runs out?'

'Jake?' He thought swiftly about something Mr Slattery had said that held his interest.

'Well...flooding? You might want to get people to take out flood insurance. I want to build proper flood defences and the like, which is expensive, yeah? Rich white people not caring about New Orleans, and that. If we can't agree, what then?'

'That's an interesting example, Jake, but surely we need to come to agreement sooner or later if we are not to come to blows. Politics is...' Mrs Gregsbury paused and leaned forward for the dramatic effect she had known to work on other occasions (including one television appearance *The Times* had described as "a remarkable tour de force that won the audience over") '...the art of finding compromise.'

Zadie couldn't be sure whether her brother's nods during this were meant to be sage or were code for 'Help! Can't find the answer in my notes!'

'I suppose,' she chipped in again, 'that we reach agreement by being as open as possible to many different voices, otherwise what we end up with isn't agreement, not really. If we don't consider all sides then isn't compromise, consensus whatever, just whatever those in power think the rest of us should sign up to?'

'Well, in that case, we are not really talking at cross-purposes, Zadie. In a free society we are *all* in power. I mean, we all have a say and the opportunity to contribute. Not all governments will listen equally perhaps but this one certainly will, I guarantee it. Any more questions, Jake?'

Brother and sister were both caught out by the suddenness of the question. Out of the corner of her eye Zadie saw the journalist lady make a discreet note. 'Ah, only a few. Yes.'

'I'll tell you what, let's see how many we can get through.'

'Okay, well, one thing was about health.' Jake spoke carefully as he retraced the arguments he had overheard during revision period. 'You, the government I mean, speak lots about the importance of healthy living. Getting people to exercise, yeah? Give up booze and all. But lots of people dislike, you know, the stress, the travel, the pace of life. So does healthy cooking and so on go deep enough?'

Mrs Gregsbury lingered and this time spoke more directly to the young man.

'Hmm, well, there's that verb, "going deep" again. "Deeper changes" and so forth. I have to confess I either find that impractical or else just meaningless. We surely have a responsibility to do what is do-able. Encouraging people to smoke less, drink less, and so forth, is responsible. It helps them by improving their health and it helps the country. Isn't that,' she shrugged slightly, 'as "deep" as we need to go?'

'Ahh...mmm...'

'Isn't there a question about whether we should be leaving it so much to individuals?' Zadie's new intervention once again seemed to throw a hint of frustration across Mrs Gregsbury's face. Zadie was conscious of doing more talking than she ever managed in class. Who was she showing off to? Her brother? 'People have some freedom over themselves, sure, but a lot of the pressures on them, and on the environment I suppose, are what my tutors call "structural" and "institutional", things beyond personal control. If that's true then by putting everything on the individual level don't we detract from some of the real causes of problems?'

'Alright, well, you say that but then there are two problems I can foresee which challenge that kind of position. Firstly, it's not clear what those "deeper" or "real", or whatever you want to call them, problems are. You say it's structural but others – and there are lots of research papers I could show you – say that it's cultural, that some people haven't been properly educated about healthy living, or that they haven't had the available opportunities, or that they just don't care about ruining their lives and expect the rest of us to take up the slack. So, can you really show that environmental damage, or poor health, or whatever it is, is what you call "structural". What does that mean, really?

'The second thing is, even if there are these structural elements they change only very slowly. Let's say that too much pollution comes from industry. Well, the job of government is to point them in the direction of less polluting alternatives. Sometimes through friendly encouragement and sometimes through incentives and penalties. But we can hardly reinvent the economic basis of our society all at once. So, wouldn't it be irresponsible to throw up our hands and say "It's structural!" as opposed to doing whatever we can do?'

With Jake still making more notes than ever before in his life Zadie replied slowly, rolling the various arguments around in her head, unsure of her ground.

'I suppose we need a discussion about what causes something. Lots of people are going to disagree, yes, and that's a good thing. They will have different ideas that explain sort of how the world works. We probably can't reach a consensus, where everyone agrees about everything, but better to talk about these things openly. And so I suppose it could be said that this is the job of government, partly, as well. Not just to make the trains run on time but to help get the discussion moving. To think about where we need to go and not just how we get there.' Zadie hoped she'd got from A to Z effectively, but wasn't quite sure she was speaking the same language as Mrs Gregsbury anymore.

'The problem, Zadie, is that the battlelines of old are gone, some of them for good and some have been replaced. We live in a new world. Liberal, democratic capitalism is the only game in town. I mean, I know lots of people still quarrel about religion, and there are real choices to be made between liberals and conservatives and so on, but the electorate wants good government, efficient government and not a debating seminar. They pay the bills, after all.'

A loud rap on the door startled the brother and sister though not, Zadie noticed, Mrs Gregsbury.

'Yes?'

Permanently-raised-eyebrows had returned. 'Ma'am, your 9.30 has arrived early.'

'Thank you, Jeffrey, I'll just be a minute. Well, you can see I have the life of a politician, ha ha! You know I have enjoyed our little chat immensely. So sorry it couldn't have been longer. Feel that I learned more from you than you from me. Still, hope you have something to write about in your project, Jake. If there is anything you want to follow up about please contact my aide and he'll be happy to help. We both will. Give my best to Professor Yates. Jeffrey will be happy to show you out. Cheerio!'

The door closed behind them. Zadie had to get her bearings for a moment. She remembered standing up, smiling, smoothing down her conservative blouse and smart stretch linen trousers, turning, walking, shaking Mrs Gregsbury's hand, smiling at the journalist and stepping into the hall. Truth to tell, she couldn't remember having done any of these things with her own free will. Mrs Gregsbury had been polite, effusive and practised. They'd been schmoozed out of the room!

There was the faintest impression of a Jeffrey-shaped vacuum in the hall but no sign of the man himself. Zadie had been right to worry that they'd be left on their own. Should she knock on Mrs Gregsbury's door to ask for directions? Or try one of the other offices or perhaps waylay someone? Zadie had always been nervous about that kind of thing, though. With one hand Jake was already happily texting again, oblivious to her dilemma. With the other he was actually managing to loosen his clothes some more, as if in reward for enduring the torture of wearing a uniform for all of thirty minutes.

If the decor had seemed designed to slow their pace when they were entering it seemed equally designed to 'tut!' and tap its feet impatiently if you dawdled on your way out. Zadie thought it best to try and retrace their steps and break cover if they spotted daylight.

'So, what do you think? Interesting? Helpful?'

'Sure. I mean, thanks. Project'll look impressive when I hand it in.'

That was as much gratitude as she was going to get. 'But what did you think of what she said?'

'It was incisive, cutting-edge and contemporary.'

'Glad to hear it. And could you actually summarise for me what it *was* she actually said?'

Pause. Distracted. 'That's where I'd have more trouble but no way am I changing my mind that it was incisive, cutting-edge and contemporary. Besides, you did most of the natter. Some observer! You'll have to remind me. Or better still, write the essay for me.'

'I'd love to but some of us already suffer from sleep deprivation. You won't have heard of this, it's the opposite of your well known condition: being-awake deprivation. Look, how do we get out?'

'It's left and down the stairs, right, then right again.'

This stopped Zadie short. 'How would you know? This is the first time you've looked up at anyone since the obstetrician slapped you at birth – not enough times if you ask me, but there you go.'

'OK. You stop here and we'll all come and visit you over Easter. Will you be wanting a change of clothes?'

Zadie allowed him to lead the way, knowing already why she'd have the last word. 'I'm glad I bullied you into doing this but what she said seemed too…complacent to me. All that stuff about getting things done is fine, but shouldn't we know more about why we want certain things done? A conversation about where to go and not just how to get there?'

'Well, these are all smart people, Zades. You've been at university for six months! Who are you to say?'

'You mean if a fascist dictator had a PhD the rest of us should just shut up? Who are any of us to say? That's my point, oh short-legged one. As the people who get affected by these decisions, we all have a right to speak and to have our opinions about them heard. That means all of the "why" questions as well. The normative ones, they're called. I'm sure these politicians and civil servants are smart but do they really think about the deeper issues? Maybe they don't have the time and so it's more important the rest of us help them out. Thank God's mother for that!'

They were outside at last. Zadie realised she'd been taking small, shallow breaths inside the building. Whatever the opposite of hyperventilation was, she felt she'd contracted it.

'Whatever, you know. But you keep going on about things being "deep". As the lady politician said, what does that really mean, anyway? Are we getting the tube back or what?'

Jake made off down the drive towards the main road. Zadie called after him, savouring the moment. 'You know who we should ask about this stuff, don't you?'

You could practically see Jake's shoulders and neck wince. Zadie grinned and lengthened her stride.

CHAPTER TWO

'How are you, Cramps?' asked Zadie.

'My life consists of one crushing disappointment after another, with nothing to look forward to except disease, decay, death and decomposition.'

'Same as usual, then?' quipped Jake, squeezing his way into the narrow lobby.

'No, really, you're fine?'

Cramps accepted his granddaughter's kiss and smiled. 'Surprisingly happy. I don't know what's wrong with me.' They linked arms and squashed awkwardly into the living room. 'How are you, sweetheart? How is university? Is my name still whispered down the chambers of academe in hushed, revered tones? No? Well, we both know that God's got it in for me.'

Zadie made her jolly 'oh-you're-in-good-form-today' face and settled onto the sofa next to her brother. He had already snagged the seat where some of the original fabric was bravely fighting a losing battle against the onrushing hordes of stains, burn marks and bald spots. Their grandfather's pension left him far from destitute but he preferred to spend his money on music and books rather than on heating, new clothes, new furniture, cleaning materials or personal grooming products. Cramps seemed to have cut his white hair recently. It now only fell to his shoulders but still soared upwards into straggly flight-paths around his dome. He wouldn't have left the house, she knew. He always cut his hair himself using his hazy reflection in the glass sideboard rather than something as mundane as a mirror. A quick glance confirmed that his crested eyebrows were still sending occasional avalanches of dandruff screeing towards their final resting place on his beard.

The living room had not changed since their last visit at Christmas. It was stacked with towering columns of books that almost seemed to be holding up the ceiling, a struggle with gravity that at least diverted attention away from the new lifeforms evolving in the carpet. The few bookshelves had long since waved a white flag under the strain of so much weight and in her worst moments Zadie worried that one day the neighbours would notice a cheesy smell, peer through the window and find Cramps buried beneath a landslide of seventeenth-century metaphysical poetry. That was, if they could see in. The bay windows did not permit much light to enter even on sunny days. Today it was like being at the mouth of a deep cave. At least the heating was on. The small coffee table was the only piece of furniture that remained fairly clear. Standing on it today, unusually, was the thin, coppery palm-sized box that had stood for years on the highest shelf and which she'd always imagined to be a music box. Zadie had never seen it this close. As a girl, puzzling over whether the surface was plastic or metal,she had once tried mountaineering up the shelves in order to reach it. Discovered, marooned near the Virginia Woolfs, unable to go up or down, she had received such a telling-off from her normally laidback, hippy-trippy grandfather, one that had started a row between him and her grandmother, that she had sobbed and vowed never to go near it again. And she never had. But now there it sat, and she could see how plain it really was, except for some swirls and curves incised into the double-hinged lids. Yet the coppery surface almost glowed, enhanced by the room's general murkiness.

So this was the room, Zadie thought, not for the first time, that their grandfather had retreated to after the death of his wife almost a year ago. She knew that the rest of the house was spotless and well-maintained, in homage to their recently deceased grandmother, but this room-cum-library had always been his space and he had slowly allowed it to fray and crumble. In truth, it had never been that pristine to begin with. 'I've seen mice throwing themselves onto the traps in suicidal despair,' had once been Cramps' running joke. 'Weapons of Mouse Destruction!' had been Jake's proud offering; one he still resurrected from time to time.

At least Cramps had ... spruced himself up a bit, she reflected, by chopping away at his hair. Gran's death had been a doubly painful blow, coming less than a year after the death of their father, Cramps' son-in-law. In rapid succession their mother had lost a husband and a parent. For a time the family had been brought together, each comforting the others in an extended wake of sadness and disbelief.

Often a distant figure before, Cramps had filled the void left by their father.

Then it had come time for them to repay that kindness when their grandmother died. Zadie had never seen Cramps so fractured, so vulnerable. At first their grandfather had been saved from the isolation they'd sensed he would otherwise crave through their family get-togethers. But then, in late autumn, he and their mother had apparently argued. They had barely talked since. Away at university Zadie had only heard about this, belatedly and unhelpfully, from Jake. Repeated calls to parent and grandparent had failed to shed light on why, nor would either talk about it during an unhappy Christmas. Zadie and Jake had had to endure two Christmas dinners – 'frozen pizza, kids?' Cramps had announced – and two New Year celebrations. Nor had the months since witnessed any thawing of the frost. Zadie couldn't believe it. Why were they acting like this?

Zadie kept asking for details in her weekly letters to him but Cramps refused to say anything about the matter. He had entertained her for a fortnight with his Attack of the Sock Drawer story. He'd packed his socks so tight into just one drawer that he'd struggled to open it one day. Then he'd pulled so hard he had fallen back onto the bed and half a dozen socks had landed on his face like cotton missiles. Other than that, she would relate news about her classes and as much gossip as she could overhear in the campus refectories. She represented her social life as being much more lively than it really was. She didn't want the grandfather she had worshipped since childhood to know she was often as reclusive as him, and with much less of an excuse.

Despite adoring his granddaughter, Cramps had always shared an absurdist humour with Jake. Jake had had to be dragged here today, as always, yet once he arrived the two of them would share jokes that could leave Zadie frowning like a puritan. It was Jake who, as a precocious youngster, had christened their grandfather with his nickname. Grandfather. Gramps. Cramps. It had been funny for five minutes, twelve years ago.

'Still managing to pack it in then, Cramps?' Jake pointed at the older man's belly which did seem to have spread outwards since Christmas.

'Jakie, you only have to worry about developing male breasts if they come with a cleavage.' Cramps shoved his face down his jumper, paused and looked up again. 'Uh-ho!'

Jake laughed at this so much Zadie swore she could see him spitting bits of breakfast onto the already abused carpet. Their grandfather's girth had long been a subject of amusement, for the boys in the family anyway. 'Nineteen seventy six,' Cramps would proudly intone, 'I was the first man in the UK to be arrested for topless sunbathing.' At least it was a safe, familiar topic.

'I've heard there's a clinic in New York that puts you into a coma for several months. Coma diets are supposed to be wonderful for your waistline. And how is your mother? Still disapproving of my bohemian lifestyle? So, my ambassadors from the real world, what can I do for you? Money? Or wise counsel?'

'Money – oww!'

'Zadie don't hit your brother. You'll bruise yourself. Smack him with whatever Henry James novel that is propping up the mini fridge.'

'She sends her love and, no, we don't need ulterior motives to visit you.'

'So you don't want me to help persuade Jake to go to university?'

Zadie froze. How had he managed to sniff out the excuse for her visit so soon? 'No! Of course not!'

'Yeah, right,' Jake grunted.

'Okay, Zades, I'll give it a go.' Cramps cleared his throat. 'Jake, you should go to university.'

'Nope.'

'There, don't say I didn't try.'

As usual, Zadie wasn't sure when her grandfather was serious or joking. 'Any chance you'll try again later?' she asked. Cramps blinked and stared at her. She always felt that beneath his sardonic humour and gentle manner her grandfather harboured the resurrected soul of a particularly impatient owl.

She quickly related a few details about university life before detailing that morning's event and saying that it had left questions in her mind.

'Which are, exactly?'

'Well, at university we are supposed to be learning critical thinking. But when I said that we need to go deeper I felt like a bit of an idiot. I sometimes feel like my lecturers have access to secrets that they won't show us yet. But since you're a famous academic and you did offer, as you put it, to "tolerate any irritating questions you have from time to time", then you're my saviour.'

'Are you staying for lunch? I'd order some pizza but the phone was disconnected weeks ago.'

Jake waved his mobile and, to his silent horror, Cramps snatched it away with astonishing speed.

'You can get onto the internet with this, no? And it probably plays games, videos, and shouts at you if you walk on the grass. A useful combination of advanced and primitive civilisations all rolled into one.' He tossed it back to Jake, to his consternation, in case it landed on the carpet and was kidnapped by some extraterrestrial species.

'The Visigoths didn't have them, Cramps. And if he'd had one Honorius could have contacted his centurions earlier and ordered them to go kick some Visigoth ass.'

'Why, Jake. Deep down you are still that remarkable seven-year old who could recite Shakespeare and pick his nose at the same time. I was never famous, Zades. Besides, vultures don't congratulate the corpse on the quality of the meal. Is this visit about Jake's project, or yours?'

Jake was desperately trying to wipe his grandfather's finger smudges from the mini-screen. 'Exactly.'

'Both. Jake's project is about the future of social problems and isn't a million miles away from what we've been doing in social science. By going to university he could study them for real. You know, Mrs Gregsbury was all, well "We have to make the trains run on time" but I think politics has to be about more than that.' Zadie was conscious of getting some details wrong but didn't think it mattered.

'Spoken like a true convert. OK, what does it mean to look at things deep down?' Cramps settled back in his chair. 'Perhaps you should be physicists, like me, hmm? Physicists have always looked for what is going on at the bottom of everything, though some have concluded that there is no floor to the well; no point at which we can stop and look up and see everything in its entirety. Atoms gave way to protons and electrons which gave way to quarks which gave way to muons, zuons and whateverons…which gave way to branes…'

'Brains?' Jake pointed at his head.

'No, listen closely. BRANES.'

'Much clearer, thanks.'

'Many in this age still dream of a theory of everything. They wouldn't be physicists otherwise, but…'

'You don't think they'll ever be able to write it all down on a t-shirt?' asked Zadie, remembering a phrase he'd used before.

Jake sighed inwardly. His sister was never happier than when she was being lectured to.

'Lots of important things can be written on a t-shirt. "Circles are not Squares". "Who Cares about a Solution to Apathy?". My point is that anyone who wears just one t-shirt is dumb. So what about other claims? Lots of mathematicians think that reality basically consists of numerical relations. If maths describes how information is trans-mitted and transformed then it might well lie at the heart of so much else: chemistry and biology, computer technology, economics. But then there's that single t-shirt problem again.

'Let's say my consciousness is in some way a set of algorithms and numerical codes. Does that mean I am basically no different from Jake's phone there? Inferior, indeed, since my brain doesn't consist of porn, self-indulgent rants and images of celebrities in rehab. Well, sometimes it doesn't. In any event we can only establish the truths of mathematics by reaching beyond mathematical truths. Are you with me so far? Where's my favourite cushion?'

'Here, Cramps.' Jake had been using it to protect his elbows against the sofa's most infamous black stain, the one everyone thought looked almost, but not quite, like Gandhi.

'Maybe we should turn away from the sciences then,' Cramps continued. 'What about the arts? '

For all its mess their grandfather knew with the instinct of a homing-pigeon where everything in the room was located. Jake knew that no computer would ever be quicker than Cramps at finding a particular book or sweeping away dust tumbleweeds it was best not to look at too closely. 'Look at this.' He opened an art book and showed them. The painting depicted five crudely drawn figures, holding hands and dancing wildly in a circle. They were coloured a disturbing pinkish-red, as if their flesh reflected the flames of an immense fire that wasn't actually in the paint.

Cramps was now on his knees, peering into the CD case which his granddaughter had given him for his last birthday. Zadie had known that it would contain only a fraction of the discs scattered around the place but also that, like the guy whose job was to comb through the draft manuscript of *Finnegan's Wake* and censor the naughty bits, she had to start somewhere. 'Music also has that instinctive embrace of the unsayable,' Cramps announced over his shoulder. 'Most great artists are either left-wing, insane, or gay, of course. Preferably all three. Sane right-wing heterosexuals have nothing left to do except go into politics, business or prison.' He gave up searching for a suitable CD and rolled back athletically onto his seat.

For all his moans at growing old Cramps could be surprisingly energetic. Zadie suspected many of his grunts and groans were deliberate, intended to supplement the growing-old-is-terrible yarns aimed mainly at Jake. 'This is your future, you know,' he'd joke from time to time. 'You start losing hair from places where you want it kept and start growing it in places that surely contravene the laws of physics.' But Jake was still young enough to feel immortal.

'So which is best at understanding society? Art or science?'

'Ah, Zades. That's a question for the ages. Is it about the motion of matter and information or about the creation of meaning, of social consciousness, discourse and culture? What do your lecturers say?'

Despite getting excellent marks Zadie wasn't even sure she understood what he was getting at. How was this meant to help Jake? 'I'm not sure they have expressed things quite in that way, Cramps. So far, it's really been about the founding fathers of social science.'

'Yes, but the founding fathers had founding fathers, didn't they? Trace any idea back far enough and even the most brilliant is quite simple because it was inspired by brilliantly simple questions. What is society? A system of interdependent institutions. How does history develop? Conflict. How does the self come to have identity? It exchanges symbols with other selves. Why do I feel hungry right now? Forgot to have breakfast. See?'

'But that just shows Mrs Gregsbury was right. If lots of smart people disagree, then surely we have to leave most of that stuff to one side as a distraction?'

'Or perhaps conversations don't have to come to an end to be purposeful, Zades. Perhaps the discussion is part of the point. Lots of theorists in social and political studies believe that they occupy a space which straddles the depths and the surfaces, the philosophies and the railway timetables.'

'Such as?'

'You're interested in interventions, right? How do we make the world a better place? OK, then, what do we mean by "government"? How prominent should government be in social life? How much money should government spend? To what extent should we leave individuals alone to sink or swim according to their own efforts? How much control do people have over themselves and their societies in the first place? Those kinds of questions are concerned with practical realities but they also imply some fundamental issues about what we *can* do as social actors and *why* we should do them.'

'So who has said what about what?'

'All depends on where you start from when you look around you. Politics is about decision-making. How should we organise ourselves and why? How can we reach agreement while ensuring that everyone's voice is heard? When does government wield authority legitimately? When are we allowed to resist the state and disobey laws? But none of these questions can really be addressed thoroughly without understanding power and social conditions. That's where sociology comes in. If power is distributed equally then we can assume government is representative simply due to formal mechanisms like elections. But if some groups hold more power than others, especially if they possess it unfairly, then we might need to alter social conditions accordingly. But what do we mean by power in the first place? Is it economic, personal, political, legal, cultural? And to what extent can we alter social conditions anyway? How can we bring about justice? What *is* justice?'

'Tell us the answers and you can treat us to an early lunch,' pleaded Jake.

'There *are* no easy answers. There are often bad answers and we can work to screen those out. And there are sometimes plausible answers that we can work to refine. That's why I said that it's the conversation which is valuable. It's like wading cautiously into a fast-flowing river whose currents started upriver, long before you were born, and will disappear downriver to a place you'll never see. All you have is your narrow strip and you can only make marginal changes to the flow of the water.'

'Sounds depressing.' Jake made a point of glaring at his sister. 'Why. Bother. With. University. Then?'

Cramps shrugged. 'There's no guarantee it'll be rewarding, but if you are truly interested in something you don't pursue it for the pay-off.'

Outside the morning skies were even lower and darker than before. If anything, the city was slouching backwards towards winter. Though the equinox had come and gone and the days had been noticeably lengthening the spring was, like their grandfather, still hiding within the lingering shadows of a colder season. On their way from the bus stop the late winter winds had ripped at them. Zadie had been thankful she'd decided to wear trousers.

The teenagers fidgeted. Remembering the journey here made Zadie think of the journey home. They shouldn't stay for lunch. The weather report had said it would get torrential this afternoon. Cramps obviously wasn't going to help her persuade Jake to send out some university applications. And although she sort of followed his thoughts about society they didn't seem to help Jake's project.

Yet she also hated the thought of leaving Cramps here in this over-cast house. She'd promised to come and visit him anyway but now felt guilty for having done so on a pretext. Perhaps she was expecting a miracle, hoping that she and Jake could somehow bring the estranged father and daughter together again. Their grandfather had always behaved a bit like a hermit, using his patrician scepticism and ironic aloofness to keep people at a distance. It was their grandmother who had kept him in touch with the real world. Now, since her death, he had added physical isolation to his emotional coolness. Zadie didn't know what she could do about it, or whether she should even try. She dreaded saying goodbye, though, conscious that the image of their grandfather, waving farewell from a doorway, would weigh on her mind for hours afterwards.

I'll come back lots of times over Easter, she reassured herself. And I'll reassure Cramps of that too.

'Are you interested in learning more?'

'A reading list would be great, Cramps.' She knew that he hated lending books, even the ones he hated.

'No,' he replied slowly. 'No.' The old man switched on his reading-desk light. 'I don't mean a list.' Brother and sister waited.

Cramps leaned forward in front of the light, his eyes now lost to them in cavernous shadows.

'What if I told you that I could give you an experience like no other.' Cramps nodded towards the next room.

Jake shifted uneasily. Oh God, had he become unhinged? A pervy perv? Jake could imagine all sorts of torture instruments awaiting them.

'What do you mean, Cramps?' reconnoitred Zadie.

'A game. Of sorts.'

'A game?'

'Yes. Listen. Since your grandmother died I haven't been as inactive as you've no doubt imagined. In fact, I've been applying the results of over thirty years of hard work. In there.' He nodded towards the next room again.

'In there? In the closet?'

'Not any more. It's actually a very large room and I've made it even bigger.'

'An even bigger closet?'

'Zadie, please recover from your closet fixation as rapidly as possible. I've been experimenting with digital and holographic technology.'

Jake hoisted his eyebrows. 'Really? I thought you were a super-conductor thingy?' As a kid, Jake had heard this and pictured his grandfather as a conductor on a train, tunnelling through sub-atomic particles at the speed of light.

'I have many talents Jake-o. I've designed a prototype of the next generation of wraparound, 3-D entertainment. Much more advanced than your phone there. This is what everyone'll be interacting with in a few years. If I can get in first, patent the technology and make a fortune, then think of your inheritance when I pop my clogs.'

'How much money you reckon?'

Zadie glared at her brother.

'I believe the technical term favoured by financial experts is "shed-loads". Interested?'

'Cramps,' smirked Jake, 'is this what you've been doing with your time instead of finding a lady to have chubby geriatric sex with?'

Zadie grimaced at their mutual bad taste. She was also lost. Cramps had always enjoyed spinning out almost-plausible stories, getting them to take the bait and then seeing how much he could reel them in. It had been half an hour, once, before they realised that, no, he couldn't have refereed the cricket match between Jewish and Arab armies at a brief cessation of hostilities during the Antarctic War of the 1970s. But they had been much younger and much more gullible then.

'You mean we can battle giant insects or something?' Jake bounced excitedly and Zadie felt the sofa's springs dig into her behind.

'Not quite. I freely admit that the giant insect idea was an opportunity wasted but, no, I've devised an educational program.'

Jake soured. Put 'holographs' next to 'education' and he could imagine something which was meant to be charming but was actually incredibly tedious. They'd probably have to build a civilisation or something. Jake didn't fancy the idea of carrying logs to a clearing and then having to fight off other tribes with weapons that he had to cut from the same effing logs.

'This is the program's access pad.'

Cramps picked up the mysterious box that had once so fascinated Zadie.

'That?!' she exclaimed, 'But I always thought that was a music box or something!'

Grruummph.

'Coming or what?'

At his grandfather's insistence Jake called his mother and told her they'd be a while yet. You're staying for lunch and dinner and maybe supper, Cramps called. Jake groaned at this but passed on the news anyway.

'Hang on. Hang on. Mustn't forget.' After a few minutes Cramps re-emerged from the kitchen with a canvas bag he flung over his right shoulder. 'Some bottled water.'

'What? Why?' Zadie frowned. 'Why can't we just pop out here if we're thirsty?'

'You'll be too absorbed.'

Cramps then led them into the no-longer-a-closet. It had been years since either grandchild had seen that normally locked door open. Now the room, perhaps ten or twelve metres along each wall, was not only empty but had been scrubbed and polished. The walls, ceiling and floor were all made from the same type of wood . Zadie didn't recognise it but was sure it didn't match the dusky pine in the rest of the house. Cramps closed the door. It was now pitch black. 'Don't be frightened,' they heard their grandfather say.

Suddenly, a series of pinprick lights sliced upwards through the darkness, like miniature searchlights scanning the sky for tiny enemy bombers, though Zadie was sure she hadn't seen any machinery. Red, blue and green light illuminated the silver hairs of their grandfather's double chin. He had opened the box, though Zadie couldn't see where the lid had gone. A music box it was not. Cramps pressed a button and what was unmistakably a screen, about three inches square, glowed into life. Beneath it was a small keypad; some of the characters were standard but Jake didn't recognise the others. The room was now half-lit, though their eyes took a minute to adjust to its ghostly artificial glow.

'I can activate the holo-program and the entire room will take us into a virtual, simulated environment.'

'What happens then?' Jake's interest was stirring again.

'Well, there's a series of seven environments programmed into this machine. You have to discover something in each in order to pass on to the next level. It's meant to be educational but also enjoyable. I might not have dragged you in here today but it seemed propitious. Jake, it might tell you something about the joys of learning. Zadie, it might address some of the questions you've been asking yourself, especially about today's visit to what's-her-name.'

"How does it work?' Jake wondered.

'I just press this button. Don't worry; you may not know how all the bits work but, luckily, it'll all be over a lot sooner than you expect. Bit like sex.'

The siblings glanced at each other, knowing that the punchline was coming any second now and they were the ones going to be punched. He'd always teased them with his zoned-out other-worldli-ness. A favourite and recurring tease had been, 'Honestly! You earth-lings! Oops, I've said too much.' Still, they felt the need to play along because *he* seemed to need them to. And the gag had gone a bit too far for them to claim boredom or incredulity now. Best to get it over with and think up a quick retaliation before they had to leave. The glance turned into a joint nod.

Wayhayyy.

There was that sound again.

24

'Should we order that pizza now?' Jake asked.

'Nahh, why worry about food?'

Suddenly there was a crash outside the door, like a picture thumping to the floor.

'What was that—?'

'A cat or a bat or something. What does it matter?'

'A cat?!' Jake shuddered.

Cramps shrugged and pressed a button.

CHAPTER THREE

As an infant Jake had daydreamed about walking into a television. What would it be like to plunge off stratospheric cliffs with Wily Coyote? To torture Principal Skinner? And now, here he was.

On the opposite wall a dot sparkled at them. As though he was looking at a tiny screen through the wrong end of a telescope, Jake had a vague impression of a city street. The dot swelled. The flat image raced towards and swallowed all three of them, as they plunged from orbit at a thousand miles an hour, sideways into the world. A sudden explosion of reality froze and stuttered forwards again, splintering into layers, enfolding and assaulting them, into objects solid and round. Then their senses, erased momentarily, responded once more to colour, sound and smell and they sensed, even in that first rushing instant, that this world responded to *them* also.

This world was cold. And it whiffed!

'Noooo, no, no, no, no, no.'

Honestly! Zadie was always so nervous of new experiences. Jake sometimes imagined she'd taken one look round the delivery room, burst into tears and then tried to crawl back up the umbilical cord. He did his best to reassure his sister. 'Dumb-arse! It's a holo-projection room.' He snatched the copper box from Cramps, examining the screen. 'Don't you ever watch *Star Trek*? Or do you think we've been miraculously transported somewhere? Wait, erm...' Jake was standing on a severed tail. He felt sorry for whichever animal had owned the thing. While also praying it was now safely somewhere else.

Zadie wasn't listening. They had been deposited on a city street and although the thin chilly sunlight suggested it was morning there was no traffic. Everywhere was eerily still and silent. The road and pavements were cracked, disjointed. Not that you could see much of either past the small mountain ranges of litter, tumbling together into landslides of cans and newspapers, plastics and rancid rotting waste, everything resettling around them as they lurched their way, like giants, through the valleys towards a clear bit of the pavement. Zadie kept her lips tightly shut, brushing away the midges, until they found a relatively insect-free zone, though she continued to wave her arms frantically whenever a bug wove into sight. The air itself seemed full of litter. Murky and liquid. Tattered buildings swayed above them, sucking away much of the thin daylight which managed to penetrate this far down. Most of the shop fronts were barricaded, though a few had been vandalised and looted, their broken windows revealing dark, empty interiors.

'Is *this* the education program you mean? Where's the door?'

Hah!

Brother and sister spun around. That voice again. Had it come from behind the now invisible door, she wondered? There was no sign of anything other than the street. The siblings shuffled away in opposite directions, uneasily, expecting any second to crack a nose on the closet's walls. Nothing. Then they realised they'd strayed at least thirty feet away from one another, yet surely the room they'd entered hadn't been that big! 'Cramps? What is this? Are we still in your house?'

Where else would you be, watersack?!

As the device he was holding cackled those words Jake jerked in shock. Fumbling, he almost dropped it.

What's wrong with you, monkeynuts?

'Great, impressive,' said Jake, recovering. 'The ornament speaks. So can my Play Station. Did you invent this as well, Cramps?'

No he didn't, wormfood, and I ain't your damn games console. I'm a synthetic intelligence. A million times smarter than you, a billion times wittier and I know how to satisfy the ladies with all the latest upgrades! Your grandpa and me is old friends, and I owe him a favour for allowing me to create all those worldwide computer viruses when I was bored. I'll be your guide for the day. Voilà!

'Guide?'

Guide! That's right, genius. And if I wanted an echo I'd shout into your ears. Name's Virgil.

'Virgil?!'

Yeah, as if I would have picked that name for myself. What a craphound you are! The gig is this. Because you spend so much time, you know, being stupid, it's my job to protect you from yourselves. The thing you have to discover from each environment is a keyword. That'll take you into the next one. Once the program ends you can go back to your totally pointless lives.

'So you *are* a games console!'

27

Shut the hell up!

'Cramps,' said Zadie, sounding puzzled, 'is it that you installed this uppity iPhone inside a music box or wh—'

'Ahhwwww!!' Jake had pulled out his phone, thumbed a few keys and then sobbed. 'Shit! There's no network signal!' He started to stomp around again, pointing the phone into the air and staring intently into the screen. 'Are you...hey, Virgil, are you blocking the network?'

No!

'Why should I believe you?'

You should. Even though you can't.

'Wait, we can end the program any time we want to, yes?' Virgil remained silent. 'Cramps?'

'Don't give up so soon, Jake. Why don't you tell me what you think we should do?'

'There's nothing here and we might get mugged by the looks of everything. I say we walk. This way!'

Oblivious to the fact that neither Zadie nor Cramps were following Jake stormed off, zigzagging his way past mounds of rubbish. He couldn't walk away so far and still be in the same room, Zadie fretted. Was it all an elaborate optical illusion? What was going on? She knew her grandfather was brilliant but.... A hundred feet down the street Jake paused. Looked down. Then retraced his steps. 'There's an insect the size of a rat down there. I wonder if this way's any better.'

'Jake, Zadie, trust me. This is all part of the program. I want to see how good you are at figuring things out without too much help. Only Virgil can jump us from one level to another. I might cheat, you see, because I love you whereas Virgil is a fairer referee because he pretty much despises having to be here.'

Damn right.

'And remember, it's supposed to be enjoyable! The holo-program won't give us the information we need automatically. We'll have to act a bit like detectives.'

Zadie and Jake looked at one another doubtfully. They didn't see much opportunity for enjoyment in this armpit of a road. Still, their grandfather's words *were* reassuring. He'd devised this simulation program, he was hyper-intelligent and they were still, somehow, in his house and only needed to pass a few tests to return to normality. Anyway, he wouldn't put them in any danger would he? And it was a chance to connect with him, Zadie supposed. Besides, there was bugger all on TV, thought Jake.

'But how come we can move about so much?' Zadie asked.

'The holographic images move around us to give the illusion of motion and distance. Right? It's like the Tardis,' Jake said.

'Jake, will you please...oh, I suppose it is like the Tardis, yes. But where do we even start? How do we know this keyword when we spot it?'

'Let's start with those people over there.'

Down the road there was a large cluster of people leaning against a wall, slouching and shuffling. Somehow, Zadie hadn't seen them before.

Though much of the pavement was now clear of litter, they still had to move slowly to avoid the splatters of faec...Zadie recoiled from even voicing the word in her head. She tried to orientate herself. It wasn't that they were moving down a street. Instead, the simulation of a street was moving *past* them. That was better.

From a distance the queue looked ordinary. Adults chatting and stamping from foot to foot in the cold. Children running around and shouting. But as they moved closer Zadie could see the destitution. The 'toys' the children were playing with were rusty cans and wads of rotting debris. Others, more subdued, observed the world from behind the shelter of their parents' legs. There was nowhere to sit except on the ground. Clothes were ill-fitting, torn and faded. The men were tired-eyed, the women pallid. Everyone looked exhausted and bored. There was little laughter. Zadie had seen deprivation before but not quite like this. Not shifting its weight to mark time, or chatting the derelict stillness away. Anything to distract them from the muddy air they were breathing.

Some of her fellow students would have been wary, she thought, but Zadie, as shy as she often was, believed strongly that only distance made strangers unsympathetic to one another. Besides, they weren't real people anyway! Detectives? Oh, well.

The men, though, and one synthetic intelligence, held back. They were afraid of getting mugged.

Go for it, sister!

'Excuse me.' As she approached it many in the line became even more sullen. Carefully, Zadie moved towards a young woman with dark curly hair, perhaps only a few years older than herself. The woman turned her back angrily, shielding a young boy, pressing him against the wall, murmuring something that sounded like 'Frotvid.'

'I'm sorry...what was...?'

'Frotvid!!' Zadie was aware of surly voices rising from further along the line. She was still three strides away from the queue. Was she being accused of pushing in?

She's telling you to get the hell away because you're just here to gawp. You don't want to know what 'frot' really means, do you?

'You can translate that?' she asked Virgil, suddenly realising that, if Cramps had programmed this electronic guide, then of course Virgil could.

Didn't I say that I'm smarter than you? Oh wow, I did!

'Then can you tell her that we are not here to hurt them in any way? That we need their help?'

'Frow much?' demanded the boy, stroking one hand against the other.

'Taze, hush. I'm sorry, you're not really t-vid? It's just you are dressed...'

'I'm not even sure what you mean...erm...'

T-vids are wealthy day tourists who come down to places like these to scare themselves, tut-tut and feel superior.

'Your toy is correct.'

Hey! Damn organics!

'Not for free, Aon!' the boy whined.

'He's right.' snapped a young man at Zadie's side. 'T-vids or not, they can't expect something for nothing. Thirty-five cents, girl.'

'Kayne! You can't moan about the system one minute, then copy it the next. Anyhow, not if you want to stay my friend.'

'Aon!'

'Hush, I said.'

Zadie saw she'd have to proceed carefully. Most of the people in the queue were now gazing at them, absorbed in their halting conversation but very suspicious. She thought it best to talk to the woman – Aon? – who appeared harassed but also educated and not unfriendly. Zadie noticed a small birth defect on the corner of her mouth, turning it down even when she smiled. It was noticing little imperfections like that which sometimes helped Zadie to overcome her natural shyness. 'Look, we don't have much to offer you but if we have anything you value...'

'What about the talking box?'

'Kayne, please. The Buzzers?!'

'Jake,' Zadie whispered, 'give me your watch.'

'Huh?'

'You're getting a new one for your birthday. We probably don't have any of their money and if we're only in a computer projection of some kind your watch will be lying on the floor once it ends.'

'Bog off!' Jake glanced hurriedly at his grandfather, who merely smiled sweetly back. 'It's not as if *we're* rich. Single mum, no? Give 'em *your* watch, why don't you?'

They'd been overheard. Aon made a great play of refusing any payment and some of the others repeated this dumb show. Kayne still looked hostile and morose, though. 'Do you need directions?' Aon asked.

'If it's not a strange question, where are we?'

'All the Grey Districts look pretty much the same. You're in 6Z.'

'And this is?'

'The work queue.'

'A...job centre?'

'What's that?'

It took a while but they were slowly able to piece together what was going on. Many in the queue still assumed they were here to make fun, so much of the information came dripping with irony and vitriol. When they wanted to share a joke they spoke to one another in the slang that none of them but Virgil could understand. 'It's how we keep the rest of the world away,' Aon explained. Jake was uncomfortable. They might be sims but his precious if malfunctioning phone suddenly felt very vulnerable in a jacket pocket. However, Aon and a few others seemed pleased to have a distraction, willing to indulge the curious ignorance of the strangers.

They were commonly known, even to themselves, as Noughts. They were barred from seeking work on the free market because their Agency Chips had been logged I.I., or 'Inadequate Identity'. Having an income of less than a certain amount was what characterised them as Noughts. Once that happened, they came to a queue like this every morning. Their Agency Chips, inserted deep under the skin in their palms, were scanned when they arrived and when they left. Being in the queue for long periods was what demonstrated their willingness to work. Noughts were paid a fixed amount, pennies only, for every hour they queued. Not a lot of actual work was handed out. The money was transferred onto their Chips and then they had to head off to another queue somewhere else. They might stand in three or four of these queues per day, for maybe twelve-fourteen hours in total. If they did get some regular work, and it paid, they might just be reclassified from Noughts to Norms. But it didn't seem to happen often.

'I don't get it,' Zadie confessed, glancing sidelong at her grandfather. 'There must be some community work to be done? What about all this rubbish for a start?'

'Not allowed,' replied Aon. 'If you don't play their game then this alerts the police who can find you easily enough.' Aon frowned. 'Are you really here to learn or are you having fun with us after all?' Their I.I. classification meant that if they strayed outside authorised areas their Agency Chips would flare up on some positioning computer like a lighthouse. 'And haven't you Norms seen Buzzers before?'

A faint metallic whine filled the space around and above them, like a soft swarm of electronic mosquitoes. Zadie had only been faintly aware of it before, mentally brushing the sound away as if it were distant city noise. But now, looking up, she saw at least a dozen dots in a jagged line all the way down the street, hovering several metres above the rooftops. Squinting, she could see they were shaped like small eyeballs, as if ripped horrendously from some disfigured alien robot. They were not cabled to anything. They were pretty much stationary but seemed to be riding the wind currents. Spinning constantly, they blinked signals at one another.

Smart surveillance cameras. Every road out here has its own virtual police force.

'Then this isn't a free society?'

If I had shoulders I'd shrug. In case you hadn't noticed some of the natives are getting antsy. Want that watch you promised.

A few of the younger men were looking more and more threatening. Jake was fuming and not hiding it very successfully. 'Is that the reason they're downers? Greed? Theft?'

'Look,' murmured Zadie, 'keep your voice down. This is all inhumane. They're just a bit desperate, that's all. Wouldn't you be?'

'Desperate maybe. But I wouldn't do anything to get myself here in the first place and if I did I'd fight back at those insect things up there. Wouldn't have any micro-ID under my skin either. Chop my hand off to get that fascist parasite out. What about you Cramps?'

'I think we're in trouble.' Their grandfather's gaze was still fixed on the sky. Following his stare Jake saw that the Buzzers no longer seemed to be monitoring the street. The several now huddled together seemed to be observing them!

'Sectexs here soon,' announced Aon.

'What about your child? Doesn't he have school?'

'Not my child. Nephew. My sister ill, in one of the charity hospitals. Besides,' she lapsed into slang, 'Norm reclass upwork less subgift.'

Most children have to tag along with their parents. Maybe they think it'll improve your motivation if your kids are affected.

'Motivation? What has motivation got anything to do with this horrible place? God, this is terrible.'

Forget God. Whenever What's-His-Name needs to make a decision he always asks, 'What would Virgil do?'

Just then they heard a screech of tyres, the thump of metal, the iron clatter of heels and a loud snarl that vibrated the air around them. STAY THERE!

Oh bollocks!

The black shapes pouring out of the two trucks were tall, broad, masked, armed and quite obviously pissed off. Zadie, Jake and Cramps found that their arms and shoulders were no longer their own, while their feet had learned how to levitate. Zadie would be more frightened afterwards than she was at the time. But what really ached later, when she slowed down the pace of events that swept them away, was that no one stepped forward to help them. No protest. No movement. No sympathetic call. No one but Aon. For the briefest of moments the two young women locked eyes. Then the contact was gone. As she was bundled into the back of one of the trucks Zadie was able to translate a word she had heard barely a minute before. The guards' uniforms bore a shiny insignia stitched above a breastplate. Sectex.

As the trucks roared away the turbulence left in their wake gradually subsided. The garbage settled into new yet familiar contours. Its distraction stolen, the queue tallied time again as the slow minutes crept into long hours. The Buzzers returned to their aerial dance.

They had been driving for twenty minutes. Practically glued between two guards apiece the prisoners had been thrown around violently as the truck constantly decelerated, cornered and accelerated again, crashing through mounds of litter. Immobile as trees the guards' arms felt like hard wooden trunks. With every passing minute Zadie's doubts magnified. They were sitting down! No holographic images could be this real, could they, no matter what Jake said? Yet surely there was no plausible alternative. Why would their grandfather deceive them?

'Cramps?'

'Yes, Jakes?'

'We're not going to be visiting any racist or KKK places in this program, are we?'

'No.'

'Because you know why that would be a really bad idea, right?'

'Yes Jake.'

At the beginning, Zadie had demanded to know where they were going and, when this didn't work, demanded to speak to someone in authority and, when this didn't work, relapsed into a silent sulk. First a holo-program that was bigger than the closet she desperately hoped they were still in, then a bolshie talking computer that apparently had them trapped, then a rat insect, and now all this! Yet Cramps was still exuding a trusting interest in it all and this calmed her. Zadie was reassured by her childlike faith in him. To some extent. Jake, too, seemed unfazed. Grasping Virgil to his lap, he seemed fascinated more by the changing scenery, though the small skylight did not afford much of a view.

There had been little at first. Patches of grey blue, more Buzzers and the occasional tops of decaying brick buildings. But before long he could spot architecture that looked impressively futuristic. Sky-suspended walkways and monorails. Angled platforms hundreds of feet in the air. Floating wafer-thin screens and streams of words and images, like vapour-trails, that reeled out of, and into, nowhere. Towering arches, bridges and skyscrapers. And something else. Not Buzzers, but an indistinct...haze he couldn't pinpoint. And then, as if this wasn't enough, something that made him squeal like an infant.

'Zades!'

'What?'

'Zades!'

'I said "what?"'

'A flying car!'

Great, we're going to be Buck Rogerred to death. By the way, Lothario, the next time we are kidnapped by goons can you either switch my olfactory sensors off, or else not press me into your sweaty crotch. Failing that, some flowers and chocolates to make it worth my while?

'Sorry, just excited.'

I feel so cheap!

After a final, bone-twisting deceleration they were hauled out of the truck, into an underground garage, as unceremoniously as they had been hauled in. 'My grandfather is old, will you stop pulling and prodding him?' Zadie was getting tearfully frustrated at the absurdity of it all. The tiny lift they were squeezed into rocketed upwards, making her feel queasy. Hadn't Cramps promised them this would be enjoyable?

Although she couldn't see it Zadie sensed the Earth plummeting away.

'Who are you?'

'We've told you that already, young woman,' Cramps averred.

'Where did you come from?'

34

'Oh...nearer than you think.'

'Why are you here?'

'That...is not something we can easily explain.'

'Let's see, then. In the last ten minutes you have variously claimed to be tourists and charity workers...sorry, homeless charity workers.' Interrogator Dearbrook sighed and leaned back, her broad shoulders causing the chair to creak in protest. Zadie blinked away the image of a long cobra slowly and contentedly swallowing a puppy that this formidable woman prompted. She had never seen anyone look so stern and yet so quietly amused. They were figures of fun for her. 'Shall I spell out why none of that is plausible? Because we are not reading an I.I. code from any of you.'

Zadie exclaimed. 'Look, it's more likely to be a machine error, don't you think?'

'It's more likely that you belong to one of the Rad factions and have found a way to screen yourselves from the BioWeb. That would explain your interest in...those people.'

'The Noughts?'

This time there was real distaste on Dearbrook's face. 'Yes.'

'But why? They're just ordinary people who deserve respect.'

Cramps was very impressed with the animation in the voice of his normally reticent granddaughter.

'Rubbish! They are failed people. Nozoomers. Sub-agents. Why do you Rads push the same tired arguments all the time? Do you see many people agreeing with you? The Noughts are as rational as anyone else. They just choose to misuse their abilities and opportunities, that's all.' Dearbrook leaned forward in her chair. Zadie guessed she'd delivered this talking-to many times before.

'They are given enough to live on in return for demonstrating at least minimal motivation and the willingness to respond rationally to incentives. People who refuse to maintain contracts like the rest of us have to be forced to reciprocate. Those who decide not to waste their opportunities any more can enter Norm society through enterprise and hard work. Those who don't can remain as they are. Those who choose not to do even that evidently prefer to sacrifice their freedom and go to jail.'

'Where they no doubt have to pay for their own jail cells and jailers.'

'And why should the taxpayer fund their incarceration?'

'You...I...that's forced labour. Slavery!'

Jake was puzzled. Was this his sister?

'And that, girl, is Rad hyperbole. Jail is merely an extension of a market contract. Don't be dense! Someone chooses to disobey the rules. But why should anyone else be asked to fund that decision? If I decided to...bang my head violently against this table, why should you be required to pay for my healthcare? Therefore in jail you are put to work, yes. You have to be forced to work. After all, if you hadn't chosen to be lazy you wouldn't be there in the first place.'

'But those people we met weren't criminals. They were just down on their luck.'

'Being unable to maintain standard relationships of production, transfer and consumption is a sign of criminal inclinations. An unwillingness to play by the rules means you lack worth. Therefore those nozoomers you were talking to, illegally, were demonstrating they possess at least the rudiments of the correct motivation. That's why the taxpayer is not unhappy to supply a liveable income and opportunities for upward mobility. We're the ones who believe in opportunities. Unlike you Rads, who would make everyone equal to everyone else, despite the obvious fact that individuals are different from one another!'

'They are paid pennies. How is that a liveable income?'

'Low pay in return for low motivation and effort, I suppose.' She clapped her hands, almost joyfully. 'However, my motivation right now is very high!'

Zadie struggled to summarise what she thought she'd just heard. 'You mean...we have to pay you for interrogating us?!'

'Obviously! Why else would I be spending time on you? If you want me to sit here, debating social principles and values that you refuse to accept, that's fine with me. But shouldn't I be paid for it?'

'But we are strangers here.'

'So you keep claiming. Why should I care about your motivations for quizzing me in this way? So long as he pays up, the zoomer is always right. And it goes without saying you also have to reimburse the guards who arrested you. And for the price of the petrol it took to transport you here. And for the wear on the tyres; rent of the seats you are sitting on; the glasses of water you have all chosen to drink; and various other sundry items as well. You will receive itemised bills after you have seen the judge. Who will also need to be paid for his time and effort, obviously.'

Hah! Sweet!

Dearbrook glowered at the device Jake was still holding. 'You chose to do these things. Just as you choose to wear those layers of clownish clothing when every day inside the White Zones is a balmy

25°C. Why should anyone else have to pay for the decisions you freely make?'

'That's insane!' Zadie cried. 'First, we don't have any money.'

'Not believable; you can obviously afford this handheld computer. Still, we will find suitable work for you.'

'Second, who gets to decide the going rate?'

'Ahh, so now you see the virtue of a fair market price mechanism. Ironic!'

'Third! If we have to pay you for asking us questions don't you have to pay us for answering them?'

'Good one. Besides, you haven't answered them. No matter. Why should I care? In a free society you have that right, so long as you are prepared to accept the benefits and burdens which flow from your choices. If you don't, that's where we step in.'

'Sectex. Security technicians.'

'We give you back the freedoms you have irresponsibly chosen to relinquish. Only by enforcing the obligations of *each* individual can we secure the freedoms of *all*.'

'But why can't freedom mean the freedom to do anything?' asked Jake.

'Because that would be anarchy! A market society isn't the same as an anarchist society, boy. Markets need order, laws and structure. And therefore, it needs enforcers like us to wave decent zoomers away from a line they shouldn't cross and to discipline the undeserving ones who cross it anyway. Some extreme libertarians argue that people should do absolutely anything they want to, that even laws are oppressive. But most of us don't go that far. And you should be pleased, Zadie.

'We require Norms to take out decent minimal levels of health and accident insurance, unemployment insurance, education insurance (should your child's school go out of business), housing insurance and so on. A Nought is a person who cannot afford even these basics. But rather than leave them to sink or swim, as some libertarians would, we provide for them. There are charities which raise funds to offer shelter and the like. So you Rads should thank us. We are trying to integrate everyone into market society. Can we be blamed if not everyone wants to come?'

'Where does the state get off—'

'The state?' Dearbrook hooted. 'Oh my. You mean the TAC? Why, this company alone has an operating budget ten times bigger than the TAC's. The "state", if you prefer that archaic term, runs the army, the courts, the police force and renews compacts with the corporations who compete to run core services! Rads don't seriously think "the state" is capable of doing anything more than that, do you?! This must be what happens when you leave the BioWeb. Having no Bioweb Prescence makes you stupid.'

'Then the TAC...?'

'Issues contracts for almost all public services to the firm who can run it for the least cost. It also amends the terms of the Post-Democracy Constitution.'

Zadie was now fishing for the keyword, eager to be away from this frightful woman.

'Then what about political parties interested in running things differently?'

'They're tiny and, not being CEOs, can't run for election. But they are free to try and persuade people of their case – I'm talking to you, aren't I? – but few Norms are interested. We believe in the freedom to be idiotic, so long as it doesn't interfere with business. If a society isn't run efficiently then it won't run at all. The tax rate rose above 5% several years ago and tens of millions clicked a petition to complain.'

'5%?' Zadie had never paid tax, but wasn't that percentage awfully low?

'I know, I know. Still shockingly high.' Interrogator Dearbrook stood up, her knees cracking in sympathy with one another as her long legs uncoiled. 'Now, as much as I enjoy debating with Rads I have other tasks to perform. You are to be transported to a judge, re-netted into the BioWeb and then you can start to repay us for our patience towards you. I suggest we get going. Time is money; your money!'

They were on their way again, walking between guards down a long corridor.

'Cramps, this has got me nervous,' Zadie mumbled underneath her breath. 'It's *too* real! There is no computer in the world that could make all this seem so real. Can't we pause this program and come back to it another time?'

Cramps saw that his granddaughter was genuinely worried. He hadn't wanted this, of course. Perhaps they could try and jump back already. *If* Virgil would let himself be reprogrammed, that is...

'Jake, can you—'

Jake nodded furtively and, ever so slowly, ever so quietly, lifted Virgil to his mouth and muttered.

'Computer, pause holo-program.'

WHAAAT??? WHY IS EVERYONE WHISPERING? DID I MISS THE BIT WHERE WE ALL DECIDED TO TALK LIKE HANNIBAL LECTER?

'Christ, Virgil, are you here to help or what?'

Take a look around, your royal doughiness. No one cares. You're the customers after all.

Virgil was right. Neither the interrogator nor their guards seemed worried by their desire to escape.

'Your toy is quite correct...'

The next person who calls me a toy...

'Perhaps you keep thinking of us as the bad guys here. We are not. We only want to help. You are the ones who have somehow wiped your I.I. codes, were detected in a restricted area and seem to imagine you don't have to reimburse anyone for the trouble you have caused.' Their interrogator sighed and stopped. The rest of the group stopped behind her. 'I am so puzzled by minorities like you that we may even do this free of charge. Only kidding, guys,' she said over her shoulder to the guards. 'Look at this. We are higher up than even most Norms get to go.'

Dearbrook touched a faintly glowing panel in the wall. Jake goggled. They all did. The wall was no longer a wall.

CHAPTER FOUR

The corridor was now an observation platform. Much of the outer wall had dissolved into a window, though not one made of glass. The floor nearest the edge of what had become a dizzying abyss shimmered. They were perched atop one of the tallest buildings in the city, with a wide view of the metropolis below. The clouds seemed to be only a few metres above their heads. Jake moved close to the edge. Zadie's heart swelled inside her throat, kidnapping her voice. Some kind of magnetic field pushed Jake away the closer he got to the edge, keeping them all safe from whatever layer of the stratosphere they were now suspended against. The few glimpses he'd snatched earlier had not prepared him for this.

Unlike the gloom they'd experienced before, the air here was crisp and he saw much of the city as it spooled away for dozens of miles around them. No countryside was even distantly visible. Hundreds of skyscrapers lanced upwards. Pillars of glass, vertical icefalls of light, gleaming and unreadable, reflecting one another, turned the city into a towering hall of dark mirrors. The streets he could see, immediately below, contained hardly any pedestrians but plenty of tiny vehicles streaming in perfect, ordered lines as though directed by some invisible conductor.

The ground traffic outnumbered the hovercars that soared above, but there they were! Darting, scurrying, sweeping among the columns and structures, they were squat and compact two-seater affairs. Jake's insides tingled. He would have given anything to be able to fly one. Above the hovercars, strips of digital images and text floated in mid-air. Jake could read news banners flowing among what looked like advertisements for products he'd not heard of. The scripts were not stationary but unfurled sedately among the city's spires, like electronic ribbons adorning its shoulders. Walkways connected many of the buildings. Could you spend your entire life above ground, he wondered?

There were few patches of green but contained within the small parks were numerous statues and monuments. The city's celebration of itself. Far off a...what was it?...a sculpture, it had to be a kilometre high! A möbius band, a figure eight, soared into the heavens, arcing gracefully in a curve hundreds of feet long and looping around in its descent towards the earth again. It seemed to be suspended on nothing.

The city was alive, powering the people who bustled within its energy lanes. It chorused a restless, relentless hymn of affluence, power, extravagance and ambition.

'It's...it's amazing,' Jake spluttered.

Dearbrook softened. 'I wish I could see this view for the first time again. You see, Zadie, even those on middle incomes live lives of opulence unparalleled in history. Those on lower incomes aspire for better lives. And the underground apartment blocks go down hundreds of metres, and are quite liveable I'm told. The Infinity,' she gestured at the figure eight, 'have you ever seen it from this high up? Our proudest symbol, standing for infinite growth, infinite riches and infinite possibility. Multiple dimensions formed out of one, symbolising how everything good flows from unregulated freedom of choice. Is this really what you Rads want to overthrow?'

Zadie was unnerved. She too was awed by the sight before her and her arguments from a short while ago now felt like a precocious child's performance before indulgent adults who possessed secrets she could never understand. Then she spotted one or two familiar landmarks and a twisting, familiar river. Was this a futuristic vision of London? She'd have to ask Cramps.

'What's that?' Jake was pointing at the sky. The air, he only now noticed, was an orangey-blue. It was nebulous but the crown of the city was shimmering and bubbling.

'The Ezone layer. Hardly visible from ground-level, I suppose. We long ago realised that growth can never be entirely waste-free. Just as our bodies shed and excrete so the social body has to store its inevitable waste somewhere. Obviously, it can't be where people work and live.'

'You mean,' Zadie pursued. 'you export your pollution outside this Ezone in order to keep things nice and clean inside?'

'Crude but yes.'

'And where we were arrested. Was that outside the Ezone?'

'My, no. You'd be fatally diseased by now. You were just inside the Grey Districts which are between here and the Black Districts. No offence, children. That's another reason why we can't allow the Noughts to wander where they will. We're looking after their interests, see? As it is, we'll still have to detox you when we re-net you into the BioWeb.'

'So our health has been affected?' asked Zadie. 'And what about the Noughts? Are they part of the waste that needs to be disposed of too? What does it do to them to be in the Grey Districts all the time?'

'Gives them an incentive to mend their ways, I would hope.'

'But if their health suffers then what about equal opportunities?'

'Who said anything about equality? You're confusing equality with fairness, girl. Of course, people don't have equal chances in life. How could they? We're all so different. Do you think that the person who wants to learn how to paint should have an equal chance to learn compared to the person who is naturally gifted? Should the rest of us be required to fund his art lessons? Where would that end? What would the taxpayer *not* be asked to fund if that were the case? No. Instead, we don't prevent people from learning how to paint and in a system like this...' once again, Interrogator Dearbrook swept her arm to encompass the view before them, '...if they work hard they can earn a good income and choose to spend it on whatever they wish.

'Perhaps this was a bad example on my part. Painting is a specialised talent and skill. But to prosper in our society you don't need anything similar. You just need a willingness to work and not be a burden to others. Unless, I suppose, relatives or charities or someone decides to subsidise you. If so, that's a matter for them but hardly the basis for a political philosophy!'

'But you didn't answer my question about the health of the Noughts,' insisted Zadie. 'We saw children out there. If they grow up in that environment, if their parents can't provide very much for them, then where's the justice? You're just a victim of circumstance.'

'My granddaughter is surely right!' Cramps chipped in, 'You keep emphasising rationality and choice. But my freedoms end as soon as someone with more power than me appears on the scene and acts in a way that constrains my choice. How much social mobility is there here? I'll bet that if you are a Nought then so were your parents and so were their parents before them. If that's true what you have is not a system based upon choice, but one based upon class!'

'Nonsense! Look, two points. First, there is *always* choice. I may not be able to stretch out my hand and touch the moon *but I am free* so long as no one is preventing me from stretching out my hand. I may be completely unrealistic about what I can accomplish, but that doesn't mean my act is not a free one. Perhaps it is more difficult for the Noughts to become well-off – perhaps they will never touch the moon – but there is no one actually constraining them from trying.'

'Second point—'

Jake almost shouted the words. 'Even the Noughts gain from all this wealth. Isn't that right?' He had his back to them, still staring out into the wonderland below.

'That's exactly right, Jake. Well done! The Noughts still gain despite their laziness and poor choices. The affluence the rest of us generate reaches them eventually. Inequality creates wealth and incentives. People compete against one another to raise their skills and so improve their earning potential. Employers compete to attract the best workers. This happens at the bottom of society, as well as the top. And, besides, few people actually starve.'

'Except they get left behind.' Zadie insisted. 'You even call them "Noughts"! What is that? No identity? Not worth bothering about?'

Dearbrook checked her watch. 'You are racking up quite a bill, you know. I suppose you want to blame that on the rich as well! Follow me,' she sighed. 'I'll show you a group of low-income individuals who find your ideas as bizarre as I do!'

As everyone moved away the energy field solidified behind them. 'Crap!' murmured Jake. The wall was a wall again.

They were in a large classroom. Most of the seats were taken by children of different ages, though at the back Zadie noticed some young adults too. In the hallways outside she had observed advertisements for dozens of products stapled to the walls. Commercials blared from the large wafer-thin TVs mounted periodically along the ceiling. Everywhere she looked someone was trying to sell her something. One logo predominated.

Their journey had been a frosty one ('You can't have flying cars *and* economic equality, Zadie!'). Even Virgil had lapsed into a huffy silence. Yet he was still 'on'. The little icons and dashes still flickered across his screen. Would a keyword free them from this...Zadie didn't know what to call it. She'd been overwhelmed, they all had, by the city which now enveloped them at street-level, which seduced them with its relentless logic and impersonal wealth. From the obscenely large car they'd been closely escorted to Zadie had seen further evidence of unbelievable prosperity.

It wasn't hidden. Instead, the inhabitants seemed to covet the gaze of others. Townhouses were painted with a substance that shifted

colours across the spectrum as they passed; swirling, decorative
materials that morphed constantly into different shapes; sim-courts
that could be reprogrammed to accommodate dozens of sports;
roof-top gardens with tall glass-sided swimming pools, like enormous tumblers, that people could see into from the street. Endless
boutiques and emporia. And, everywhere, adverts and more adverts
in every flashing blinding blinking colour and graphic imaginable
crying 'Here, this is all you've ever wanted, right here. Take it!'

It *was* remarkable.

But wasn't the price too high? Wouldn't it be worth having less
wealth in one place so long as it could be spread around more evenly?
Nor could Zadie see many public spaces. Some very large private
gardens, yes, but few parks. Marketplaces and malls, but few plazas
or public squares. No one just lounging and enjoying the day. People
rushing, but no one strolling.

Yet there was no prejudice here, Dearbrook claimed. If they wanted
something then someone would sell it to them. Why reduce profits
by discriminating against potential customers and good employees?
There was sexual and religious equality. And ethnic equality, they
were patronisingly reassured. Jake had bristled at that. Want to paint
your face green and wear a tutu? Fine! Be who you want to be. Invent
yourself! You can conquer desire by endlessly fulfilling it!

Zadie frowned, churning the arguments over in her head,
becoming more bewildered as she did so. Was arguing constantly like
this making it harder to find the keyword or easier?

'This is a charity-funded Technical College,' Dearbrook informed
them. 'As you know, children from low-income backgrounds can be
educated here. Normally, visitors are not allowed in to gawp but the
director is a friend and she is always willing to be entertained by Rads
like yourselves. So, here you are. Question them; they're on a break.
Are these people oppressed and dissatisfied? You tell me.'

Zadie wondered what this would prove. Maybe the pupils here
were as happy as bunnies. Maybe that meant Zadie was wrong to be
sceptical. Or maybe any happiness was just compensation. Another
sign of their oppression.

Well, she would at least try. Zadie cautiously approached a sandy-
haired boy, perhaps fifteen years old, standing at one side of the
classroom. What's he going to charge me for talking to him, she
wondered bitterly? And indeed, smiling broadly, the lad handed her
a menu of items:

- asking teacher a question (10 cents)
- rent of seat for lesson (25 cents)
- charge for disrupting lesson with inappropriate behaviour (50 cents)
- cost of having assignments marked ($10 per item)
- charge for notification of marks ($2 per item)
- stress counselling ($2.50 per hour)
- bathroom break
    non-flush (30 cents)
    flush (75 cents)

On and on it went. Oh Lord, she thought. However, the young man was grinning at her.

'You look horrified!' he chuckled. 'Don't worry, you can talk to me for free.' He leaned towards her, a mock conspirator. 'Only don't tell the teachers I said that!'

He was flirting, trying to impress her. *Her*, the older woman! Zadie couldn't help but grin back. She half crouched, half knelt beside him, making sure he could only see her better profile.

'There, that smile will buy you more minutes! I'm Eric.'

'Zadie,' she replied. 'Do you like this place Eric?'

'Sure. It's helping me to get on.'

'Get on?'

'Me and everyone else I suppose.'

'I'm not sure what you mean by "get on".' She smiled again. 'Could you explain? Make me feel less stupid?'

'I mean...I don't come from a rich background, none of us do. My parents and I have been Noughts time to time but always managed to work our way back up. They managed to get me in here for a term and now I receive a scholarship from these guys.'

He held up a textbook. It proudly displayed the same logo that adorned the school's walls and ceilings. It's on the spine, the front cover, the back cover and probably everywhere inside, Zadie reflected. EduSols. The Norms had their own slang too, it seemed.

'Once I graduate I only have to work for them for seven years to repay the scholarship. I'm working like a monster to make sure that I never become a Nought again and if I can help my folks too, I will.'

'You don't use the Nought slang?'

Eric narrowed his eyes. 'No,' he said softly, 'I did once but it's a habit I forced myself to break.'

'Sorry, I didn't mean to embar— Do you think that it's all down to choice? That the Noughts like being where they are and so don't deserve our sympathy?'

'I'm not sure. I'm still learning.' Eric lowered his voice even further. 'I don't want to say that people choose *everything* about their lives. But a lot of it is choice, isn't it? My parents have been Noughts but managed to haul themselves back up. If they can do it, why can't others? I'm thinking perhaps what we find ourselves born with is a matter of luck but we have to respond as best we can, don't we? If we can't make a living for ourselves then why expect other people to do it for us?'

'But how many of the Noughts agree with that? Isn't there anger? About those with all the economic and political power? Don't the Noughts want to fight against that?'

He frowned. 'You're teasing me. Sure there are some Rad factions but they can't campaign in the Grey Districts. Isn't that why you're under arrest? You belong to them, don't you?'

'Not quite.' Eric didn't appear convinced. 'What are you studying?' Zadie asked to change the conversation.

'Social Analysis 101. Here.' He slid over the textbook and flicked through a few pages. Zadie had been right. The logo was on every page. Twice!

Eric started reciting. 'If some people want to buy goods at a certain price and others are prepared to sell them those goods at that price then we should let them get on with it without interference. Prices will fall to their market clearing rate, set by the level of demand relative to supply, and profits will be both consumed and reinvested. Either way, economic activity satisfies needs and drives the next cycle of production and consumption.' Eric looked pleased with himself and was obviously awaiting a compliment or two.

Zadie liked him. She didn't want to hurt him. But he'd rattled off those lines as if he'd rehearsed them. Perhaps she could simply get him to recite something else?

'That's great, Eric. I'll bet you're a quick learner. What about different views though? What does the course you're doing say about those?'

He looked unsure of himself now. Hell! She was upsetting him. 'Well it does mention them, sure. There was Marx. We did him yesterday. He was wrong about what makes an object worth something and so wrong about everything else.'

'Is that what the book says? What about you? What do you think?'

'Me?' he looked frustrated. 'What can I say about any of this? These people are smart. If this was a science book and it said the sun was at the centre of the solar system would you expect me to come up with an argument to say it isn't?'

Eric's frustration was upsetting him. God! Zadie hated herself sometimes. The lad was just trying to improve himself and impress her. What was wrong with that? Why couldn't she ever just accept people as they were? She tried smiling again but the magic had worn off. Great, Zades, you repulse men. Time to buy some cats and a rocking chair, yes?

'OK, thanks again Eric. I really am impressed. Hope the rest of your learning goes well.'

'Well, Zadie, have we convinced you?' Everyone drifted back out into the corridor and towards the building's main door. Jake's mocking grin told her he'd witnessed her failure with Eric. 'Oh dear, Flirty Gerty strikes out again.' Embarrassed, Zadie wanted to let rip.

'Be real!' she spat at Dearbrook, 'They have very few opportunities and you are only teaching them one way of looking at the world. Does EduSols care about people or about profits? How can differences of opinion exist in an atmosphere like that?'

They were almost back at the vehicle before Dearbrook turned to her. 'Zadie, let me ask you this—' But the question never came. The world froze.

'You're here to rescue us?' Zadie asked.

Shortly after leaving the college their escort had been paralysed, literally, with some kind of subliminal mental detonation. They had been partially stunned as well and so had felt groggy for several minutes. As their rescue van pulled away they could see Interrogator Dearbrook still striding in mid-question. Hypnotised. Immobile.

They sank back into their seats.

'It's Aon! The women from the queue.' Zadie cried when fully herself again. She hugged Aon as if the older woman was a big sister. Her rescuer. To her delight, Aon returned the hug. 'I don't think they mean us harm.'

The thin-lipped glare being directed at her in the rear-view mirror made Zadie think twice about this. Kayne was driving wildly. Was he still suspicious about them? Or was he jealous of the hug he'd just witnessed?

'Are the three of you here to help us?' Aon had to shout over the screeching tyres.

'You belong to the Rads, yes?'

'Yes.'

Great, they want you to lead a revolution and create a better society for them. All before teatime.

'But how can we possibly help?' asked Zadie.

'Sod this,' Jake interrupted. 'Time to find the keyword and get the Elmer Fudd out of here. If only my sodding phone was working we could Google the answer.'

'They need our help, though. We can't just abandon them.'

'Zades, I say this with all the feeling a brother can have for his sister. WE'RE INSIDE A HOLOGRAM, YOU MORON!'

Zadie was abashed. What alternative was there? She hated to leave Aon, though. Not with that needy, desperately hopeful look on her face.

Cramps entered a code onto Virgil's screen.

'What do you think?' said Jake. 'It's got to be a word, right Virgil? Something related to what we have seen today.'

You got it.

'Ok. What about "choice"? They kept going on about choice, right?' As Zadie and Cramps nodded, Jake entered the word onto Virgil's keypad. Nothing happened.

Oops, you got it wrong. BIG surprise, I can tell you.

'Bugger! Let's try "rights". Rights to property and all that.'

Nothing.

Their rescuers looked on this with impatient bemusement.

'Markets,' suggested Zadie. Nothing.

Freedom.

Individualism.

Duty.

Nothing, nothing, nothing.

'Oh, holy crap.'

Listen birdbrains! All of these could be right but I've been programmed to respond to only one keyword. What's the common denominator?

Jake and Zadie thought about it for a moment. Wealth? Nothing. 'Crap!'

Cramps made a suggestion. 'If you buy something from a shop and it has a warranty, what kind of relationship is that?'

At last! An animal who is 0.000036% as smart as me!

'Got it,' shouted Jake, 'remember her mentioning it too.'

'What is it?' Zadie demanded.

But before he could answer Jake had entered the word and the world began, once more, to dissolve around them. Aon, Kayne, the van, all fractured into digital shards. Sparks and motes flew into and around them. Then the fragments also fractured, again and again, over and over, until they were centred in a tornado of whirling pixels. The cyclone spun ever faster.

Help, I'm gonna be sick!

Jake held Virgil upside down and away from his shoes. 'What are you doing?' hollered Zadie into the maelstrom. 'A machine can't vomit.'

'Sod it, I'm not taking any chances.'

'What was the keyword?'

'Contract.'

She thought about this. Damn him! Time to be gracious, Zades. 'Ah! You only got that because you fell in love with the place, you little fascist.'

Before it disappeared for good Zadie shouted a few remaining words into the binary hurricane, to where Aon had been. 'Thank the rest of the Noughts for us!'

CHAPTER FIVE

They were wedged inside a very small toilet.

Ugghh!

Jake found himself holding Virgil above a toilet bowl.

Why do humans have to leak so much? You're like walking garbage disposal units.

'The kind of loo you get on an old-fashioned train,' Cramps said. 'Not moving though.'

Someone knocked on the door. 'Camarade?'

'If you kids don't mind...' Cramps intimated.

'Oh granddad!'

'Sweetheart, remember you said that when your bladder is 25,000 days old. If we're on a train, please go and find us some seats.'

Zadie frowned. 'I have about a zillion questions for you, you know.'

'And if you want to ask them while you've still got dry shoes I suggest you follow your brother!'

Toilet? Zadie frowned as the door clicked shut and they squeezed passed a startled woman. How can he be going to the toilet if we are still in his closet?! She didn't like where that thought might lead and pushed it away.

As they awaited their grandfather Zadie and Jake saw that the train had obviously been assembled by a mischievous child, gluing together parts from other toys and other train sets. The Victorian lace curtains bowed gracefully to the Dickensian coat-stands and mahogany luggage racks, who were wary of, but still elegantly charming towards, the lush Edwardian railings and faded carpeting. These, in turn, were positively hostile to the hard, upright, aluminium chairs, the mottled brown metal walls and the ornate brass clock with electronic hands and numerals.

The train seemed to have detoured into the twentieth century, decided it was better off returning to the nineteenth and then become hopelessly lost. It was all the wood-burning furnace in the carriage's central square could do to keep the peace! Thankfully, on such a warm day, it was off. The passengers, about forty in all, were not sitting in rows but faced inwards towards the furnace, with the cramped seats running in a square around the inner surface of the carriage. They could see and be seen by everyone else. Their clothing was peculiar too. Bright, even lurid, colours and straight, simple lines. Not much jewellery. Woollen slacks. Woollen slacks? And sandals. Lots of sandals.

And mutton-chop whiskers! One jowly elder had grey mutton chops the size of Jake's hand, like dead ferrets glued to the side of his cheeks!

Mutton-chops was grinning and casting sidelong glances. Others too. Zadie could feel people peeking at them surreptitiously, not wanting to be rude.

Through the windows opposite Jake spotted what looked like part of a station wall through a drift of steam. A large, flamboyant clock peeked through the mist. By comparing it to the nearby brass clock Jake noted that it was broken. What conked out nightmare *was* this? Were they on a steam train? FIN, a station sign announced. Hope that's not ominous, he thought.

'Looks like we made it out of prison,' mused Cramps, sitting down with a renewed glow in his cheeks. 'Virgil, are you still with us?'

Do I look like I've sprouted legs, wings or any other appendages I could use to get the poop away from you beanheads?

'How reassuring. Hmmm? What's that...?'

Zadie was trying hard not to be overheard. Mutton-chops was taking an interest in them. 'Am I crazy or what?' Cramps followed his granddaughter's nod-wink-shrug across to a woman immersed in her thin, ink-smudged newspaper. 'Social Wellbeing Rises for 36th Consecutive Year', read the headline. Only part of her face was visible, but... The hair was tidy and recently washed, the makeup was smart and the suit seemed new but was it?, yes, indeed...Aon!

Zadie had been surprised but what made her uncomfortable now was the look of puzzled alarm on her grandfather's face. No way had he been expecting this.

'So what?' said Jake. 'I'll help you expand the software later, alright? Eh?' He nudged his grandfather. 'Is that alright? And look. My watch says it's almost 2 but that clock says it's 11. Isn't that the time we entered the holo-room? Is that right Cramps? Will it be 11 a.m. in every level?'

Zadie also looked at her watch. 2 p.m. Cramps had not replied to his grandson. He was still gazing uneasily at the Aon lookalike.

'Should we get off this train or stay on?' she quizzed him.

'Wouldn't be surprised if we ran into a few celebs too,' Jake exclaimed, 'eh, Zades?'

'Oh, be quiet!!' Zadie's exclamation sank the carriage into a shocked silence. Heads craned around. Foreheads cringed. She suddenly felt again like the earlier five-year-old version of herself who'd been caught weeing in the school playground's sandpit.

Cramps composed himself and said, *sotto voce*, 'I suggest we go with the flow, just as we did last time. Despite a few bumps and bruises we came through the first environment okay and it is all kind of exhilarating, isn't it?' He took Virgil from Jake, tapped the keyboard and examined the screen.

'Aren't we due some food soon, though?' Jake said, accepting Virgil back. 'Lunchtime's come and gone. What about it, Virge?'

Do I look like an underpaid waiter with his snotty thumb in your soup? Chew your hair.

Just then a tin voice rattled over the intercom. 'Fraternals! Attention, fraternals! Prepare for departure. We will arrive at the Finland Estate in approximately thirty minutes. Salute!'

From their left someone started nervously reciting a brash if discordant song. Someone drunk this early in the day?! Then to Zadie's dismay this was taken up by everyone else, the volume rising into a raucous din. Within seconds they were sitting, embarrassed and conspicuously mute, amid a communal orbit of chanting, warbling, tapping feet and swaying, rhythmic handholding. Great! Zadie hated sing-alongs. Of all the things she hated this was one of her favourites. Her brother and grandfather were also at a loss. Should they mouth some words just for show? Whistle?

Then she noticed that one of the voices, managing to get practically every note deliberately out of key, was Virgil's.

> *We plough the soil of foreign lands,*
> *And grasp the hail of strangers' hands,*
> *For as we toil we must implore,*
> *No one will be a stranger more!*
> *The earth now free from human greed,*
> *As we are free from rich man's need,*
> *There are no limits to endure,*

No one will be a stranger more!
        History has begun at last,
One all as one, lament is past
Into the future we will soar,
No one will be a stranger more!

Then the same verses just repeated. Five more times!

Ahh, the old ones never fade. Doesn't it bring a tear to your LCDs? You didn't join in, you mumps.

And with that the train chugged forward and they were off.

This couldn't be right. Was there something wrong with the tracks? The carriage was rising a foot or two...falling...then rising again, then....Outside the countryside undulated up and down as if they were on a stiff ocean and the fields and trees were solid, inflexible waves. It was as if their mischievous child-engineer had gone rapidly insane, laying the tracks across a series of regularly spaced hillocks.

What the sweet baby hip-hop is going on? You know my circuits don't have the stomach for this kind of thing!

Mutton-chops now leaned across, aiming a yellow-toothed smile at Cramps. 'Your grandchildren? Their first rail journey?'

'Er, yes,' Cramps replied.

'Ahh, such excitement!' He doffed his cap. 'My name is Williams.' He pointed at Virgil. 'That device—'

Cramps headed the awkward question off. 'This Finland Estate...'

As the elderly men sank into conversation Zadie spotted a magazine rack against the nearest wall. Balancing very carefully, learning how to roll her feet with the train's fantastical undulation, she staggered across, grabbed a large thin book and tried to get a closer look at the woman buried in her newspaper. Drat! It might be Aon and it might not. Should she say something?

Plonking herself back next to Jake, who was once again staring forlornly into his dead phone, she looked at the book's cover. *A Child's History of the Revolution* by Finlay Fugson. Good. This would give them some quick information about the kind of society they were now in. She dug her brother in the ribs, indicating that he might want to read along. He sighed but nodded. Zadie opened the book.

Let me see too!

The paper was stiff and the printing was in large type. On the left-hand pages some quite abstract drawings were presumably meant to illustrate the story. Jake planted his chin on her shoulder the way he used to do when they'd read Philip Pullman together. Zadie tingled as warm memories gathered in her mind, ruined only occasionally by her brother's fake snores.

Virgil started humming the revolutionary song to himself. At Zadie's urging Jake muffled the sound with his hand.

Forget the actual history for now. She turned to the chapter entitled 'Please Explain'.

'It is much easier to explain why history develops than our pre-revolutionary sisters and brothers imagined,' they read. 'Humans are labourers. We leave our mark on the world around us. We act upon the materials that nature makes available to us. But we labour together, as common members of a species. We are therefore *social* beings. Nature becoming conscious of itself. The society we live in is in large part shaped by the tools available to us. During the earliest, primitive stages of human association we had only basic instruments – rudimentary axes and shovels, etc. Because we couldn't do very much with such tools we had to spend all our time in the business of survival. That's why the stone, bronze and iron ages lasted for such a long time. Technological innovation grew very slowly.'

Goody, thought Zadie. Standard Marxism. Did this last term.

On the left page a palm with eight thumbs presumably illustrated the slowness of history. She turned over.

'As our tools and skills – known as "labour power" – gradually grew more sophisticated the wealth created was not distributed evenly. Those who, because of inheritance, violence, theft or sheer luck, occupied positions of power were able to control that wealth and oppress and exploit those who lacked such power. They were class societies. Those who had property used it to accumulate more by ensuring that those who had no or little property were able to accumulate none. As we extracted more from the earth we became better able to convert natural materials into items we could use and trade with one another. We created wealth! But the powerful, who controlled the rules, laws and institutions, threatened violence against those who would challenge them and thus grabbed most of this wealth for themselves. So although wealth is created by everyone, collectively, it was appropriated by just a few.'

A broken pyramid symbolised social inequality. Next page.

'This couldn't go on indefinitely. The dispossessed began to notice the gap between the amount of wealth their society had and the extent to which it was not distributed evenly among all of that wealth's producers. They became dissatisfied, agitated and organised for change, and eventually overthrew the system of unequal property which was oppressing them. Unfortunately, for most of human history this only led to new forms of inequality and exploitation.'

Some destitute-looking farmers walking upside down, their feet in the air.

'By the nineteenth century the latest manifestation of this was capitalism, the like of which had never been seen before due to its capacity to create incredible affluence. The industrial revolution saw the creation of machines able to extract massive amounts of material from nature and able to convert those materials efficiently into lots of goods that people would want to possess and exchange with one another. Those who owned these machines were also able to own those who had no choice but to work on them. The proletariat, in other words. This capacity to produce wealth is what we call capital and so those who owned machines and factories were capitalists. Very quickly, capitalists overtook and replaced aristocracies and the landed gentry as the real power in society.'

Top hats. Miserable children were being thrown into it one while, from the other, champagne bottles were falling out and being caught by a bunch of partying, self-congratulatory, dead-eyed hoorays.

'But those they exploited became aware of how unfair this all was; of how everyone could live a comfortable life, a life without self-ishness, competition and aggressive rivalry, if the wealth was shared around. The capitalists resisted, of course. Because of their economic power they were able to control the state. The police, the courts, the army, basically did whatever the capitalists ordered them to. And because they owned the media and because the churches were greedy and eager to serve the powerful, capitalists tried to turn the class of the exploited proletariat against itself. Some deluded workers argued that there was no need to overthrow the system. That trade unions and political parties could help to distribute affluence more fairly without having to abandon capitalism and its ability to create abundant wealth. Others argued that God, the "Arch-Capitalist", had ordained that this life is less important than the next, so that the poor and oppressed would be rewarded in heaven.'

A politician in bed with a monarch, a soldier and a policeman, with what looked a crozier and a mace poking out the bottom of the covers.

Ahhh-haa-haaaahh-haaa-ha-ha. Priceless.

Jake had been examining Virgil's screen and his cackling had attracted attention.

'However, these voices did not prevail. As other chapters relate, capitalism was vanquished over eighty years ago. The worldwide conflagration lasted a decade or so and those who resisted change were either converted or eliminated.'

And that was the end of the chapter. The final picture was of a flag waving in the breeze. On the cloth, two hands were grasping one another by the wrists.

'Hang on,' said Jake. What was it that Interrogator Dearbrook had said earlier? 'None of this makes sense!'

'You weren't even reading!' But Zadie had to admit she was sceptical too. Was this any better than that dreadful EduSols textbook?

Williams overheard this. 'What's the problem, my young friend?'

Jake had been reluctantly impressed by his normally quiet sister's passion. Can't let that go, can I? 'Aren't people basically self-interested? Don't they desire power and wealth for themselves?'

'No.'

'No? Why not?'

Relishing the challenge of educating young minds, Williams slid onto the floor, crossed his legs and stared at them intently. Some of the other passengers leaned in, listening. Jake squirmed, feeling he'd suddenly wandered into a church and now couldn't back out again.

'Because as they organised the workers realised something that none of the exploited classes in previous societies were able to realise, that real wealth comes from sharing and cooperating with others. Previous exploitations happened under conditions of scarcity. Those who rebelled wanted to control rather than put an end to a system *of* control. But industrial workers saw that capitalism had solved the problem of scarcity. There was now enough to go around so no need to replace one class of oppressors with another.

'It is true that during and immediately after the revolutions we had to consolidate progress by centralising power upon the state. You'll remember that we call this period one of "socialism". After all, capitalists didn't disappear all at once and they worked to reverse the gains of the revolution. We therefore had to control the institutions of the state in order to turn them to other purposes. But this was done and the government departments who organised everything during this period of transition began to abolish themselves. The state itself began to wither away, the last one disappearing almost forty years ago now. What we are left with is a classless society of self-organising, democratic, common ownership. Communism!'

Jake now knew what a fly must feel like stuck in a web. Everyone was looking at him expectantly, even Cramps. Message to brain. Just keep bloody quiet in future or it's all over between you and me. Got it?

He shook his head. 'I just find this goody-two-shoes story difficult to accept. What about human nature? What about greed? Everyone wants different things.'

'Indeed, history shows that humans can do terrible things. But it mainly reveals that we are creatures of our environment. By over-coming our negative instincts and creating a just society we are able to keep those negativities at bay. So people still compete, for sure. Sports are popular, as you know. But why does competition have to be aggressive and demeaning to the losers?

'And we are all different, you're right. But why should that be inconsistent with communism? The idea that only competition and selfishness are the real expressions of individualism is a discredited one. In capitalist societies people had to spend most of their lives in pointless jobs, obeying the boss and the state, in order to earn an inadequate wage which they spent on consumer items they have been trained by the advertisement industry to think they really needed. Not much individualism there! Under communism people don't work for some faceless corporation, they work for each other! They apply their skills wherever they'll be useful, according to the goals they have in life. And they do so in and for a community of equally free women and men. What could be better?'

Applause rippled outwards from some of the nearby passengers.

Others were puzzling over the unmelodic noise coming from Virgil. Cramps pressed what Jake guessed must be the mute button and slipped Virgil into his grandson's jacket pocket. Zadie frowned at this. So what if a bunch of holograms noticed Virgil?

'Wait, wait, wait,' she pleaded. 'What has this got to do with the train kangarooing up and down? My backside is beginning to bruise.'

Williams chuckled. 'Sorry. Well, obviously we still need adminis-trative committees to run things. Those occupying offices can serve for no more than one year during every decade, so elections for each committee occur every year; that's 318 elections per year or one elec-tion every 27½ hours.'

'You...I mean we...hold elections every 27½ hours?' Cramps was blanching.

'Well, certainly,' Williams and some of the others were perplexed at the older man's question.

'So how can candidates be properly assessed at that speed?'

'Ahh, you're playing Capitalist's Advocate. Good teaching tech-nique. But everyone wants to do their best for others. Real democ-racy is not about just voting. It's more a constant debate about the health and direction of society.'

'And the train?' Zadie was finally learning how to rock from side to side.

'Sorry sorry! Shortly after the revolution the 1935 national transport committee believed that much of our infrastructure should embody revolutionary principles. This drew upon the science of praxis, or the notion that ideas and actions should be fused together in the service of social emancipation. So instead of centring the carriage's axle on the wheel's hub it is slightly off-centre. As we rise our motion symbolises the forces of production (the tools by which we convert nature into value) giving birth to production relations (the system of ownership). As we descend the relations give way to new forces that carry us further along the track of history. You see?'

'That's insane,' exclaimed Jake. 'You mean we are bouncing up and down for the good of the revolution?! Not exactly efficient.'

'Perhaps. But principles of democracy and solidarity are obviously more important. If you are obsessed with efficiency, as capitalists were, then people are treated as units of efficiency, like objects, and become alienated from themselves, their neighbours and their society. Besides, you can hardly claim we are inefficient. The first robot probe leaves for the moon only next month!'

Next month? Before Jake could pursue this thought the train slowed, the incessant bouncing ceased and the passengers around them began to rise and gather their coats and bags.

Before it was too late Zadie leaned across to their former rescuer as she was folding her newspaper. 'Excuse me. Have we met before?' But, no, there was a welcoming smile but no recognition from the Aon lookalike as they climbed down from the carriage.

'Ah, sod it,' Jake suggested, 'why don't we blow out of here already?'

The several hundred people who had descended from the other carriages were now wandering slowly up the gentle slope of a small hill, continuing to chat and chuckle. Their grandfather was among them, deep in conversation with Williams again and failing to notice his grandchildren left behind.

'What do you mean?'

'I mean, we've already had our lesson about Crazy Society Number 2 so why wait around? Let's guess the keyword and go on to the next level!'

'But don't you think all of this is just implausible?'

'Nahh! It's just wraparound, hyperreal, interactive TV. Every home'll have a room like this in twenty years. Cramps is just the John Yogi Bear of the twenty-first century.'

Zadie hestitated. 'Well...I suppose.'

Jake unmuted Virgil. 'Ok, "class", right?'
Wait a damn minute, Sherlock. It's too soon.
'What's that mean?'
I mean that you ain't heard everything about this place yet.
'Bollocks to that. So what?'
Because if it was just a question of guessing a word then you wouldn't learn anything, would you? According to my program I have to be satisfied not only that you have the keyword but that you understand what it means. You might not survive the later societies if you haven't understood the earlier ones fully. Or do you think just repeating what you hear others say is how you learn? No wonder you're so thick. Why else do you think I'm blocking your access to the Internet?
'Why you fuc—'
Zadie interrupted. 'What do you mean "survive the later societies"?'
Ahhhhh ahem. Cough. Cough. Nahh, forget I said anything! Yeth?
'What?' Jake asked.
Excuthe me. I thuffer from a lithp every tho often.
'Freak'
'Why are you kids dawdling?' Cramps shouted down at them. 'Sixty-seven, but I'm still fitter than you children!'
The path was now empty. Everyone else had vanished over the crest of the hill. At their grandfather's urging Jake and Zadie followed.
'I made up a hopefully plausible story about who we are. It seems this is some kind of delegation that is going to mediate a dispute that has arisen on this estate. An estate is apparently a combination of agricultural, industrial and residential units. Like the administrative committees we heard about it's run on a collective, democratic basis. The dispute has arisen because some members are demanding the freedom to engage in private enterprise and others are demanding religious freedom. Normally, disagreements like this could be sorted out internally but on this occasion things have become a bit fraught and this delegation is supposed to hear all sides and try and reach an accommodation. Interesting, nay?'
'Oh, yeah, sure.'
'Williams is going to accompany us. He used to be a teacher. You know the type...finds it difficult to shut up.'
'Cramps,' Zadie nudged him, 'how long is this going to take. Shouldn't we call Mum again?'
Her grandfather brushed this away. Though it was a warm day Zadie felt a sudden chill.
Before they disappeared over the ridge Jake glanced back at the train. It *was* steam-powered. Pudgy, ugly, misshapen and already

small in this vast, unruly landscape. How he already missed his flying cars!

The countryside had never been one of Zadie's favourite experiences either. Especially this one. There were no roads she could see, no charming stone walls, no hedgerows, no signposts, no tourist gift-shops with a coffee bar and waitress service. In fact, the wood they were stumbling through showed no sign of human occupation what-soever. The backs of the other passengers showed faintly through the dark trees ahead and Zadie worried they would be lost if they didn't keep up. Then she remembered what it seemed incredible she could forget.

She was in an enclosed space that seemed to stretch for miles in every direction. Before today Zadie had not thought it possible to experience claustrophobia and agoraphobia at the same time! Now she felt as if an infinite world was closing in on all sides around her. It was an effort just to keep the vertigo away. Yet here was the breeze on her face, the breath of overnight rain and the scent of flowers and grass. And, yes, thank you Virgil – globs of mud on her shoes. Even Jake was hopping from grass clump to grass clump.

Yet Zadie couldn't suppress her doubts. Wraparound, hyperreal, interactive TV? Maybe. It had to be holograms, though. The other possibilities nagging at the edge of her thoughts were too scary to contemplate.

CHAPTER SIX

After a few minutes, they emerged into a wide, shallow valley. Nestled within it, stretching more than a mile in every direction, were hundreds of buildings. The Finland Estate.

What immediately struck Zadie was the patchwork quilt look of the place. As on the train, different styles fidgeted alongside one another, as if an indecisive artist had layered several different landscapes onto the same canvas. Windmills beside towering, skeletal machines. Tractors and horse-drawn ploughs. Chimneys and sprawling, humming generators. Simple cottages and spiralling, skyborne architecture. Tree-wild thickets of dense vegetation and large, well tended civic clearings.

And it was clean. There was that faint haze above the rooftops which always indicated human presence, but no smokestacks, no belching black funnels, no sky-sawing pylons, no cars that she could see. Most of the structures hugged the ground. The buildings were scattered irregularly, with few straight lines, grids or corner blocks. There did not appear to be any paved roads, though several ran in and around a section of the town occupied by the larger constructs, with one road leading out of the estate and disappearing across the valley.

There were no parks as such – the entire place was a park – but in several glades the tree population had been thinned. Fountains. Tents. Children's swings. Stages. The tallest structure seemed to be an arena. There was nothing resembling a shopping mall, in fact nothing that even looked like a shop. Dotted around the valley were a series of farms, corrals, sties, barns and paddocks. The estate seemed to be moulded out of the land. Zadie had the impression of a playful giant scooping his gargantuan hands across the land, squeezing nature between his palms and hurling the results back into this valley to become these compact patches of greens and browns.

61

What a dump!

Williams had dawdled and now joined them on their ten-minute descent into the valley. He seemed more eager than ever to educate the youngsters.

He told them stories about his father's experiences in the pre- and post-revolutionary days and from this they inferred something of how this society functioned. The estates had been modelled on the garden city design that had been proposed over a century ago and were midway between old-style rural villages and industrial cities. This meant they were integrated as much as possible into the countryside.

Estates were not self-sufficient and so trade between them was fairly extensive. Those commodities an estate could not manufacture for itself were the subject of negotiation with other estates. If that didn't work then a request was lodged with what Williams called 'Centralised Stores', some kind of national warehouse system over-seen by one of the 318 administrative committees.

The rail network had been enlarged considerably, as had the water-ways. Since the emphasis was upon people living, Williams said, rather than on them ruining the earth in order to consume it, the big roads were reserved for essential transport, only some of which was motorised. (Zadie slipped 'motorway' into the conversation but it got no response, though 'London' did.) Why travel quickly when there was so much beauty you might miss along the way? If people wanted to visit other places they journeyed by train if the distance was long, otherwise they walked or bicycled. Air travel had been restricted as an anti-pollution measure, though now more and more of the new solar planes were being built. 'Some of them can hold over twenty passengers!'

A truly global consciousness was still developing but was already well advanced. The question 'what is good for me?' was inseparable from the question 'what is good for others?' and this applied across estates, across nations and now across the world.

'That's where we're headed,' Williams pointed at the arena's circular roof. 'But we have a bit of time. Why don't we look around?'

Bloody hippies, thought Jake, as he traipsed behind his grandfather, sister and newest tormentor. Where were they going to end up next? Hitler's bunker?

Their first stop was an 'industrial commons' where many of the estate's workshops and plants were located. Jake, so used to noise, much of it created by himself, was oppressed by how quiet it was. He felt edgy, as if a screen was blank and the remote control missing.

Some of what they could see were recognisable factory floors, with simple machines, but no assembly lines. Instead, there were lots of storage depots and conference rooms. Everywhere the pace was leisurely and the atmosphere relaxed, with men and women – in equal numbers, Zadie was pleased to note – often setting down what they were doing to chat with those around them. There were no admonishments. No angry foremen storming towards them. In fact, almost everywhere he looked Jake saw meetings and gatherings. Work here seemed to consist mainly of talking. Wasn't communism meant to imply Stalinist whips across your shoulders?

Since Cramps was pretending this was all familiar to him Williams was again speaking mainly to the youngsters. Who is this guy? moaned Jake to himself. I'm gonna have to tell Cramps that his education program sucks tomatoes. Teenagers just don't respond to this stuff! Why not some car chases for the lads and some, you know, furry animals and whatnot for the girls?

'Work has to involve some element of play,' Williams was saying. 'Why work when it isn't enjoyable? What you produce for yourself is surely more valuable than what others might produce for you. The best work involves craft and creativity. Like your, erm, interesting clothes! The more repetitive the task, the less time we ask people to commit themselves to it.'

But weren't some jobs so difficult that the people doing them deserved extra rewards, Jake asked? Doctors, for instance? Inwardly, he gave his brain another kicking for defying him.

Williams repeated that efficiency was less important than job satis-faction. If people were talented what reward did they need other than the pleasure of exercising their talents for the benefit of others?

'But some doctors are bound to be better than others,' Jake persisted. 'Don't some deserve to be paid more?'

Williams shrugged. 'How could money substitute for esteem? True freedom cannot exist outside a classless society.'

'So you can work whenever you want in whatever job you want?' Jake could suddenly see the advantage of this!

'No.'

Crap!

'Surely your grandfather and others will have discussed this with you?'

Cramps jumped in. 'We haven't really discussed economic matters, no.'

Williams continued. 'Well, each comrade owes one month's work per year so that the Centralised Stores are maintained. As well as replenishing the estates this also ensures that we can import what we need from other nations. Such trade is overseen by a global executive committee, the closest thing to a traditional state organisation that we still have.'

Jake tried to imagine what Dearbrook would say if she could see all this. If the products industry produced were decided according to the needs of the workers then were consumers receiving what *they* needed?

'Consumers? What are consumers?'

'The people who use the stuff you build or grow.'

'Ahh, you mean "emptors",' said Williams. 'But worker and emptor are merely the same person at different stages of the cycle of production and consumption. Therefore, the works' councils agree production targets which supply all the basic goods that people need.'

No wonder there were so many meetings.

'But,' Cramps suggested, intimating that he wanted to help Williams educate the kids, 'what if some jobs are so dull that no one wants to do them? Doesn't that mean some goods are not produced? And what if you end up manufacturing too much of the same thing?'

Williams winked, playing along. 'There are coordination subcommittees to reduce the possibility of that happening and weekly general meetings where such matters can come to light and be discussed.'

'That's a big coordination problem, though.'

'Perhaps. If we have too many goods then they can be stored until they are needed or traded with other estates.'

'This must mean that what you send to another estate is equivalent in value to what they send to you. How are prices set, then?'

Prices? This required another round of explanation. The monetary value of something. A rate of exchange. What that thing is worth to producers and emptors.

'You mean the labour-hours involved in its manufacture?'

'Not only that. What people are willing to pay for it.'

'Hmm! That's partly what we are here to discuss, of course. But many of us feel that the idea of exchange-value is archaic. Marx talked about the freedom to fish in the afternoon, remember? That people should receive according to their needs. To ask people to pay for their goods places a potential obstacle in the way of their receiving what they need to live a fulfilling life. If this estate needs 10,000 potatoes and can trade these with an estate that needs a spare tractor then why worry about whether their value is equivalent? The priority is to help your comrades and help them to help you.'

By now they were meandering through a residential part of the town, not that Jake saw much difference from the factories they'd left behind. There were no pavements, because there were no roads. No street-signs, no private gardens, no fences. The 'streets' were just the open spaces between irregularly spaced houses. These homes seemed to have been planted around the trees rather than vice versa. There were no window-fronts, no billboards. The 'shops' were large communal meeting places and dining halls that doubled as stockrooms. Their few signs made simple announcements. Furniture. Food. Clothes. Library. Occasionally, they saw larger clearings and thoroughfares in which fairs and carnivals were being held.

Who built this place? A drugged-up hippy with no taste?

Williams bristled. He obviously wanted to ask about Virgil but Cramps kept distracting him.

The tall lampposts seemed to be gaslit, though Jake was sure that a few of the bigger ones would be powered by electricity. Sometimes the grass had been cut and sometimes they had to wade through chaotic waist-high kingdoms of ferns and scrub. There were no motor vehicles other than some tractors, few engines of any description really, but lots of bicycles, wagons, buggies and wheelbarrows, as well as horses and even cows and goats wandering aimlessly about.

The people they passed were invariably smiling, bowing and greeting them with a friendly, clenched wave. But they were far from mindless drones. In fact they debated and argued with one another animatedly and endlessly, sitting at fountains, leaning in doorways. People gathered everywhere, the children too. Some played board games. Some, of course, were singing.

And many were using phones. Jake's eyes lit up at this. Mobile phones! These were easily the most advanced part of this society he'd spotted, though the phones were surely nowhere near as sophisticated as the model now clattering uselessly against his thigh. It seemed people used them for voting and for official broadcasts as well as for simple communication. 'In a democratic society,' they overheard someone say, 'what is more important than good communication? Scientists are slowly creating a Nomad system so that Transcomms can become even more interactive.'

An internet, perhaps? Jake nudged his grandfather. There! Not such a useless toy after all!

The furniture they could see was basic, the furnishings and deco-rations were often elaborate if amateurish – homemade rather than purchased. Jake noticed something else, that house interiors were remarkably open to view. There were no obvious locks, no doors in many cases. The dwellings seemed designed to present no barrier to social interaction, in the same way that it was possible to stroll freely through the wooded areas. But what if you wanted privacy, Jake wondered. Were you expected to do the dirty with your lady while a heifer drifted into your bedroom and mooed at you? He tried to imagine a diplomatic way of asking that question later. For now he tried again to pick holes in what Williams had been saying. Not because he wanted to impress his sister any more. More because the place irritated the bejesus out of him. What was to stop someone from doing work of little value and then going down to the shops and demanding the most expensive items?

'That doesn't happen,' Williams replied, patiently. 'Work is one means of fulfilling your potential. It was capitalism which first made it difficult for people to find satisfying jobs and then insisted that the unemployed were lazy and corrupt. You don't have to compel people to do what comes naturally to them. Besides, everything here is an object held in common for the good of all. To cheat others is to cheat yourself.'

'But do the criminals know that?'

Williams chuckled again. 'Crime was in many ways a protest against unjust circumstances. If there is no injustice then there is no need for crime. If you can have what you want then why would you need more of it than your neighbour?'

'Nobody just going a bit mental? No crimes of passion?'

'If you are talking of the family, then we are all one family. I may have stronger ties to kin but those don't have to exclude the ties I bear towards others. People consent to be together. If someone doesn't consent then being jealous about it will not win them over to you.'

Jake gave up, confirmed in his long-held view that intellectual discussion was too hard and about as enjoyable as pulling on nostril hair. The phones aside, this place was simply less impressive than the city they'd visited earlier. Sure, it had a laidback quality he appreciated but even their idea of leisure was a bit too sedate for Jake. There was no excitement or urgency. No luxuries. Frivolities, they called them. The shops they looked into were just provisioning depots that people visited when they needed to. If what you wanted was not available (if it had been 'underproduced') then you put your name down on a list and could reserve it. But from what Williams hinted, and here he was a bit less forthcoming, you could be on the list for months. Fine, except what if the item you needed was a winter coat for your child or new...well, new goddamn sandals?!

Could this sense of community, this happy-clappy feeling of belonging, ever compensate for a standard of living lower than the wonders he'd experienced just hours earlier? In his bones, Jake rejected the idea. It all seemed fairly medieval and pious. People here seemed to spend half their lives in meetings. Common ownership and democratic cooperation had to be extremely time-consuming. You might not want to pig out in front of a TV or computer your entire life, but it was great to do that from time to time wasn't it? The word 'computer' didn't register. However, their building-sized 'calcula-tive engines' did help the coordination committees match supply to demand. How bureaucratic and clumsy! Jake wondered what you could do here on your own initiative without having to worry about what others thought or wanted.

Just then bells reverberated across the valley. The people around them began to drift in large congregations towards the long rooftop that curved above the trees.

'Good, the meeting has been proclaimed.'

Williams set off, Cramps and Zadie following. Hell, Jake asked himself, when is Cramps going to pause all this and offer them some food? Sighing, he pursued the others towards the arena.

It had taken an hour for the tens of thousands to congregate in the tiers that surrounded three sides of a pitch, not much bigger than a tennis court, on which a speakers' platform had been constructed. They had rushed to the centre of the arena but twigged, too late, that this left most of the stage out of view above them.

Luckily, it turned out that Cramps had not only packed water in his bag but some ham sandwiches too. True, they looked like the ruins of a demolished building and contained no butter, no mustard...nothing but bread and thin ham. But since it had been so many hours since breakfast they swarmed on them like a feast. Zadie swapped one for the apple which a neighbour proffered. It, too, tasted delicious.

So how could a holographic apple taste like a real apple? To her dismay, Zadie thought she'd worked out what was really going on.

Williams had remained glued to them but he was sat on the far side of Cramps and their discussion was drowned in the noise of the densely-packed crowd. Virgil started to join in with one of the nearby songs but Jake, forgetting where the mute button was, quickly shoved him under his shirt to muffle the din. Zadie found herself looking at him enviously. For all his bluster, his who-cares attitude, Jake always seemed to belong to the space he occupied. Zadie sometimes feared she was trapped in someone else's version of her life.

Perhaps they could get out of here after this event. Both young-sters wanted to leave. Jake was still hungry, and now tired too. The novelty of this bloody educational program had long faded. Honestly, he'd have to pitch the giant insects idea to his granddad again. Zadie, meanwhile, was increasingly afraid that they were in danger.

The crowd was shushing itself. Craning their necks they could now see an elderly gentleman perched at a cumbersome microphone. He welcomed the visiting delegation. They were going to hear opening statements and were being asked not to interrupt at this time.

'Zades!? Should we try and get a Mexican wave going?' Virgil emitted an electronic fart.

There! That's what I think of you.

'And back under my armpit we go!'

Mmmmmfff!

The first speaker was a young man. Confident and self-assured, he quickly had the vast audience captivated.

'Neighbours and friends! What has arisen is merely a debate about the application of the principles we all hold dear. Those of us with doubts do not wish to abandon tradition but simply to update those traditions for new times.

'The old divisions between the political left and right have long since disappeared. One era of history has closed and another opened. The new must replace the old. No one in their right mind now imag-ines that society should be organised according to market profit and self-interest. Who would want to return to that kind of society, I ask you? No! The world has moved on and we have moved with it. There is no turning back, no alternative to the common sense, communist values of cooperation, equality, common ownership and democracy.

'But the fact that we have resolved the contradictions of the past does not mean we have resolved *all* problems. Ours is a free society. It is not based on the idea that disagreements between individuals are counter-revolutionary. Such were the views of some who treated Marxism as a kind of religion and themselves as infallible priests of a new faith. We all know how close Leninists came to scuppering the communist dream. Healthy disagreements are the lifeblood of our harmonious community.

'Yet some of us have begun to wonder whether the borders of consensus are drawn too tightly. Markets and unequal wealth alienate comrades from their brothers and sisters. But does this mean that *all* commerce is unwarranted? If I fashion a wooden figure in my workshop and a friend admires it then I may, of course, offer it to her as a gift. But if I requested an exchange for something of equivalent value, would that be so wrong?'

Jake could sense people behind him beginning to shuffle uncertainly in their seats.

'We have long since distinguished between goods of production and goods of consumption. That factories, machines and tools are commonly owned and controlled does not allow me to enter your home and walk away with your furniture. It does not allow me to claim that your home is actually mine, however much you are happy to share your domicile with me.'

That puts an end to The Great Heifer Question, concluded Jake.

'So, cannot such examples of private property not also generate a more formal kind of exchange or contract?

'Or if I wanted to invite friends to dine with me would it be so wrong to ask someone else, someone with greater culinary skills than mine, to cook the food in return for a fee of some kind? Is that not possible without resurrecting the discredited employer-employee relationship?

'Let me make the point less abstract. You are aware that our communities face coordination problems. No estate is self-sufficient and therefore trade organised on democratic lines is widespread. But agreement by consensus can be lengthy and does not always ensure that everyone receives what they need when they need it. Would it not therefore *support* the principle, whereby each receives according to their needs, to allow some distribution according to price?'

Chatter and even some boos swept around the arena.

'Friends!! Friends! Please...can I...comrades! I can hear your unease but let me stress that setting a fair price is not the same as allowing markets to set a price blindly, on the throw of a dice. I am not advocating the latter at all! I am only proposing that that principle of equal value be given a unit of exchange, and thus a more solid foundation, and combined with the principle of need. We should not confuse a limited use of prices with capitalism and the socialist tradition is replete with those who have argued as I have.

'These are weighty issues, I know. Thank you for your time, camarades, and let us look forward to a healthy discussion.'

The applause was polite rather than rapturous.

The next speaker was a nervous and hesitant woman, clinging to her notes like a lifebelt and more than once feedback spluttered out of the microphone.

'I don't need to repeat the comments of my inestim...colleague about the virtues of our way of life. It goes without saying in what I am going...to say. It may seem absurd for someone like me, anyone I mean, to stand here and make a case for relig...that is, spiritual belief. We know that belief...spiritual...has been a source of oppression throughout human history, both as a source of consolation for the downtrodden and because the Church either sided with the rich and powerful or became an oppressor in its own right.

'Why, then, you might ask...will ask, should this case be made? We are creating a heaven on earth. A real heaven with real freedom and justice for all. And it is not as if religious belief has been outlawed. So long as they do not impose their beliefs on others anyone is free to believe in a divine power if they so wish. But some of us worry that there are limits to which we...us...believers...are allowed to express our opinions in the open or to commune together and share our views. This is a very tolerant society but amidst its great diversity there are few churches or places of worship. There are no laws against calling any space a church but the community does frown upon it.'

Here, again, the crowd shifted uneasily.

'There are several reasons why we call for debate. Number one, I am talking about spirituality rather than religion. Communism does not and cannot offer a metaphysics. The Bolsheviks used communism to explain everything that moves in the universe and we have rightly rejected such nonsense. So some of us believe that a creative force in the cosmos may account for why we are here in the first place. This is in contrast to pre-revolutionary societies who thought of God as a warlord or as a cigar-chewing, fat-cat capitalist.'

The crowd hooted appreciatively.

'Secondly...finally...we know from some brothers and sisters abroad that religious practices are not simply tolerated but woven into the life of their community. So in parts of Asia Buddhism continues to flourish because it was...is... a humanitarian ethic that is similar crucially to we...our beliefs. Why then should we imagine that there are no elements within Christianity that can be incorporated into these more enlightened times? Thank you.' She bowed quickly and disappeared.

More polite applause rippled around the arena as the elderly gentleman appeared again.

'Colleagues! Much appreciation to our speakers. We now receive a brief, preliminary response to what we have just heard.'

A fourth person now stepped to the microphone above them. Difficult questions to raise. Debate is what we are about. Burden of proof lies with our critics to show that reform would not recreate old ways. And so on.

Zadie wasn't listening. She couldn't believe who was speaking. The sounds evaporated into the air as Zadie gaped, disbelieving, at the figure above her. Okay, wait. The angle *was* difficult. She could see a chin, two of them actually, and some gaping nostrils. She was wrong. But the voice. The voice she remembered from only hours before...

'Jake!' Jake wasn't listening either. Though in his case it was because he was cleaning Virgil's casing with his shirt.

Ooouuuhh, fantastic. A little more to the left, you slut.

'Jake!!' Zadie practically wrenched her brother's head upwards. And then he saw her too.

'Holy Christ! Mrs Gregsbury!'

'Whhaaat?' Cramps shot to his feet. 'Your politician?'

'Yes.' Zadie's thoughts had scattered, clambering across one another like the Keystone Cops.

'Hey, friend, we can't see!'

Zadie remembered. He'd been startled before, on the train, at the newspaper-reading woman who had resembled what's-her-name, Aon. If Cramps is startled then he can't be in control of whatever this is and if he's not in control...

'What's happening?' Mrs Gregsbury had vanished and they were suddenly shadowed in a forest of bodies as everyone around them rose. 'It's over?'

Williams leaned towards them. 'Those were just the opening statements. The actual debate begins tomorrow and continues for up to five days. Did you recognise the last speaker?'

Zadie ignored him. She had to catch up to Mrs Gregsbury and discover whether this really was the same person or not.

The stage was already empty.

Zadie plunged into the loose drapes covering the base of the platform, half expecting to smack her head on something. But, no. The wooden slats gave her just enough room to squeeze through. The crowd was thinner on the far side but Zadie still felt guilty as she elbowed and shouldered her way through the shuffling figures towards the exit. She sort of liked it here. Far more than that horrible free market wasteland of a metropolis. All the same, she ignored the complaints and one very un-communist curse as she jostled people out of her way.

The exit led down some steps towards a junction. Which way? At this point in the film the pursuing hero always worked out which direction to take. How? Smell? Echoes? Instinct? Disturbed flurries of dust? She dashed down the corridor to her left.

Zadie knew that this was no longer a bizarre technological game. How could she still be in the same room as Cramps and Jake? She felt her sense of reality slipping away. Mrs Gregsbury defending communism? The same Mrs Gregsbury who, hours earlier, had been defending private enterprise? Couldn't be. But here was a mystery and a half.

Damn. Nothing. Some detective she was.

She wound her way back to the junction and tried the other routes but by now it was she who was buffeted about by the exiting streams of humanity. It wasn't worth scouring the town. What, she reflected, would they ask anyway? Excuse me, are you the junior minister we interviewed earlier today in, you know, that other, non-communist society? Discouraged, she went back outside to where they'd been sitting.

Good, they had waited for her. Not so good, Jake had a look of near panic on his face.

'Jake, I told you, he's just in appercept mode. You can still enter the keyword.'

'What happened?' Zadie feared the worst.

'Virgil winked out on me. Cramps entered some code and now he's gone into some kind of scan thing.'

'I invented this little fella. I know what I'm doing.'

Would everybody shut the hell up while I'm trying to work?

'What's going on, Cramps? ' Zadie implored. 'Please?'

'The appearance of that politician spooked me. Probably just a coincidence but thought I should check the holo-program. This scan does that. I made an excuse to send Williams away.'

'It's not Mrs Whocares which is the problem.' Jake spat. 'I can explain that to you if you give me all of ten seconds. But Virgil's our only way out of here.'

'I can explain it too,' Zadie remarked.

'Virgil!' Jake shouted.

Good Christ, what? Do I interrupt you when you mysteriously lock your bedroom door for all of five minutes in the middle of the day?

'Can we still get out of here?'

Yes!! Didn't the wrinkly one just tell you that? Blimey, guv'na!

'OK, what's the keyword? Zades?'

'Communism?'

Jake entered this onto the screen's keypad. 'Nothing. Too obvious. Next?'

'Equality?'

'Nope'

'Solidarity,' offered Cramps.

'Solid-ar-ety-ety?'

'Oh for pity's sake. I now see you're more worried about the spell checker being unavailable!'

But 'solidarity' didn't work either.

'Wait! Productive forces and relations!'

'Don't be a nutzoid.'

'Common ownership? Cooperation?'

'Hah, hang on!'

Jake typed another word and, sure enough, the arena collapsed sideways into the whirlwind of melting colours they'd experienced twice already.

'Classlessness!' Jake shouted triumphantly back at her as he dissolved into the storm.

How is the little brat managing to get the right words? Zadie wondered, before the whirlwind swept through her too.

CHAPTER SEVEN

'Oh, good. Biscuits.'

The kitchen, caked beneath layers of rust and slime, had room for barely one person. Jake swept up the packet and began to munch, remembering to look as if he'd genuinely forgotten to offer it around.

'My turn to tinkle,' he said, his tongue vacuuming crumbs off his shirt.

Uh-uh, not with me, you don't.

Cramps took Virgil as Jake stepped into the bathroom.

And there it was again, Zadie pondered. An unseen toilet in the holo-room they were supposed to still be inside. 'Has Virgil finished his scan yet, granddad?'

'No, sweetheart, that'll take a while yet. But really, there's nothing to worry about.'

Zadie found it increasingly difficult to believe him. She decided to wait until Jake returned.

The flat was obviously vacant. No one here could have failed to notice their arrival. The kitchen opened onto a living space, poorly lit by the dingy light that dribbled in through one solitary window. Only the bathroom possessed a thin connecting door which, they couldn't help noticing, did not stifle the cheerful noise of splashing, chewing, humming and some bold rat-a-tat farting. Zadie's childhood had been plagued by her brother's attempt to play the latest hits using every orifice at his disposal. She shuddered at the unwanted memories of the family's summer holiday to Greece in 2003.

The entire apartment couldn't be more than fifteen feet long and as many wide. They had materialised crushed toe to toe. Zadie wondered whether, if the ceiling vanished, they'd shoot into the sky like toothpaste. A tumbling two-seater sofa faced a threadbare chair and a jittery dining table on which a small, old-fashioned television was perched. Much of the walls' paint had flaked onto the floorboards.

Since Cramps was intent upon Virgil's screen, Zadie moved to the window and looked out through gaps in the yellow newspaper pasted to the glass.

They were perhaps seven or eight floors up. It was a rundown part of a large city though, looking across the rooftops, it at least resembled the world Zadie knew, and which she hoped was still awaiting them beyond the closet's unseen door. The pavements and street corners seemed to be blanketed in street signs and Zadie caught only occasional glimpses of the few pedestrians below, some of whom seemed to be walking awkwardly though she couldn't make out why. Exposing as little of her skin to the mouldering wood as possible Zadie levered up the window and now light and the hum of distant traffic flooded the room. After their rural wandering the noise felt alien and acute. She leaned out carefully.

More signs were welded onto the sides of the apartment buildings opposite theirs. Obedience Breeds Respect! Work Is Its Own Reward! Earn Virtue! Indigence Excuses Nothing! There were dozens of them attached to every building she could see. Zadie leaned out a bit further. Similar signs were bolted to this building too. We read the signs opposite and those living opposite read ours. And there was something else.

Cramps had stopped fiddling with Virgil and closed his eyes. He needed a minute. When should he tell them what was actually happening? Zadie was obviously suspicious. Jake somehow just accepted it as a computerised game. There was no point in alarming them if there was no danger. Hopefully, Virgil would eventually work out whether anything had gone wrong. Besides, why would they believe the unbelievable? Then again, if there *was* danger ahead then didn't they deserve to know as soon as possible? He might not be able to get them home unaided. Cramps replayed that sentence reluctantly. He might not be able to get them home.

And that's your dilemma, you old fool. You're letting them down, and for what? The memory of a woman you knew forty-two years ago? A duty you swore in another place? No, it's more than that. There's so much at stake, including the very existence of my family. If I don't return, might someone follow me? Intercept me? Prevent my family from ever having existed? I'm not just being selfish, surely? By leaving them I leave a void they'll have to cope with, but I can also protect them from people like me. At least then they'll be safe. I'm not just being selfish. Am I?

Cramps snapped upright, suddenly aware he'd half-dozed and been muttering to himself. Zadie was now perched on the sill, her back to the world, staring at him quizzically. There was a hardness there now. Behind them, pipes rattled, hissed and squawked.

'Don't do it, Zades,' said Jake. 'You might land on someone. Best slit your wrists. Though there's no bath, only a shower. So you'd have to do it standing up. Not that it's very hygienic in there so perhaps best use the sink.'

'Even less hygienic than it was two minutes ago, I'll bet. And you've eaten all the biscuits? Congratulations. We could have shared those later. I'm sure you'd like to see me die from hunger, but your grandfather too?'

'Thanks for the image, Zadie,' quipped Cramps. 'I'm worried about you, though. At my age relieving hunger creates as many problems as it solves. Is there anything left for your sister, Jake?'

'Errrmm,' Jake pivoted rapidly into and out of the kitchen. 'Just some cheese flakes and an anchovy which looks as if it turned rancid only recently. And there's a couple of spiders but they look feisty. Aren't there any more sandwiches?'

'It doesn't matter. I want to talk about what is going on with us,' Zadie said. She bent over, removed a shoe and began to tap mud onto the floor.

What the hell is that smell?! Has someone died? Was it me? Have I died?

'Virgil's right,' Jake wheezed. 'I know we've done some walking today but phoo-wee.'

'Look, oh...shut up. Mud, see? And on your shoes as well. We picked this up on our way to the Finland place. If this were holographic mud why would it have followed us here? Wouldn't it have been erased once the program jumped to the next level? And what about the people we saw? Aon and Mrs Gregsbury?'

Cramps stared diplomatically at the peeling walls. 'What are you getting at, Zadie?'

'That we are not in some holographic-generated teaching program. And I'm sorry, Cramps, but either you know we are not, or you strongly suspect that we aren't.'

'Then what is happening?'

'Hypnotism.'

Jake whooped and collapsed onto the decrepit couch. 'Boy! No wonder you're so worried about your essay marks, Einstein!' Jake dodged the kick aimed at his leg. 'If you didn't want me to read your diary you shouldn't have left it under your bed in a safe with a combination lock that only took twenty-five minutes to crack. I already told you, Professor. Aon is just a virtual person, a face that the computer reuses. She'll probably turn up again. The mud is also holographic. Since we are still inside the program there is nothing to stop it from being projected here too. Right, Cramps?'

'For what reason? And Mrs Gregsbury?'

'Ahhh, we can't be sure it was her. Besides... I'm hoping that before this is over we see Jessica Alba and that one from *Terminator III*. Preferably in bed together and completely nak—'

'And the apple I had? It was tasty! Are you telling me that we can taste holographic apples? And what about those poor biscuits you were with in the last few seconds of their existence? You can only taste something like that if someone is fooling you into thinking it *can* be tasted. I'm suggesting that our neuro...logical something brain-waves are being manipulated. We are not just inside the hologram; the hologram is inside *us* and that worries me. This is some kind of hypnotism. It has to be!'

'For crap's sake—'

'Jake!' Cramps interrupted. 'Zadie, I won't deny that something unexpected has happened but I need you to trust me. Can you do that, sweetheart? Please?'

Zadie hesitated to answer, despite the pleading in her grandfather's voice. That hesitation turned into a restive silence. She was afraid, angry and lonely, and Cramps knew that was when people most needed understanding but were often most incapable of receiving it. Besides, she was closer to the truth than he could tell her right now. And also much farther away. No. He shouldn't tell them anything until he was sure himself.

Even Jake knew not to clown away an uncomfortable silence. For a few seconds anyway.

'Damn worms. Zadie, where did you leave the can?' Silence. 'What happened? Have Zadie's socks killed the cockroaches? Are we mourning the roaches?'

'PLEASE REMAIN WHERE YOU ARE! AN EVALUATION TEAM WILL BE WITH YOU SHORTLY!'

What the sweet blue bingo was that?

'It came from up there.' Zadie pointed to a blinking red light in one corner of the damp, sagging ceiling. It resembled a burglar detection system. A system that had just bellowed orders at them. 'That's not all,' she said, 'look at this.'

The wounded expression on her grandfather's face pierced Zadie. Not for the first time today she'd launched in without thinking. But had she wounded him with the truth or not?

Cramps and Jake joined her at the window and she indicated the blanket of street signs below and opposite. 'And do you see?' Overlooking a junction to their right, perhaps five hundred yards away, was a giant screen showing a stern elderly woman with bun-tight, white hair. It was at least thirty feet high, though from this height and distance they could make out only a few, occasional words of what she was saying. It wasn't a commercial. A news report? No, it looked more like a relentless public information film aimed at any pedestrians below by a no-nonsense don't-answer-back aunt. They could just about glimpse several more screens with the same image at junctions farther away.

'Here!' Jake had switched on the television and there she was again. 'Something wrong with the colour.'

'No. It's just a black-and-white set,' his grandfather explained.

'A what?!'

'Never mind.'

The announcer's hair was obviously long but wound around the top of her head so tight you'd think her skull was being throttled for its own good.

'...ber is on the tagline for those interested in taking up this wonderful opportunity. The time is 11-oh-5 of the clock. Welcome to the Purity Channel.'

Jake and Zadie checked their watches. Almost 5 p.m., they announced. On their time, anyway. They'd been in the program for almost six hours already!

'Classifieds and Unclassifieds are reminded that there is an open-air meeting in Roberts Park tonight, where the Reverend Sidder will make an address entitled "The Virtues of Obedience: lesson 78".

'The Reverend will be elaborating on the points made in his seventy-seven previous sermons on human nature, where he established that hierarchies in nature apply to humans also. Wellbeing comes from recognising your place in an unequal order and performing the duties consistent with your social position. Obedience to cultural, govern-mental and spiritual authority is the means by which we submit to God's plan within the natural scheme of things. Possessing unrealistic expectations, such as egalitarian beliefs, therefore offends against the moral community because it represents an abdication of responsi-bility, relocating it away from individual character which is the recep-tacle of God's love and thus the only source of civic peace. Values are already known and not dependent on subjective, relativist evalu-ation. Wellbeing involves the performance of obligations within a rule-bound system of behaviour. Freedom is not about the pursuit

78

of desires or the fulfilment of base, material needs. The first duty of Classifieds, and those Unclassifieds wishing to qualify for classification, is the acquisition of property; property being a sign of one's righteousness and so an offering to God.

'Tonight, Reverend Sidder will pursue these themes with particular reference to the public depiction of pre-moral art. The subtitle of his address is, "The Sexual Promiscuity of The Venus de Milo." Showers are expected tonight—'

Jake switched over. One channel showed commercials offering chastity devices for teenagers and younger children; another sold miniature surveillance equipment. 'Worried that your servants are stealing from you? Nervous about the neighbours? Curious as to why your teenage child is showing signs of arrogance and irritable mood swings? The Probe for Probity system will solve all your problems...'

The next channel offered a gladiatorial talk show. 'My boyfriend CHEATED with my Sister and then RAPED me!' the caption said. The snarls and hoots from the audience almost drowned out what sorry-looking individuals on the stage were saying. 'Will Lacy accept her sister's apology? We'll be right back!'

Every channel seemed designed to scare the pants off them and make them despair at the stupidity of other people.

Zadie turned the sound down while Jake continued to channel-surf. Have we gone back? she asked herself. Back to the Grey Districts?

'Owweeiii!!'

Jake shook his sister's wrenching shriek out of his ear.

'Didn't you hear that? Go back!'

Zadie crouched before the small screen as it returned to a grainy image of a party. The men wore long, dark waistcoats topped by neckbrace cravats and the women were draped in straight white dresses, short sleeves and long gloves. She didn't recognise the actors but was pleased to have something familiar to latch onto at long last.

'I know this. It's Jane Austen!'

Jake peered. 'Which one?'

As with her grandfather, she honestly didn't know when Jake was dumb and when he was playing dumb. She'd asked him once. He'd started picking his nose and claimed not to understand the question.

'Jane Austen's the one who wrote this, you freak geek. I heard someone say "Darcy". It must be *Pride and Prejudice*.'

Huh, show us a bit of leg, love!

'Shush!' spat Zadie. 'Let me enjoy a bit so I can remember what life was like before I went insane.'

Jake watched as people moved back and forth. They laughed at each other's unfunny jokes. Cast meaningful glances at each other's meaningless expressions. Danced around in flouncy circles. Let's see. Blah-blah-blah. But surely you would like to dance with the inestimable Miss Bennet? Nahhh, she's a bit of an ugg-mugg, know what I mean?

This went on for several minutes before he snapped.

'Somebody do something!'

Uh-ho! She's using the angry face. Hide me! For the love of God, hide me!

'Shush! This is real literature, not that gunk you pour into your head to keep your mouth company.'

But just then the picture froze and a voiceover began.

'What's this?' Jake asked. 'Like, a DVD commentary or something?'

'I...no, it doesn't sound like—'

'Shush!!' Jake hollered blissfully. 'I want to hear what Jane Austen's got to say.'

'This is a perfect example,' a woman's voice intoned, 'of how western morals were eroding even within the best families. Although it is subtle, there was a virulent sexual undertone to the apparently casual conversations. Men and woman are being invited to offer themselves to one another. Yes, the surface context is that of banter but look at how the bosoms of the women are accentuated. These are the forerunners of the *de facto* prostitutes who came to dominate the female population by the middle of the twentieth century.'

'Isn't that the same voice as that announcer we heard?' Jake wondered, as the party faded and another scene appeared. Now a middle-aged couple were arguing about family matters in front of what Jake assumed was their daughter.

'Your mother will never speak to you again if you don't marry Mr Collins. And I will never speak to you again if you do.'

Again it froze and again the sour voiceover sprayed vinegar over everything.

'The fault lies with the parents. The mother almost wishes to sell her daughters to the highest bidder. And the father prefers to joke rather than to treat serious matters seriously! Ribaldry is nothing other than a threat to fidelity, faith and obedience to the order of things. Incredibly, the work of Jane Austen was once held up as an example of virtue and moral education! Only since the Great ReAwakening have we come to realise our ancestors' mistakes...'

Zadie clicked the TV off. 'This is a nightmare!'

Cramps wanted to avoid wherever that thought was going. 'People are on their way. Should we get out before they arrive?'

'Yes!' shouted Jake. 'Let's go find some food!'

'I suppose we ought to have a wander,' concurred Cramps. 'I don't relish ending up under guard again.'

Zadie felt tired but had no reason to disagree. If anything, a walk would prevent any furtherance of the awkward conversation they hadn't finished. Or even started, really.

Depressingly, the flat turned out to be clean and habitable compared to the rest of the building.

Zadie had taken one look at the brown streaks on the banister and decided not to risk touching it. Then, as each downward stair had sagged beneath her feet, she had clung to the wall, the banister, her brother, and anything else reasonably solid. It was as if the building was made from little more than stiff, battle-hardened cardboard. A dead dog stared at her with its one protruding eye as she tiptoed around it. By the time they'd reached the ground floor her legs were trembling. The staircase had been empty, though they'd heard the sounds of distant televisions and radios, an angry shout and a door slamming so fiercely that Zadie was certain she'd seen the walls flex. This was beginning to seem like a mistake, but no way was she going near those steps again.

The street outside was fairly quiet, though thuds, laughter and yells seeped from some of the ground-floor windows. There was little traffic other than one very old-fashioned car, like a 1950s Morris Minor, which chugg-chugged down the road before speeding off round a corner. The street signs she'd spotted earlier now prevented them from seeing very far in either direction. They all bore the same type of anodyne but vaguely bullying adages. Zadie wondered what purpose they had. They set off towards the large screen, the austere voice now somewhat muffled at street-level but growing louder as they walked.

The first person they passed, loitering on a stoop despite the brittle frost in the air, was rolling a cigarette to replace the one still dangling from his mouth. He greeted them with a long stare and a 'Yah?!' which could have been a threat as much as a welcome. They didn't pause to inquire. The man was staring intently at her legs. Jake glared at him. Very chivalrous, thought Zadie, but don't get carried away.

This place is awful, she thought. And to confirm the misery they were at that moment dive-bombed by three kamikaze pigeons. Cramps shooed them away.

I made them do that, you know. Yeah, I did.

'Jake, perhaps you should store Virgil in your jacket pocket again.'

Sigh!

A bin had been knocked sideways and lay across the pavement. Legs were sticking out. They had to negotiate their way around what Zadie first feared was a lifeless body left, abandoned and forgotten, for today's refuse collection. Then faint metallic snores echoing from the canister reassured her. There was a menace to the place, aggravated rather than suppressed by its lack of pedestrians. Weeds cracked the walls, the gutter oozed from blocked drains and the buildings peeled and slumped as if gravity was calling them early to their grave.

A passerby overtook them. Zadie had heard the clank and immediately stiffened her shoulders, expecting at any second to feel the jab of a knife entering her back. She felt rather than saw her brother tense. No. Nothing to panic about. The man was wearing a bright yellow jacket, much like the one construction crews wore on building sites, black letters on the back: 'Community Restoration'.

But it was the leg chains that mesmerised Zadie. About a foot long, hanging from beneath his trouser legs and rattling against the asphalt. The man's entire body was engaged in a rolling gait, an expertly coordinated walking trot, that enabled him to move surprisingly quickly without tripping. The chains were kept taut, only hitting the ground every third step. Zadie couldn't digest it all. She was too shocked to be outraged and even impressed by how the man had adapted to his new appendage. Presumably he had been convicted of something and here was this society's version of community service. The man continued to lollop away ahead of them.

Cramps halted and picked up a newspaper from a boarded-over doorway. 'This might enlighten us. Could swear it's warm. Recently someone's bed, I expect.' Zadie and Jake looked over his shoulder as he turned the pages.

It was a litany of human folly, corruption, aggression and selfishness. Practically each story plumbed the worst depths of human nature and social breakdown. Parents who neglected their children by spending eight hours in the pub. Street violence fuelled by binge drinking. Disabled people whose homes had been ransacked and possessions stolen. Gun and knife crime. Families whose members had not held a proper job in decades. It went on and on, page after ink-staining page. And the photos were equally disturbing. Assault victims with scars and bruised eyes. Loitering teenagers waving derisively at the photographer. Broken windows and broken lives. Cramps paused over the paper's editorial.

How Much Longer?

How much longer must we suffer? The decent, moral, law-abiding, hard working folk of this island have finally had enough. We have had enough of the underclass expecting something for nothing. Constantly taking, taking, taking, instead of giving.

No matter how often we remind them of their responsibilities, they forget. No matter how many opportunities we provide, they are thrown back in our faces. Ordinary people are getting angry. They live in constant fear of theft, of being mugged and of the simple vulgarities that fill everyday life with anxiety. It's time to crack down.

Of course, much has been achieved since the ReAwakening. Yet the dregs remain at the bottom of society, immune to morality. The government estimates that perhaps 10% of the population stick two fingers up to the ethical standards, the normal decencies, most of us live by.

It is time for a change. We have had enough. How much longer can we be expected to tolerate this? Each day this week we will be detailing the measures that need to be taken. Today, we highlight the bad parenting that...

The rest of the page had been ripped away.

'Great,' said Jake, 'we've landed in another craphole. Any chance you included an Hawaiian beach party in this program?'

'Don't be dense,' Zadie said, before Cramps could reply, 'it's a tabloid. You know what they're like. They either make stuff up, exaggerate things or else go on and on about the crimes of the poor and conveniently forget about the sins of the rich.' Even so, looking around, Zadie couldn't help but feel a fresh nervousness at their surroundings. Perhaps they ought to find a less threatening area where they could rest and figure out what to do.

They continued, hesitantly, in the same direction as before. The screen was now only a few hundred feet away, the headmistress-looking woman glaring down on them from a rooftop, her voice becoming louder and stricter with every step.

Suddenly an elderly man ran out of a door in front of them and dashed into the road. 'Free soup,' he yelled at them, pointing at a ramshackle wooden church in the corner of a deserted, rock strewn parking lot, a crucifix on its roof leaning sharply and ominously to one side.

'Free soup, anyone?' Jake asked in mock seriousness. Zadie wasn't even sure they'd been the ones addressed.

Then, from the same door, another man emerged. Seeing them he froze, then squared up to them, over six feet high, his fists cracking. Trouble. This guy was fierce. He was sizing them up quickly, looking for things to steal, checking how many witnesses were around.

Jake...glorious, fragile Jake...all five feet four inches of him stepped in front of his grandfather and sister.

The first man was almost at the church when he spun, peered down the road behind them, bellowed 'Ehh-ha?' at his companion and flung himself through the church's entrance.

Zadie, Jake and Cramps heard the sound as well, but were too paralysed with fear to react.

The second man sprinted off as a car braked heavily, screeching to a halt beside them. Jake remembered the ceiling voice that had warned them to stay put. They hadn't managed to avoid their welcoming committee after all.

CHAPTER EIGHT

After being hustled off the street they'd been escorted by two men wearing stiff business suits, like uniforms, to a squat, militaristic and unwelcoming cabin on a street corner. Zadie spotted others at street corners further away. It was an unreflective gunmetal grey, a colour that hid the stubby machine-gun barrels until you were close enough to be shot by them. 'Police Sub-q' was stencilled on one side in black letters.

Mercifully, they were given a bathroom break and some rusty water that Zadie drank with her eyes closed to avoid looking at whatever minute creatures in the water might be staring back at her. Then they'd been left to sit on a steel bench in one of the cabin's three rooms. After about ten minutes of silence, broken only by dull sounds coming from the screen a dozen floors above their heads, a woman joined them, practically a clone of the announcer they had seen earlier. She and the two unblinking men bowed in prayer, mumbling *sotto voce*.

'Sounds like Greek, Latin or Klingon,' Jake whispered.

The woman's head snapped up to see her charges in a blasphemous state of non-praying.

'That gets things off to a good start!' thought Zadie. For a long moment the woman stared unemotionally at them. Furtively, Jake had reached into his pocket to mute Virgil. Holograms or not, he didn't fancy confronting this she-dragon.

'I am Evaluator Ridley. Who are you...persons?' Ridley looked them up and down as if apologising to her shoes for ever having stepped on such muck. Here again Zadie found that her legs were being stared at. Then she realised. It wasn't her legs. It was her pants. Was she meant to dress like Ridley? With her collar propping up her chin?

'We come from another province,' Jake ventured.

For several very long seconds Evaluator Ridley looked as if she seriously might explode. A furnace blazed briefly in her face. She inhaled deeply. Jake half-expected to be lashed by the tongue of a flame-thrower.

Zadie sighed. She could tell he was as nervous as she was, but hiding his fear in bravado. Why couldn't the smart-alec ever keep his sci-fi clichés to himself? For the second time today Zadie expected to be trapped in an interrogation.

She decided to try something. 'We're Noughts.' But this brought no understanding from their new questioner. 'What on earth are you talking about, child? Since you fail to dress like a woman, it's no surprise your brain is addled. This is what happens when people rebel. The order of things becomes confused. Are you the family moral guardian of these children, sir?'

'Yes.'

'Then please hand over your functions.'

Functions? Erm, now where...erm...

'Your social licences! If you have neglected to carry them then that is an even bigger violation. Licences must be carried at all times, mustn't they?'

Erm...

'Let me give you the only chance you'll have today. Who are you? Where have you come from? Why are you here?'

Isn't that a bag of questions I'd like answered myself, thought Zadie.

Silence. Ridley snapped to her feet, the steel chair scraping painfully on the steel floor.

'Very well. I can wash my hands of you with a clear conscience. The Remoralisation Centre, it is. Don't claim later you weren't warned.'

Cramps found his voice at last. 'Urgh!' But it was too late. The door snapped shut and they were alone.

'What fib were you going to try, Cramps?' Jake inquired.

'Be silent!' a metallic voice clanged at them. 'Prior to transport you must undergo preliminary reorientation!'

After a few minutes part of the ceiling opened and a dented globe, with a camera lens protruding from one side, descended on heavy, clattering chains. As they watched a series of fuzzy slides was projected onto a steel wall. The first slides showed pictures of what a caption announced as a lawless time. Riots. Street fights. Unruly children. Someone urinating against a wall. Pornography. People enjoying themselves at parties. Voting booths.

Hang on, thought Jake, shifting uncomfortably from one bum cheek to another. Parties? Voting booths?

'You,' a scratchy recording of the by-now-familiar female voice said, 'are scum.'

Oh good.

'To be more precise, you are lower than that. At least scum has a function. You, by contrast, have chosen to break the law by disregarding your functions. You are Unclassifieds, the lowest of the low. Because you are therefore very, very stupid we need to explain things to you in the infantile terms that people of your inferiority apparently need.

'Under the Anti-Permissiveness and Moral Revival Act of the year of our Lord 1972 you are required to accumulate a stipulated number of moral tokens every three months. These are registered on your "participation cards".' The screen now illuminated a large multi-ridged oblong, the credit card from hell. 'The stipulation depends on your assessed amount of capital, income and property. The wealthier you are the fewer tokens you must accumulate. If you fail to acquire the required number of tokens then you are processed at a Remoralisation Centre. The penalties for non-compliance become more severe with each violation.

'For instance, you may be tagged and curfewed, or perhaps stocked. You may be subjected to public, televised flogging. Finally, of course, we deprive you of your function licences. This means we just give up and put you in prison indefinitely.'

The hairs on the back of Jake's neck stood up and tried to fly somewhere, anywhere else in fear. Now he realised what they'd seen. The guy with the leg chains. That was what they meant by being stocked?!

'The reason for such harsh penalties is so simple even you should understand. We gain our sense of social function from those around us. We are moral beings if the community we belong to is moral. When we obey the rules or demonstrate virtue we feel pride because others have pride in *us*. It works the other way too. If we err then we are brought back to the flock by recognising the disapproval of our neighbours. We are shamed and so feel shame and vow to mend our ways. We all blunder from time to time and such communal readjustment, although stern, is designed to help the wandering soul. Just as a parent loves the children he must thrash for their own good.

'Unfortunately, there is a sizable minority in society – yourselves – for whom normal forms of community readjustment do not work. Those who have less sense of shame and dishonour. Lacking the correct motivations and understanding of right and wrong they have to be forced to be included. Lacking the appropriate values and culture we have to adopt strict measures. Even if you don't *feel* moral within we can at least compel you to behave as if you do.'

The pictures now showed a flashing series of happy revolutionaries smiting all before them. The music switched to a faint church choir and to tinkly yet solemn organ chords.

'This was the reason for the ReAwakening. Before that time all was morally dark. The permissiveness, the licentiousness. Marriages breaking down. Adultery. Children running wild. Defying authority. Disrespect. Constant profanity. Nudity. Laziness. Blasphemy. If we did not control Unclassifieds we would regress towards the liberal dark ages.'

Isn't that condemning the poor to a miserable existence, Jake asked himself, nudging away the memory of having rolled his eyes when Zadie had said the same thing to Dearbrook.

'The liberals made the mistake of believing that equality meant material or social equality rather than equality of obligation. They wanted to punish the rich out of envy when the possession of wealth is itself a sign of virtue. Why? Because the rich automatically recognise the value of work and the valuelessness of the feckless and workshy. This applies just as much to those brought up in a wealthy household because they will also inherit the values, standards and ethics of their parents. Work confers discipline and virtue: obedience, pride, self-respect. Anyone sufficiently hard working to earn is obviously of good character and upstanding behaviour. This includes all of the Classifieds, whatever their income. For it is more important to be morally wealthy than materially wealthy.

'The liberals, communistic social scientists and weak-willed politicians almost managed to persuade us that inequalities are economic in nature. Yet inequalities are moral. Poverty is behavioural and arises from a lack of virtue! It's a cultural deprivation. Why imagine that having a low income excuses you from performing necessary social and moral obligations? If anything, it means you should be required to perform *more* obligations since you may be tempted to devalue the work ethic.

'Of course everyone should have basic opportunities to stand on their own feet. Your sins or your deserts are yours and you should be penalised or rewarded accordingly. That your Unclassified parents are likely to raise you in a culture of deprivation and low expectations is not a reason to abandon you! It is a reason to provide schools that offer an education in faith, virtue and respect for authority. So, you see, we don't say that people are immoral because they are Unclassified; we say they are Unclassified because they demonstrate less moral conduct than a decent society requires.

'Of course, many children of Unclassifieds fail to get the message and so much pauperism and immorality are unfortunately perpetuated from generation to generation. A "cycle of deprivation". For what greater *love* could we have for the morally negligent than to refuse to abandon them? No. We would abandon the indigent if we did *not* make demands of them.

'In the pre-moral era some churchmen recommended that we look after people from cradle to grave. How right they were. But some fools tried to interpret this as meaning that we should provide services and income to people without demanding anything in return. Can you imagine what would have ensued had we gone down that road? Chaos. Crime. Permissiveness. The indigent breeding their litters without permission. We help people more by integrating "the poor" into a moral culture that serves God, serves national traditions, serves others and so ultimately serves themselves. When we punish, we do it with love for the transgressor.

'If we left that crime unpunished it would risk the Unclassifieds disconnecting themselves from the rest of us, becoming even more of a separate culture than they already are. Deterrence is more important when it comes to the Unclassifieds. Those who have little or no property, and so less of a stake in society, have little to lose economically. This encourages criminal behaviour. Therefore, it is only by enforcing moral values and stressing, through punishment, what you *still* have to lose that we can keep control of you.'

Jake was confused. Were they claiming to have solved the problem of crime? Yet they also invoked its spectre everywhere. Which was it, he wondered.

'But those liberals only took their lead from the free market idiots of the nineteenth century, the people who believed that all you need is an unregulated capitalist society. How could a moral economy be based upon free markets? If profit was the only concern then what is to stop someone from producing and selling pornography and making their money that way? The very thought is obscene. That is why markets need regulating.'

The music stopped and the slides faded. Jake had tried to stop listening but that sonorous, dogmatic voice made it difficult.

'On the slim chance that you are serious about mending your ways there are five ways in which you can earn your moral tokens. Firstly, you volunteer for charity work or you make a donation. It should be evident why charity is virtuous. It establishes a more personal connection between the giver and the person to whom charity is given. The pauper can learn a lesson from the moral example of the person who helps them. If a bureaucrat were to give you money then what can you learn except to demand more?

'Secondly, your employer decides that exemplary work deserves a bonus over and above your wage. Or perhaps you simply agree to work, unwaged, for more than the required twelve hours a day. Work repays God for the life He gave us. Remaining idle is an insult to God; another way to take without reciprocating.

'Thirdly, you attend church more than the mandatory four times a week.

'Fourthly, you attend more than the required monthly number of patriotic events to celebrate our national history. It is the accumulated wisdom of the ages which gives meaning to us; the traditions overseen by our elders and betters. The nation offers a strong set of rules and conventions, unlike the multiculturalist stew that the Stupid Sixties threatened us with.

'Finally, your assigned family counsellor judges you to be an exemplary husband and father, or wife and mother.'

Those signs aren't there to educate the Unclassifieds, Zadie realised. They're like the chains. There to reassure the Classifieds that the 'less deserving' are being watched.

'How do we get out of here?' she whispered.

'Try taking your shoes off again,' Jake shot back, a little too loudly. 'We'll sneak out once they've fainted.'

The door rolled open and Ridley grimaced down on them.

'Your transportation is ready.'

Zadie lunged forward. Cramps had slumped to his right and slammed his head into the wall.

Now Zadie felt it too. And Jake's face was creased with pain. Were they being taken to the next level in the holo-program? No, that couldn't be it. Besides, this wasn't a tickle that crept into you from afar and whisked you away. This was worse. Much worse.

Zadie groaned as if a gloved fist was twisting her insides. Her limbs were on fire. As she lost consciousness Zadie had a sense of falling into herself, turned irreversibly and irrevocably towards an inferno within. Her body coiled inside out. She tasted blood.

CHAPTER NINE

'What *is* the matter with you people?'

Zadie's head hurt. She had bitten her lip. In fact her whole body hurt but, by stabbing her in the eyes from behind, her brain obviously had no intention of giving in to the competition. Had they gone on to another level? No. She'd ruled that out. No keyword. They hadn't gotten around to that. Zadie slowly prepared to open her eyes but was afraid the spikes behind them would launch and impale whatever she saw first. What she did eventually see was Jake, shaking away his own grogginess. And Cramps. Slumped and barely conscious.

They were sprawled on the cold floor of a brightly-lit cell. There were vertical bars to Zadie's right. The cell also held a couple of dozen people all seated on hard wooden benches. The shutters had snapped down behind their eyes, leaving them silent, with glum stares. They were the centre of attention, again. But no one was offering to help them up.

'Well?'

The young guard who had spoken was leaning on the bars, peering down on them with bored wariness. 'If you don't want my help, you can't be that badly off.' He sauntered away.

She nudged Jake and together they lifted Cramps onto one of the empty benches. 'I..urm...right, m'aright.'

'How are you, Jake?'

'Crap. Brain feels like a sponge. A sponge filled with crap.'

'Cramps?'

'Alright, darling...just give me a minute to adjust. Where are we?'

'In trouble still. What happened?'

'Threes you suddly slid to floor,' one of their cellmates said. 'Funniest thing e'd seen. Laughs brought u' guard lad. Side effects o' the detox jets?'

Zadie was getting tired of having to understand the ins and outs of all these new places. Why wasn't Virgil helping more? They'd have to check whether he'd finished whatever scan Cramps had thought it important to run. 'Sorry, but where are we?'

'Eeeii, you off it. Old guy lost eez fight wi floor.'

Zadie had also seen the cut on the side of her grandfather's forehead where he'd hit the wall. So much for the holo-program not being dangerous. 'You saying he did that on the floor?' she asked.

'Course. Nize trowzers.'

'Thanks. Then...how long have we been here, please?'

'Not long. Half hour. Dunno. Ain't I seen youz before?'

'Does it hurt, Granddad?'

Cramps had his eyes open at last. 'No, Zades. Not much.' He smiled, probing the cut tenderly. 'Your grandmother used to do worse whenever I annoyed her. Usually with the teapot. Don't worry about me. You've bitten your lip, sweetheart. How did we get here, do you suppose?'

Zadie sucked and swallowed at the blood in the corner of her mouth. 'Not sure. We seem to have lost time. Do either of you remember anything after what's-her-name said about the transport?' The two men shook their heads. 'Then I suppose we have to start—'

Zadie broke off. She could see part of the bay down which their guard had ambled. Two desks faced one another. The sign above the left desk was half obscured but she could make out some letters.

WELLBEI

SEC

REMORA

COMM

'We're in a Remoralisation Centre.'

'Sure?'

'I'm sure, yes. And look.' She tapped her watch. 'Jake, what does yours say?'

'Eh? Almost 7.25.'

'p.m.?'

'Yeah.'

Cramps was nodding his head delicately. 'You're right, Zadie.'

'Right? 'Bout what? I don't get it.'

'Listen,' Zadie lowered her voice. 'In the other two levels we appeared on the scene about 11am right? The same time we first activated the holo-program. But we've been able to monitor the real time outside the holo-room on our watches. When we appeared in that bedsit it was about 5 p.m., yes?' Jake grunted. 'Well, we were in the flat for about fifteen minutes, another ten or so on the street, another thirty minutes, say, in that police place. That's an hour. So what happened to the other ninety minutes? This guy said we'd been here for thirty minutes already. Can either of you remember doing anything since we collapsed?'

'No.'

'No.'

'Wait, what?' said Jake, 'Haven't we simply gone on to another level?'

'No! Remoralisation Centre, remember. And even if we had how would that account for the missing time? Zadie turned to their cellmate. 'Half an hour right?'

'Yep.'

'Did you see us with Evaluator Ridley?'

'Not 'eard o'er. You were brought in by whatsits...Steel Knickers....'

'And what have we been doing since we arrived?'

'Sat lik statues. Damn unjolly, if y'ask me.'

'That means something *is* wrong with the program,' Zadie insisted. 'It's as if we've been participating but have somehow been in a trance. That's what I warned you about earlier. It's as if we've become briefly lost within the program. Lost our sense of ourselves. Hypnotism! What if it happens again? Granddad, you need to tell us what's really going on!'

'Okay, okay.' Jake patted his pocket. 'Should I get Virgil out, Cramps?'

'Wait,' warned Zadie, 'maybe we shouldn't attract even more attention than we have.'

'No problem,' Cramps declared. 'I can keep him on mute while he talks to us.'

As his grandchildren huddled around, Cramps pushed a button and Virgil's screen lit up. Cramps tapped in a question with his podgy fingers.

Virgil, are we sytill on levl 3?

The reply rolled out across the top of the screen.

Nice of you bonebags to ask. Yeah, I'm just fine, thank you. Who taught you how to type? The Elephant Man?

Virgil!

Level 3, sure. The plain one with the over-developed sense of accomplishment was right. The 'program' (heh, heh) is f&#%ed.

Do hyounow whats wrong?

Not finished the full scan yet but can give you the preliminary.

?

A continuum rupture. How much more do you want these pinheads to know?

'Cramps?'

'Sod this.' Jake snatched Virgil away.

Hey you utter garge opener we want out here end th rograme noww

Oh, that's sweet! He's pissed! His typing's slurred. Love it!

You little asswipe

'Cramps?' insisted Zadie. 'What did he mean "how much more"?'

The man behind them slapped his leg. 'That's it! You were ose t-vids who got driv off!'

Zadie's eyes widened. She turned around very slowly.

'You said—? What did you say?'

'T-vids.'

'Are you...' she could barely manage to get the word out, '... Noughts?'

'Course, girlie.'

This man could only have recognised them because he'd been in the queue in the Grey Districts! How was that possible? Her grandfather appeared miserable and resigned rather than alarmed at this new development.

'Ridley spoke about Unclassifieds,' she reminded Jake and Cramps. 'I asked her about Noughts and she said she'd never heard of them. Was I dreaming?' They shook their heads. 'Then how come—'

Just then the cell door rattled outwards and another guard motioned them to rise and follow. The expression on his face suggested it would not be wise to refuse.

The nurse was in her mid-twenties and friendly despite her uniform looking as though it had been bleached, starched and ironed with her already wearing it. Like Ridley's outfit earlier, the skirt was a floor-scraper and no flesh was visible apart from her face and hands. It reminded Zadie of pictures she had seen of nineteenth-century hospitals. Everywhere, the stiff formality.

And she looked familiar. This was someone else they had seen before. Zadie sifted through the impossible hours. Had she glimpsed this face, too, in the Grey Districts? In the interrogation building later? The school? Or had it been in the communist society? One of the delegates, perhaps? Someone in the crowd at the arena? Zadie couldn't place it, but somewhere from the periphery of her memory that face nagged at her.

Zadie's lip had stopped bleeding. Did hangovers normally extend into the very farthest reaches of the body? They had been summoned because the young guard she had been woken by was not so uncaring after all and had reported their distress.

'Funny, all of you fainting at the same time like that,' said the nurse, soothingly. 'Any idea what caused it? Not just looking for some tea and sympathy? You sure?'

Zadie could not help smiling in return. Here at least was a comforting word and a squeeze of the hand. She shivered as she recalled the abyss she had felt herself tumbling into when they'd collapsed.

'Well, I can at least treat these cuts.'

The medical room was well equipped and what Zadie had seen of the rest of the building did not resonate with the fire-and-brimstone vision of a Remoralisation Centre that Evaluator Ridley had conjured in her mind. On their short walk she had seen the rest of the sign:

WELLBEING CENTRE

SECURITY

REMORALISATION

COMMUNITY

Because of whatever was going on between Cramps and Virgil – a subject she intended to pursue as soon as possible – the keyword mattered less right now. The missing time had to be explained. And what else? Ridley had not recognised the word 'Noughts' yet their cellmate had used it not five minutes ago to describe himself. Were they on the same level as before or weren't they? Perhaps they'd better try to ferret out some information after all.

'I'm still feeling a bit groggy. No, no, my lip's fine, thanks. But I am a bit confused as to why we're here.'

95

The nurse was applying some iodine to her grandfather's forehead.

'I'm afraid I don't know anything about that. I'm sure it will all be clarified at your interview.'

'Interview?'

'Yes. With an advisor. You know?'

'I'm not sure I do.'

'You're first-timers? Thought so. You're well spoken and well dressed...even if,' she frowned at Zadie's trousers, 'a bit unorthodox. A wellbeing advisor will sit down with you and give you a basic neurological exam, offer an assessment of your circumstances, agree a therapeutic plan of action with you, agree a timetable of further meetings and then you'll be able to pop along on your merry way.'

'No tagging?'

'What's that dear?'

'Something I heard...to do with remoralisation.'

'Remoralisation simply means counselling you about your spiritual and emotional wellbeing, in addition to your material welfare. Can't have one without the other!'

'So you're saying that the moral evaluator is here to help us?'

'Moral evaluator?' Stumped, the nurse stopped what she was doing.

'Someone mentioned something like that in the detention cell.'

'Ohh, you don't want to let those incorrigible old-timers scare you. Yes, some people manage to reappear here time and time again no matter what assistance we try to provide. Moral? I suppose it is because, after all, this is a time of moral re-awakening. But it's not moralistic in a frightening sense, dear! You're not afraid, are you?'

'Perhaps just concerned about some of the questions the...advisor will ask us. What happens if we don't pass the test?'

'The test?' The nurse, having applied a gauze wrap to Cramps' forehead, sat herself down and chuckled. 'Do you think we are going to tie you to a ducking stool? You must have jobs, yes?' They all nodded. They all lied. 'And you honour your leaders, your country and your God surely? Well then, what have you got to worry about? The advisor will simply go into more detail about those matters and whatever it was that brought you to this regrettable place will be sorted out in no time, I'm sure.'

Cramps was now clearheaded again. 'What are the Noughts to you, if I may ask?'

'The Noughts? A hangover from a regrettable time. That slang they speak to each other! Is any more proof needed that they belong to an impoverished culture? But you know more about that age than I do, sir!'

'I'd still be interested to hear what you think.'

'Well, from what I remember as a girl, in the pre-awakening era society faced moral corruption, cultural disease and collapse. People had misread the real causes of poverty. The Noughts are a remnant of that earlier, erroneous thinking. For instance, the socialists and liberals thought that poverty and injustice was about the distribution of economic and material things. Some of our politicians were of that persuasion until they realised that human salvation could not come that way. It would take time to cure society of all its ills, of course.'

'What are the real causes of poverty, would you say?'

'The fact that wealth is ultimately spiritual and communal, of course,' the nurse frowned again, puzzled by the question. 'We become ourselves by uniting with others in a community. Obeying the same social and ethical rules, worshipping the same god in the same way, honouring our parents and other elders, respecting national traditions. The Noughts still believe that they suffer because they lack "things", a decent home, a good income, when what they lack is the right motivation. They imagine it is only worth working if it results in a high income. Then they imagine that such an income is impossible and so they don't bother working. They look for an easy way out. So they steal, they cheat.'

The nurse paused, looking momentarily awkward.

'Present company excepted, of course! But they don't appreciate that work is its own reward. Working for a wage, working for acceptance in a community of God's children, working to raise a family, working to defend one's country. A decent income matters but matters less than diligence and moral abidance.'

Zadie wanted to try another word. 'So you wouldn't label them as Unclassifieds?'

'What does that mean, dear?'

'Oh, just another phrase I heard...' Zadie trailed off, trying to work it all out. Had the nurse implied that she *remembered* the pre-awakening era? Zadie wasn't sure that Ridley had mentioned a timeline but hadn't she given the impression that the moral re-awakening had happened *decades* before? Had they gone to an earlier period of the same society as before?

'But your grandfather here is a much better authority,' the nurse continued. 'You must have served in the wars against totalitarianism and liberalism, sir?'

'Oh, certainly. But I always encourage my grandchildren to think for themselves.'

Her face darkened and the nurse seemed doubtful.

'Of course, thinking for yourself is important, but not if it gets in the way of sound obedience, conformity to one's duty and submission to God. Those terms you were hearing before, in the cell. You weren't receptive to them, were you?' She looked down at her fingernails. 'Tell me you're not Rads? The Rads are still something of a danger.'

There it was! Proof! She recognised the terms 'Nought' and 'Rad' but not 'Unclassifieds'. That malfunctioning little electronic monster, Virgil, had put them somewhere which was a fusion of the first society and the third. And if the damn thing was malfunctioning then why had they been wasting time getting it to run a scan? How could it tell them what was going wrong when *it* was going wrong?!

'No, my dear.' Cramps purred. 'Nothing like that. We're not Rads. But I recall that not everything about the old ways was bad. The ability to criticise and analyse is not to be against faith or the family or the community. Our friendly discussion is hardly heretical, is it?'

The nurse wasn't convinced. Her lips were pursed and she was still avoiding their eyes.

'I won't say you are wrong, sir, but those are unorthodox views and thankfully less and less in evidence as the years pass. I hope your maker will forgive you. I know I already do. And may He forgive me if I am too harsh in my judgement of you. It does perhaps explain why you are here, though.'

She stood up and beamed again. 'But enough of that. I'm sure your assessor will clear such matters up. Who am I to condemn? Now, I've enjoyed our chat but I do have a busy day ahead of me. You're sure you're all feeling better?'

She shepherded them out the door and back into the care of the waiting guard. As they moved off down the corridor Zadie wondered when the three of them would get the chance to chat in private. There was a lot to ponder. They couldn't be headed to yet another cross-examination, could they?

The door behind them suddenly opened again.

'Look, I'm sorry if I sounded testy. You look like decent people. If it comes up, tell your assessor that I am willing to offer a reference as to your good characters.'

They halted, turned and Zadie thanked their good Samaritan for her kindness.

'Not a problem, my dears,' she shouted as the door shut again. 'Just remember, my name is Nurse Ridley.'

CHAPTER TEN

It was her daughter.

It was her younger sister.

It was a coincidence.

'It was only a younger version of the same character created by the HOLO-PROGRAM WE'RE INSIDE!'

Jake's conviction never wavered and perhaps, thought Zadie, he was right. She'd always thought of herself as being closer to their grandfather than Jake, yet it was she who had been the more sceptical of the two. Was she being unfair? Or was Jake enjoying some *Farscape* fantasy too much to care?

If the holo-program had been disrupted then they'd simply been sent to another, earlier version of the society they were already exploring. But no. They couldn't have just been rewound. People here talked about the Noughts and the Rads. If it was a glitch then it had to be a pretty big one.

But when she tried to voice her doubts Jake just shrugged and Cramps conveniently probed the bandage on his head.

The guard was taking them through a wide, windowless, neon-lit corridor that led into a series of barracks, laboratories and adminis-trative offices. The guards here were certainly intimidating but not especially hostile or aggressive. It was like being in a well-fortified airport rather than a prison. If this is was what a Remoralisation Centre looked like a few years after the ReAwakening, what would it have resembled several decades later? What had the other Ridley – the older Ridley? – been taking them to?

They seemed to be walking from the medical bay back towards the detention section of the building, presumably towards an interview with their evaluation officer. Did they need to hang around, though? Why not try to guess the keyword and jump away? Assuming Virgil was still functioning. If Virgil was the problem in all of this, then where would he send them next? Couldn't they just break whatever spell had them in its grip and find the door to the damn closet? Zadie needed to have it out with Cramps and plan what they ought to do but being rushed constantly around like this was making it difficult to take a breath.

They were parked at the end of a long queue. Several no-nonsense guards, patrolling up and down, shushed people every so often.

'Jake, does Virgil have any advice about what to do now?' she mumbled. Jake hunched over, drew Virgil out of his jacket, hugged him to his chest and whispered a question.

'He says to leave him alone you...flim...flangs.'

'What?'

'He says he's sleeping.'

'Jake, wh—' her brother opened his hands.

'He says that Jake, through no fault of his own, left him in the nice nurse's office to talk about the weather and such, and someone needs to go back and get him.'

Zadie's forehead furrowed in despair, horror, anger and...'And you had food!' Jake had been speaking into the last remaining digestive he'd hidden in his pocket.

She counted to ten. Very slowly. 'So...just to sum up and every-thing...not only have you lost our escape route out of here but you have deprived your sister and your grandfather of about seventy, maybe eighty, calories?'

'Zades? How come you know the calorie count of a typical digestive?'

'I...shut up! How long were you hoping to keep this quiet?' she spat.

'Until shortly before the world ends. Don't think I've given up hope of that happening soon either.'

'There are some days when I literally just pray for death.'

'You don't look depressed.'

'I wasn't talking about my death, genius.' Zadie raised her hand towards one of the guards who patrolled the queue ahead of them. 'Mr Guard? Excuse me! Sir?'

'You're doing what now?'

'We have to go back to the nurse's station. Fake an illness. Say a few words and he'll work out that you're mentally deranged and send us back in no time. Sir?'

First, the guard was walking towards them. Then he was falling sideways out of a flood of sparks. Then the lights went out. Then

Zadie fell too, into that same silent tunnel. Jake's wish that the world would end soon had come true.

For the second time in less than an hour Zadie had to shake her head and squeeze the light out of her eyes. This time, though, it was Cramps who helped *her* up. She gagged on the dust that had sprayed into her mouth and tried to swat at the grit that reeled around them, as though grey flour had exploded inside some monster's kitchen.

Part of the left wall had exploded and those closest to it lay bleeding and moaning. Most of the lights were out. Everyone was stunned, shocked, stationary. Then figures, vague in the smoke, crammed in through the hole and the people around them began to panic and shriek, scrambling away. She could barely hear above the whine in her head. The explosion had been so loud she hadn't heard it.

'Come on. No, wait.' Zadie shouted. 'Where's Jake?'

'I think he'd already bolted for the nurse's office.'

'Little idiot. Let's follow.' But that wouldn't be easy. Klaxons and sirens were now screaming and guards crowding in on them from all directions, behind erratic, demented flashlights. Some were assisting their colleagues, some tackling the intruders, and some detaining the fleeing prisoners. Zadie shoulder-charged a female guard and hustled Cramps along in the brief seconds the confusion gave them.

They'd pretty much marched in a straight line after leaving Rid... after leaving the clinic. They could surely find their way back but would they have time? The formerly bright corridor was now thick with wreaths of smoke pouring from the building's wound. Behind them, cries, threats and bone-crunching kicks flew beneath the blaring alarms. Shocked administrators and secretaries piled from the lit doorways, adding to the flurry and helping them to remain unseen.

The waves of panicked humanity sweeping past on all sides buffeted them, though they managed to keep up a rapid pace. Already, Zadie was worried about Cramps' heart. He was panting and wheezing. No sign of Jake. No choice. Zadie grabbed her grandfather and jostled him through some double doors. He needed to pause a second, catch his breath. Zadie felt rather than heard the whine in her head subside.

It was an empty workplace gym, poorly lit by a single skylight. Gasping, Cramps lent against the parallel bars. Through the gap in the door closing behind them Zadie could see the vague outline of fire crews, medics and yet more guards rushing towards the melee. The din was intense. Many were shouting for quiet, only adding to the commotion and increasing the sense of things suddenly being out of control.

She patted the old man on the back. 'Alright, pater?'

'That...why you...stopped? Thought Jake...was...in here.'

'No. I thought we ought to run but I was trying to make you sprint. Sorry. Especially after everything that's happened today. Were you hurt? What happened?'

'Fine...People surround...knocked down, including you...but I was OK. Saw the wall cave in...you were only down for a second or two... then this. Dozens of people hit. Explosion sounded louder than it really was. Doubt anyone killed. Hell of a mess, though.'

They shared some water from the bag still draped around Cramps' shoulder. Zadie spat the water out until her mouth felt clear.

'How are we going to find Jake in all this? Perhaps we should just hand ourselves over.'

'Need Virgil. He won't jump anyone to the next level unless we are all together. We ought to go on.'

Not together? Not in the same holo-room still, separated by a digital illusion, some kind of technological hallucinogen? It still wasn't the time for that. 'Okay, find Jake.'

Before they could move the door clicked open and the gym's weak light swept into the corridor's gloom. A man in white shirtsleeves jabbed his head around, saw them and disappeared. If they were going to go they'd have to go now.

'Glad to see you're OK.'

The woman's soft voice had come from behind them. Zadie recognised it instantly.

Aon and Kayne stood up. They'd been hiding behind one of those vault things.

Astonished, Zadie asked the question about fourteen on her mental list. 'How did you get here before us?!'

Aon indicated another, smaller door which pointed back towards the direction of the explosion.

'Then you have something to do with this?'

'A complete screw-up,' growled Kayne, as angry as ever. 'All the military discipline of a children's party.'

'So...you remember us? From the Grey Districts?'

'When we thought you could help us we wanted to come get you,' Aon explained. 'An informant said you'd been brought to this centre. We managed to get a team together.'

'Why did you think we could help?'

'Some of the strange things you said this morning. None of the Rads we know recognised you. Thought you might be a new group. That communications device of yours. You were talking to someone in the factions, yes? I insisted we hit the place today. Come rescue you.'

'You weren't at the school, too?'

'What school?'

Zadie ignored the question. 'Forgive me for asking, but how long ago were we in the Grey Districts with you?'

Aon looked puzzled. She pulled them down. Kayne crouched to one side, keeping watch on both exits. He was holding what looked like a cosh.

'A few hours.'

For them, obviously. In Zadie's time-frame it had been over seven hours ago. More proof that the holographic societies had somehow intersected and become confused.

'But why risk it? People were injured back there. Maybe killed.'

'A miscalculation. We were supposed to enter a deserted part of the building, make lots of noise and slip inside while the authorities were trying to work out what happened. We were not only trying to find you but free as many revolutionary brothers and sisters as we can. We should go.'

'Then you *are* Rads?'

'Of course.'

'Communists?'

'We are a network of groups opposed to the neo-fascist dictatorship which has taken over. This centre is an abomination which helps to keep people poor and then punishes them for *being* poor.'

Zadie fumed a little. 'The same brothers and sisters you just blew up?'

'Like I said—'

'Listen, sweetheart!' Kayne grabbed Zadie roughly by her right shoulder. 'But for Aon...' Aon now placed her hand on his, silently pleading for calm.

He trailed off. That sad look in his eyes! Zadie remembered the jealous glare the other Kayne had thrown her in the rear-view mirror of the van. She wondered whether Aon knew how fond Kayne was of her. 'There can be no liberation without obliteration,' he proclaimed.

'Good slogan.' Zadie shrugged herself free of his grasp. Wait! Jake! 'We have to go.'

'Damn true.' Bent double, Kayne stooped off towards the smaller door.

'No!' she hissed. 'My brother! You remember?'

'So what?' Kayne shot back, 'Too dangerous now.'

'We're not going anywhere without him. Aon, please!' Zadie grabbed her hand.

Aon chewed her lower lip, Zadie again noticing the slight birth defect. They had seen the shirt-sleeved man, too. It was a miracle they'd not been discovered already.

'He was heading back toward the medical bay,' pointed Zadie. 'You mentioned the device? Jake was going to fetch it. We're not much use to you unless we can get them both!'

With a short, confident nod at Kayne, Aon stood up and the four of them pressed to the wall nearest the main door.

'This is madness, madness, madness.' Kayne almost trilled the words. He was more nervous than he tried to appear. Trusting Aon.

Carefully, Aon inched the main door open. They'd only been gone a couple of minutes but the hall was now a bit more orderly. The crowds had thinned beneath pale red emergency lighting. At that moment the sirens and alarms hushed as dramatically as they'd begun, the echoes taking a few seconds to dissolve down the corridors.

'If we look anxious but otherwise normal....' Aon directed. 'You're a bunch of dim-witted data processors who got lost. Think of that.'

They slipped out of the gym to their left, huddling into the dim semi-light, Zadie leading the way, trying to look as inconspicuous as possible. Several people did glance more than once at them but the corridor was wide and the emergency services were still too busy rushing to and from the scene and the office workers were too busy sharing their non-experiences of the event to make a challenge. It was still fairly chaotic.

They came to a junction. Damn! They *had* turned a corner before, remember! Left? Right? She'd been concentrating more on who Nurse Ridley might be. 'This way,' Zadie guessed, trying to sound confident.

The medical bay had consisted of several labs, clinics and an emergency room but Nurse Ridley's office had been quite near to...yes, there was her name on the door. Not such a bad detective after all!

'Help!'

'Stop!'

'Help!'

That was a woman's voice. Who'd shouted at them to stop?

The shirt-sleeved man who'd spotted them before was behind them at the junction, no more than fifty feet away.

'Bugger! Office!'

The four of them pushed through the nurse's door with Kayne taking up the rear. The stranger made an Olympic-sized sprint towards them but Kayne swung the cosh at his head and the man slumped heavily.

Jake wailed. He was engaged in a classic, comic tug-of-war with Nurse Ridley. They were each trying to wrench Virgil out of the other's grip.

'She won't give him back!'

I didn't sign up for this! Tell these idiots to let me go!

'Who the goodness...Help!...are you people? Help! Rads! You're Rads! Help! Are you responsible for that explosion? Help!'

Kayne locked the door behind them with a heavy click. 'Won't last long. Any last thoughts before we go to jail for ten years, boss?'

'And to think I was going to speak up for you people! Oh...have your toy back.' She released Virgil and Jake recoiled, cracking his head on a cabinet.

'Ow!'

'Jake, what happened?'

'I hit my head on the—'

Zadie fluttered her arms. 'No! I mean...'

The door handle rattled behind them and a blurred, silhouette was visible through the frosted glass.

'Well, thought I'd get Virgil even though we were all to blame for leaving him here, really.'

Bollocks!

'Found her messing with him.'

And not in a nice way either!

Cramps took Virgil and began checking his screen menus.

'Help!'

There were now two silhouettes behind the glass and the thump of shoulder-charges against the wood frame.

'Would somebody gag her!' Kayne turned to Aon. 'What do we do, boss? We've got seconds. Can we make it out there?' Three small windows lined the upper edge of the wall opposite the door.

'Not big enough. It's been a complete mess from start to finish! Sorry, Kayne, you deserved a better leader.'

'Cramps?!' Zadie implored.

'I think he's okay. The scan was interrupted, that's all. Virgil, are we okay to jump onto the next level?'

Of course! Why didn't you airheads ask me that ages ago?!

'Great. Jake, you seem to be good at getting the keyword...'

'Fine! You, Florence Nightingale, say something.'

'When the authorities get you, good riddance, they'll throw away the key...'

'Crime?'

'Nope,' said Cramps.

'...scaring decent people like this who are only trying to earn a fair's day's pay...'

'Morality? Work?'

Nope.

'...don't you think we have your best interests at heart, so why do you throw it back in our faces...?'

Community? No.

'...but I suppose you can't help being who you are...'

Culture? No.

'...and that means we have to require you to act in the proper manner we prescribe...'

'Responsibility? Duty?'

'Argghh!'

'Order?'

Lift off!

'...because anarchy would result otherwise...'

'Shut up now, knucklebrain.'

Glass shattered behind them and angry faces appeared through the crack. Another smash and in a few seconds they'd be able to grasp the door's inner handle.

'Chief! We have to try!' Aon looked uncertain. She'd been mesmerised by this odd exchange, perhaps hoping in desperation that somehow the strangers could perform a miracle and save them all.

Well, it would be a miracle of sorts, but not for them. Before, Zadie had found it difficult to accept that Aon and Kayne were holographic simulations. Now, she prayed that they were.

She sensed the familiar glow and gentle prickling that would soon spread outwards and engulf the world around them. Just in time!

'Aon, I'm sorry, really sorry, to do this again. You're so kind!'

But hang on, she thought, jolting sideways. Something was not right....

CHAPTER ELEVEN

I can't believe it. How often can I take this?

For a third time Zadie had to crawl upwards through fogs of swirling lights, warped ocean-bed sounds and numb, unresponsive thoughts. Instinctively, she sensed that she'd struggle best against the shadows by surrendering to their currents. The fog *was* her and it would carry her to wherever she needed to be. The jump had felt like the earlier ones, where they'd travelled between levels, but also a bit like the nauseous attack that had hit them in the police cabin.

Zadie sensed she was lying close to the floor. Easing her eyes open gradually, she saw a single skylight running along a low curved ceiling. The room was quietly busy, pockets of subdued noise beyond her feet. A metal apparatus hung down to her left. Zadie's outward breath turned into a cough. Clearing the tubes, her dad used to call it, and she'd whack him on the back to help. Her father had made a game even of the disease that would eventually kill him. What was her mum doing now, she wondered sadly. Worrying about them? Ringing her grandfather's house?

'Doctor, over here.'

Zadie was freeing her arms from the tight sheet that wound her to the stretcher.

'Whoa, young lady. Let's see how much you're back with us, shall we?'

The doctor pressed a stethoscope to her chest. Zadie grinned weakly as her brother's face towered into sight above. She had never seen stubble on his face before. Had he started shaving? she wondered.

'How's it going, lazybones?' he asked.

'Don't talk just yet,' the doctor advised as he swung a penlight from one eye to the other, checked her pulse and thrust a thermometer into her mouth.

''m'OK. 'Ows 'ramps?'

'He's unconscious. So's Kayne.'

Zadie's eyes widened. 'Yane?'

'Yes, but Aon is alright. She woke up just a few minutes ago.'

What was...? Zadie tried to sit up but got no further than the doctor's hand. 'What did I just say?' He eased her back down. Her head buzzed and she closed her eyes until the swirls of coloured light faded again.

'It's getting on for noon but,' Jake continued after a few more moments, tiptoeing around the doctor's presence, 'can you believe my watch is still not working properly? Says it's almost 8.30 p.m.!'

So, they hadn't lost any more of their own time but the mid-morning reference tipped Zadie that they had successfully jumped away to another level. Thank god for that at least. Except that they'd somehow brought Aon and Kayne with them. More evidence that whatever this journey was doing, it was malfunctioning.

'You're shaky but fine.' The doctor finished his tests. 'A bit of shock to the system, is all.'

'Thanks. How's my grandfather?'

'Ahh...not bad but it looks as if he's taking longer to wake up. We're monitoring him. Were you caught in the blast with your brother and your two friends?'

'A blast? I don't—'

'Don't worry. You'll be groggy for a time. I'll swing by again in a few minutes.'

The doctor disappeared as Zadie strained and eventually managed to sit upright on the cot. It appeared to be the same gym they had sought refuge in earlier, though it had been converted into a make-shift ward. About two dozen stretchers and camp beds were lined together in three rows. Like her, a few of the patients were sitting up; doctors and nurses tending to the rest. Cramps was lying, insensible, several beds away, right next to Kayne who was also unconscious. At least Ridley hadn't accompanied them. Farther away, Aon's back was turned to her as she sat in conversation with a middle-aged man. Zadie saw who this was and groaned.

'What's happened?'

'We, erm, materialised here about thirty minutes ago,' Jake sat down beside her. 'In the middle of all that smoke and confusion. The explosion? You know? You, Cramps and Kayne have been out of it. We're not in the Remoralisation Centre, so far as I can tell. Aon started whizzing out but I managed to calm her. Told her you'd explain everything and not to fuss off. Maybe she's worried about the police or something. She seems to trust you, anyway. Crap knows what we're supposed to tell her.'

'You mean she remembers the nurse's office and everything? She's carried her memories with her too?'

'Yep.' Oh lord, this was new!

Jake nodded. 'She's as confused as hell but knows how to handle herself. I think she thinks we have new technology that can help her. Which is half true, I suppose.'

Zadie again looked across at the man sitting beside Aon. 'And Williams?'

'No, doesn't seem to remember us.'

'Does your obsession with computer games give any clue to what is going on? Aon, Kayne, the others...still think these are holograms?' Zadie couldn't help thinking of Pinocchio, the wooden boy who acquired life.

Jake seemed less than sure now, glancing over in his grandfather's direction. He tapped his right jacket pocket. 'Virgil won't say. Still doing his scan.'

Then they'd have to wait for Cramps. And this time she was going to have it out with him. Find out exactly what was going on, no matter what.

'Any idea what kind of society this is?'

'Can't work it out. When I came to, that doctor jabbed some kind of skullcap round my head. Then he nodded as if I'd passed some test or something. They seem friendly enough.'

'Help me up.'

Zadie lurched to her feet. Before she could totter over to Aon the doctor who'd examined her earlier intercepted them. Zadie knew the type. He had a boyish charm that he probably felt could get him anything from anyone. And for the most part, he was probably right.

'Better now?'

'I'm...yes. Is anyone—?'

'No one seriously injured here. The serious cases have been transferred to Emergency. Most of the wards are full so we've had to make this into a temporary ward!'

'We're in a hospital?'

'Still not come back to you? Surely you were visiting a patient, yes?' Zadie nodded her head weakly, uncertain what to say, as he shone the penlight in her eyes again. 'No worries. We'll get you sorted once things are back to normal. The police are going to want to interview you about the blast. But perhaps you should continue to rest for now. Do you want to take the LM Sift though?'

'The blast was deliberate?'

'Oh, some new terrorist outrage. Those conservative fanatics are getting worse. Attacking a hospital! What about the Sift?'

'If you think...'

The doctor led her and Jake to one side of the room where a portable computer monitor stood against the wall.

Conservative terrorists? But how come there had been an explosion here too? Were the program's levels jumbling helplessly into one another? Her grandfather was having his pulse taken by a nurse. He was still unconscious.

'Waaaa...wait. This won't take a minute.'

The doctor fitted a wired rubber cap over the top of her head, scrunching her hair, twiddled a dial then turned to the monitor. The computer itself seemed unremarkable, clunky even, but she didn't recognise the software.

'What is—?'

'Don't moan yet, Zadie,' her brother quickly interrupted, 'it's the proctologist after this.' Be careful, his rubbish joke and rigid smile warned.

Lines streamed from left to right on the monitor; data boxes blipping their way on and off. The screen then started scrolling out tables of information. The doctor bent over, looking satisfied. 'Preliminary is good. This'll just take a minute.'

'I asked the doctor about the principles of the LM machine,' Jake told her. 'You know I don't understand computers.' That lie must have pained him. 'He gave me this booklet, if you're interested.' When had her brother become so wily?

The doctor chuckled, still reading the screen. 'Neurolobe-Compatibilist Metricity. Of course the nickname "luck-o-meter" shows no signs of going out of fashion.'

Jake handed her a thin official-looking pamphlet. *LM: The Basics*, it was entitled.

The LM technology was developed as a means through which society's egalitarian principles could be applied more closely and successfully to some of the key events which occur in everyday life.

Most people now accept that we are responsible for the consequences of what we freely and voluntarily choose. If your choice leads to good consequences then you should reap the benefits, whereas if it leads to bad ones then you should accept whatever burdens and costs are coming your way. But if that is true, it follows that you should not be held responsible for what you *didn't* choose.

Obviously, there is much about our lives that we didn't choose. There are limits to our freedoms. It might be that you have less money than Smith mainly because Smith inherited his wealth from his parents. We don't choose our parents or the social and economic circumstances of our birth. In one sense, therefore, we don't *deserve* them. We didn't actually do anything to earn our good or bad fortune. Then why should you suffer because of bad luck that you did nothing to deserve? We are born with certain 'talents'. In a society that respects intelligence above all else Joe would prosper; while in a society which respects attractiveness Josephine would prosper. But neither Joe nor Josephine did anything to deserve their talents and the kind of society we find ourselves in is also something that we didn't choose. It was just a roll of the dice and social justice can't be determined by something as capricious as luck.

It is, of course, true that intelligence and attractiveness, and all other talents, need to be developed. It takes effort to develop intellectual ability. Someone should be rewarded for that effort. Therefore, once we have factored out the conditions we did not choose, what we are left with is both freedom and responsibility. It is perfectly acceptable to reward people differently according to how they apply themselves. Moderate inequalities are fine so long as the basic *equalities* are in place.

This means that markets must be regulated if a class society is not to reappear. Individual choice is vital so long as it does not restrict the freedom of others. Jones is happy for Smith to possess a bigger house, but if Smith's wealth becomes so big that it prevents Jones from owning a decent house (perhaps because Smith purchases all the land and charges an exorbitant rent) then that is unfair to Jones.

Choice and autonomy and freedom are important but without fair equality of opportunity, without restrictions on some choices, without limits on inequalities, then you don't *have* a free society; all you have is a system of power and class in which the fortunate get to parade their so-called superiority in front of those who have simply been less fortunate in life.

Having eliminated the main sources of injustice through fair taxation, regulation, socialisation of the economy, etc. it was deemed necessary to address many of the day-to-day injustices that are governed by luck, accidents of birth and chance. Philosophy Technicians spent years developing the LM.

The LM scans your neural pathways, looking for what are called cerebral echoes. Volition, what we do without coercion, tends to leave trails across the conscious mind which are different to activities which are involuntary and determined from outside our conscious selves. For instance, a dream is involuntary whereas your choosing to describe the dream to a friend is voluntary. The neural path of the dream will therefore be dissimilar to those of the recollection and the LM Sift can detect those differences.

Critics point out that there are degrees of volition. True. But the technology gives a fairly good reading of when we chose or didn't choose to do something in the previous twenty hours. Cross-referencing that against events we know occurred in the external world means we can assess your level of conscious, willing participation in them.

If you are simply scratching your nose to relieve an itch then that would register on the LM Sift as an unremarkable flatline. But if your scratch was in fact a signal to someone to rob an old lady then that would show up as a distinctive pattern because its cognitive significance would be so much higher.

The LM is not a lie detector. More of a freewill detector. It has many applications but obviously helping to fight crime is one of them.

So with LM Sifts becoming a regular feature of our lives it ensures that our egalitarian values can finally breathe something other than the foul air of injustice!

Zadie finished reading just as the doctor finished his scan. 'Everything's fine. Looks like you're not a terrorist!'

She tried smoothing her hair down again with her fingers. Though she really wasn't up to playing detective she managed to ask, 'You know, I've never understood this. How can a machine make a meaningful distinction between choosing and not choosing?'

The doctor was distracted, filling in a form. 'For that you'd have to ask a PhilTech. It's all probabilistic. There's a kind of uncertainty principle. Something that can't be read. But the LM is only meant to give an approximate reading anyway.'

'Harry? On a break?' One of the other doctors glowered in their direction.

'Just finishing the LM for these two. Be there in a mo. Tetchy bugger,' he said, turning back to Zadie. 'You kids are too young to remember what it was like but go down to the Right Quarter some time. All those redundant bankers and stocktraders sitting in their themed cafes with those digital boards on the walls showing mock share prices. They look harmless but if we allowed people like that to get back in charge we'd be in big trouble!'

'Then they aren't the terrorists?'

'Ouch, why don't more kids read newspapers? No, for all their faults at least the market liberals recognise the importance of freedom. No, the real lunatics are the moralistic conservatives. Don't give a hoot for individualism or equality. Idiots want to take us back to the middle ages when everyone knew their place and you had to bow and scrape to the powers that be your entire life. Mike's giving me dirty looks again. Any better now?'

'But it seems fairly clumsy,' Zadie persisted. 'Requiring people to be scanned every time something important happens. Isn't it impossible to gauge *all* the effects of luck?'

'You know, I don't disagree. You looking to go into politics?'

'I think it's all crap,' Jake threw in. 'Don't know what that machine records but it can't be free choice. There have to be endless things lying behind what I do. The idea that you can be judged responsible for this or not responsible for that is fu—...it's rubbish. You said yourself you don't know how it works.'

The doctor frowned. 'I also said that it gives an *approximate* reading of neural pathways. And apportioning responsibility is something that every society has to do. Who knows?' He squeezed her arm. 'Zadie, I have work to do. Give me a shout if you need anything.'

'You didn't have to be so rude,' Zadie said, once the doctor had left.

Jake seemed to have regained his blind confidence in Cramps and in technology. 'Puhleez, big-knickers, will you stop treating these computer projections as real?! Once we persuade Cramps to add some nudity and lots of violence it's gonna make us rich as Larry.'

Zadie didn't argue. Her brother's ability to appear both smart and dense at the same time was nothing new. They wandered over to Cramps. He seemed a bit more relaxed now and a nurse reported that they expected him to awake fairly soon. How am I supposed to explain this to Mum? He got hurt when a holographic wall exploded? They'll throw away the key!

They now saw that Kayne was awake and sitting next to Aon. Huddled together, whispering, they both stared fiercely at Zadie and Jake. 'What on earth are we supposed to say to them?' Jake shrugged, uninterested again.

As they walked across they saw that Williams was arguing jovially with two other men who had also joined the group. It *was* Williams and yet it wasn't. Physically the resemblance was identical, mutton-chop whiskers and all, yet there was perhaps less of the sunny optimism, the banter, the bonhomie that had worn them down a few hours earlier.

Kayne rose quickly to meet them.

'What the hell is going on, you two?!'

'Keep your voice down,' hushed Aon, coming up behind him.

'Are you feeling okay?' asked Zadie.

'I'm...yes, thanks. Where are we? Is this your technology?'

Zadie had quickly worked out a plan that involved being almost, but not entirely, honest. 'We aren't sure. What has just happened to you happened to us as well, hours ago. That's when we ran into you the first time.'

'In the Grey Districts?'

'Yes. You see, we found that device. The computer. The one we call Virgil? And we were messing with it and it transported us to where you were and now obviously it's brought us all here. We don't know why or how.'

'Buuulllshit. Transported! You know more than that, girl.'

'Hey, arseface. Lay off.' Jake squared up to Kayne's chest and looked up fiercely.

While trying not to make a scene, Aon had to hold Kayne back and Zadie had to do the same with Jake. 'Boys! Boys! People are watching!'

'I'm just saying I don't accept this, no way,' maintained Kayne, soothed by Aon's touch. 'One second we're in that clinic. Then here? It's bollocks. Where's that device?'

'Getting out of there was what we asked them to do, but...' Aon's stare was cool but accusatory. 'This gym is identical to the one we were in! Ideas and politics have changed completely! You owe us an explanation.'

'What can I say?' Zadie responded calmly. 'You saw how disoriented we were this morning. Now you know why.'

'I asked where the device is,' Kayne growled.

'Doesn't matter, does it?' Jake barked. 'Not as if you exist or anything.' Zadie groaned. Why did he do these things? One minute he could be so sweet, and then...

'Not real? Listen, fucknuts, you'd better start making sense.'

Zadie squeezed the arm she was still grabbing and felt her brother flinch. 'It's just the disorientation. I mean, we began to wonder what was real and what wasn't. You haven't said anything to anyone, have you?'

'No!' Kayne was waging a staring competition with Jake.

'What about Williams?'

Kayne turned to her, suspiciously. 'Yeah? How'd you know 'is name?'

'Someone we recognise from our travels, that's all.'

'Then I'd better get some answers, kiddies. Where's. That. Device?!!'

'My grandfather has it,' Zadie lied. 'Only *he* seems to be able to work it. I suggest we sit down and stop being the centre of attention.'

Neither Aon nor Kayne looked happy but a glance between them confirmed that they didn't have a better plan of action. Not yet. Aon pushed and cajoled Kayne back towards the beds.

Cramps probed the inside of his head, massaging the nerve endings, smoothing the synaptic filaments and tendrils. It had been a long time since he'd received his neuro-g training but he'd practised the basics over the years while pretending to be meditating. He'd worn his hair long to maintain the image of an ageing hippy, endearingly out of tune with changing times. He remembered how first his daughter then, later, his grandchildren would imitate him in both bemusement and affection. A swizzle-haired, round-bellied Buddha still worshipping Dylan or whatever! But now.

It wasn't the faint, maroon light washing his closed eyelids that made it difficult to visualise and repair nerve endings. It was his divided motivations. It was the memory of those irreverent children. Dancing to a music they'd thought would never end. The best he could do was to preserve them in their past, like flies in amber. The alternative might be non-existence, a wiping away of the last four decades. That left nothing. No resin. *I* wouldn't even remember them. I wouldn't even be *me* anymore. I have to leave for their sake. It was the weight of this responsibility which now kept him pinned to the bed, in a self-enclosed darkness.

Yet it was also what *she* had said all those years ago. Return to me. I don't care what happens. You owe it. You owe it to all the people depending on you. She had brought him to himself. Made him live for the first time. Helped him on his way. Made this possible. Made the lives of his children and grandchildren possible. And his now dead wife. Had he not married her because she reminded him of that earlier love? Wasn't it her void that he needed to fill, calling him back to the beginning of his journey?

But how can I be happy in that future life by betraying the people I am clambering over so eagerly to leave behind? I have to make sure they're safe. That's the overwhelming priority. It's time to tell them. We must have jumped forward this time. It's time to tell them.

What should they do once their granddad woke up? Williams and the others hadn't questioned them too much, sympathetic to their worries about their grandfather. That hadn't stopped the stares, though. In the last few hours Zadie had been stared at more than in the rest of her entire life. It's the clothes, she thought. Accents don't seem too different but the clothes…. Here, everyone was wearing some light pyjama-like material. Zadie now felt overdressed.

If the police were interviewing witnesses outside it wouldn't be easy to slip away. Zadie tried to think about their options as the conversation went on around her. Hours earlier she, the new impassioned Zadie, would have joined in but now other things were on her mind. Aon and Kayne sat silently too. She noticed how they brushed their hands against one another. A simple act of mutual faith.

Only Jake took an interest in the discussion. Using his talents for finding food he'd managed to grab a banana from somewhere.

'This society is still obsessed with individualism and competition,' Williams was saying, 'when solidarity and cooperation are what give meaning to life. Trying to distinguish between what we do and don't choose! Why should that even matter?'

'Why should it even matter?' The speaker was one of the newcomers, a short, heavy-set man whose name was Myllan. 'Wouldn't communists try to make us all think alike and act alike, hmm? It's choice – genuinely free choice, of course – which helps to distinguish us. If some inequalities result from that then it's a price worth paying.'

'Rubbish! People can only be true individuals when they don't have to worry about their place in the pecking order.' Williams was smiling even as he jabbed his finger at Myllan.

Friendly adversaries, thought Jake, saying farewell to his banana and working out where to throw the skin. He already recognised it as pub-bore talk. Recognised it because a month ago he'd begun sneaking into the boozer with a few of his mates and hiding the liquor-breath from his mum.

'Listen to yourself, boy!' Myllan playfully ducked around his old friend's arguments. 'People are just people. Why do you have to judge them against some perfect version of what you think they should be?'

Williams now started clenching and twisting his fists, jabbing some invisible sword through the air. 'It's not us doing the judging, old mate, it's you! The LM Sifts? They're fascist!'

'Ohh, nonsense. All we did was to eliminate the sources of social injustice. Once you've done that then you have to let individuality breathe. The LM device is just an extension of that basic principle. We are not trying to run people through an ideological grinder. Not like you communists. And wh—'

'Hold off a bloody—'

'And why?' Myllan pressed. 'Because communists always smack down anything which speaks of what they call bourgeois feeling. You know, family emotion, simple enjoyment, private property. All that!'

Williams spluttered with ironic amusement. Zadie looked up. With most of the patients now recovered the makeshift ward had become quite noisy. They were reasonably inconspicuous. A doctor and nurse were bent over Cramps. He seemed to be breathing properly.

'In a strange way I have to agree with our communist friend here,' the other newcomer leaned over. 'Name's Anders,' he announced, coolly. 'I agree that the distinction between choice and circumstance has been carried too far. I mean, sure, we want to give everyone an equal chance in life. But doing it this way invades people's dignity. The LM machine is invasive and even if it finds in your favour it labels you as a victim, as someone who didn't deserve the factors which shaped a portion of their life.

'We have tackled poverty but at what cost? We prop up the least advantaged at a level of minimum entitlements as if they are not allowed to fail, as if they are incapable of looking after themselves. "Your abilities are lower than an acceptable standard but, hey, you weren't responsible for this so have some money as compensation." It's demeaning!

'Wasn't it our conservative enemies who always distinguished between the undeserving and the deserving? Well, how have we moved on from that? Doesn't the LM scan do the same by determining how much you chose that something would happen?'

'So what's your alternative?' asked Myllan. Williams shook his head wearily.

Anders smiled to himself. When it came to debate he was a bird-of-prey whose feathers were difficult to ruffle.

'OK, OK. The problem with communism is that it wouldn't solve the problem. You, sir,' he indicated Myllan, 'have already stated why. It would presume against individuality and freedom. No, we need to preserve basic social equalities but make room for more personal freedoms without worrying about all this free-will stuff.

'I want to eat chocolate ice cream. Who cares whether I have a genetic predisposition to desire chocolate ice-cream? Or maybe I'm compensating for something by stuffing myself with calories. I didn't get the job I wanted. I mean, so what? Just sell me the damn ice cream and don't judge me!'

Myllan stroked his chin slowly. 'And if your ice-cream eating habits lead you to become miserable or poor or whatever? What then?'

'What then? That's my business!' said Anders. 'It can't be a matter of public policy. There have to be limits to state intervention.'

'The consequence of your view,' Myllan replied, 'would be to allow more inequalities back into society because once you distribute according to luck you are not only allowing a roll of the genetic dice to determine individuals' social position, you are risking a permanent division between the powerful and the dispossessed.'

'No, no.'

'Of course you are! One circumstance that none of us are responsible for is our parentage. If we allow parental background to stand then I inherit the good or bad fortune of my family. That, my friend, involves reintroducing class structures into the picture.'

'No, you are simplifying what I'm saying. We continue to bear down on inequalities and unfair—'

Williams bellowed, 'Sure! Social markets! We've heard it before. But unless political equality is accompanied by social equality, then you are trying to base democracy on uneven foundations. The rich have only managed to control government for, I don't know, the last five thousand years! Dahh! The only way to have political equality is to have social equality and that means getting rid of the affluent and sharing wealth around evenly.'

'I have a question. Where do the women come into all of this?'

Aon's query was so soft and yet so forceful that she silenced the testosterone-fuelled jousting. Kayne continued to stroke her hand, lost somewhere inside himself, not caring about the discussion.

'Women often see the world differently from men. When I have children I would want them to care for others. Freedom shouldn't crowd out other values. I respect the choices people make but that's because it's the respect which comes first, not the choice.'

Myllan broke the thoughtful silence which followed.

'Exactly. We wouldn't be egalitarians unless we cared for one another.'

'Where I come from—' continued Aon.

Detecting trouble, Jake stopped sucking strands of banana from between his teeth. 'If people are responsible for their choices doesn't that mean treating those who lose out pretty harshly?'

Myllan was still puzzling over what Aon had said. 'Eahh, no. Why?'

Jake closed his eyes and concentrated. 'Well, if I was brought into this hospital cos of a traffic accident, a pedestrian knocked down by a car, I'd receive the best treatment it could provide, right?'

'Obviously.'

'What if I was the driver? What if I was injured as much as the pedestrian? Would I receive as much care as the pedestrian?'

'Well, the LM Sift—'

'Yeah, OK, OK. Let's say that the car didn't fail or anything like that. Let's say I was careless. I was rooting around in my pocket when the accident happened. Would that make me as entitled to the same medical attention as the pedestrian?'

This brought Zadie out of herself. She was impressed again. Then she felt a pang of jealousy. He'd be better in university than you, she said to herself.

'It's an old argument,' Myllan mused. 'As egalitarians we try to provide for everyone's basic needs.'

'But if a decision has to be made about who gets treated first, then would it be me or the pedestrian?'

'If your injur—'

'Nahh, no. Injuries the same, remember?'

'Then I suppose we would see to the pedestrian first. Who wouldn't?' Williams and Anders nodded in agreement.

'But if I am entirely responsible for the accident then shouldn't I be entirely responsible for patching myself up?'

Myllan shook his head. 'We believe in social insurance, not private insurance. Companies should not be able to make a profit out of people's misery. People should receive it without having to worry about the size of their bank accounts.'

'Though I must say,' Anders coughed ruefully, 'some of us think that the young man is right to propose limited forms of service charge and personal insurance. The entire point of distinguishing between choice and circumstance is to assign liability. Shouldn't more of the actual cost fall on culpable individuals, then?'

'I wasn't arguing anything,' Jake glanced ruefully at his sister.

'I've already told you,' said Myllan, defensively. 'We wouldn't make an issue of freedom and choice unless we already respected people. That's why we're egalitarians in the first place. Holding people responsible for conditions they did not bring about is a right-wing con-trick. The emphasis on freedom only makes sense in an egalitarian environment.'

'But if we also say that we will care for others...' Aon started.

'In itself that's meaningless, though. We ought to care for others, sure. But decisions have to be made about how responsibility is apportioned. Otherwise—'

A shadow loomed over the group.

'...otherwise, care becomes little more than sentimental attachment and that takes you back to conservatism again.'

'Cramps!'

Cramps grunted as his granddaughter instinctively launched herself into a hug. 'Y'OK, Jake?'

Zadie spluttered. 'We need to talk! How are you feeling?'

'I'm fine, sweetheart.'

'You are?' Zadie held him at arm's length. 'You've been out for ages. Are you really OK?'

'Just a deep sleep. At my age it's better than sex.'

Jake indicated a spot near some climbing bars along the gym's nearest wall. Kayne made to get up and follow but Cramps leaned over, whispered something and Kayne, hesitant, sat back down next to Aon. 'Has Virgil...?' he asked once they were alone.

Jake tapped his pocket. 'I've been checking. Scan's finished I think. Can we get out of here now?'

'Yes and no. Gimme. Oy, wake up.' Cramps released the mute button.

Owww, stop slapping me around! I've been slaving over a hot spacetime continuum while you three have been (a) dozing, (b) picking your nose, and (c) talking inane drivel with complete morons. You ain't putting me back in the grotty one's pocket. There's dead skin, bogies, and all sorts in there. I insist on being washed at the earliest opportunity!

'Hell,' Jake exclaimed, 'Doctor Floppy's got us in his sights.' Many others in the gym were peering around at them too.

'Zadie?' the doctor called over to them, 'Now your grandfather's well again the police will want to talk to you all.'

Zadie stepped towards him. 'Doctor, could we just have a minute or two more alone? My grandfather is just a bit dazed.'

'Two minutes then.'

'Aon and Kayne are gonna be over here soon. What did you tell them?'

Cramps grimaced. 'That we are working on a way to get us all safely home but need some privacy first.'

Zadie looked into her grandfather's eyes and hoped it was true. Besides, she'd been lying to Aon and Kayne herself, hadn't she? She sensed their eyes boring into the back of her head. 'OK, we have two minutes. What's the plan?'

Cramps finished reading off Virgil's screen, looking satisfied at last. 'Plan is to fill you in on what I now know. You're not going to like it, even assuming that you believe it.'

Or can understand it. We should have brought along some sock puppets.

'Try us.'

'Not here. Not if we're about to be arrested for the umpteenth time today. We have to jump.'

'More keyword crap?' groaned Jake. 'Keeps landing us in worse trouble than before.' Cramps shrugged apologetically.

'It's got to be "equality",' suggested Zadie. Cramps typed the word into Virgil.

'No.'

'Luck.'

Cramps sighed. 'No.'

'Fairness? Justice?'

'Redistribution' Jake said.

None of them seemed to work.

'Cops!'

 What's that got to—'

'Heading our way, dumkopf!' A constable and a detective had entered the gym and were zeroing in on them, winding their way through the stretchers and camp beds. They had only seconds.

'Damn effing shitbelly machine,' cursed Jake.

'Not helping!!'

'Choice? Freedom? Solidarity.'

'Needs,' Jake said. 'No! Disadvantage!'

This time there was no tingling, no nausea, no swirl of pixellated colours. Zadie didn't even have time to feel jealous, yet again, of her brother's intuition.

They just winked out. There and then gone.

Everyone left in the gym gasped. They'd vanished into thin air! They would maintain this later, refusing to change their stories. We were there, damn it! We saw it! To the reporters, to the investigators, to the cynics, to themselves. Nowhere but into thin air!

CHAPTER TWELVE

Aon feels the damp soil on her cheek,
her lips and between
her clenched fingers as
she clings to the ground. Whimpers.
She opens her
eyes.
Dark
daytime
dark.
Cold wind
invades
her nostrils
her ears.
'Kayne?'
Nothing. No answer. Her
voice. Cavernous.
'Kayne! Please?'
She gets to her
knees. Raises her
head. Muscles protesting every
movement. Ruins.
She is alone.
Stone blocks litter every
direction. Rocks. Nothing green. No
trees. No seas
blue. No colours.
A burning darkness.
Except her.
She is this landscape's only colour.

Soot layers
most of the mud. Mud
sucking
her hands
into the black earth.
'Zadie!' No one.
No distant shouts
of reassurance. No minutes.
She sits.
The
sky is lightless grey. No clouds. No
stars. Grey eclipses the world. Seared with lightning
flashes.
Shattering light down to the debris.
Flashes. Devastated. The
world's wreckage.
Aon closes her eyes.
Not alone. Not here. Not inside my head.
Kayne!
The shadows skulk and
resettle.
Grey everywhere. Rain
soon. No horizon. The horizon lost
behind me the
ruins stretching everywhere.
Scraping.
She scrambles to her feet. Scraping. Behind
me. Wrong. How wrong was I?
Something there
after all. Something there
with me. Moving.
moving
the dark. Behind me.
Wrong. How wrong. Oh, Zadie! Oh God!
The dark moving. The dead breeze.
Aon screams.

CHAPTER THIRTEEN

They were standing on a white plain in a blinding sunless light.

At first Zadie thought it was another room. A bleached, snowblind version of their grandfather's closet. But the whiteness wasn't paint. It wasn't lit. Its emptiness drew in the eyes but gave them nothing to focus on. Above and below. No ceiling, no floor, no walls. The horizon might be an arm's-length away. It might be a million miles distant. They seemed to be standing on nothing, in a depthless radiance, filling the space that stretched out endlessly around. Zadie would feel as if she was falling, then, a second later, as if she were still and it was the pale universe expanding away from her.

She was reminded of those featureless landscapes she had read about, of how on the Antarctic plateau it was impossible to visualise distances as you were the only figures moving in a boundless, horizonless blur of sky and land. Or the moon. The way rocks that seemed to be within touching distance were actually house-high boulders a mile away. Zadie felt that she could stretch out her arms and reach between the worlds. They were standing there, alone, the only shapes and shades on an infinite white moon. It was only those familiar forms, nearby, which were preventing her body from following her mind floating off into a shadowless universe.

'Zadie?'

'Mmm...'

'Zadie!!'

'Ye—'

'Don't drift. Concentrate! Look at me. Nothing but me. You too, Jake.'

Zadie gazed into her grandfather's eyes. Normally so shy! Why? So shy? Why? Why? Why? So shy so shy why why so so sh—

'Zadie! Did you hear me?! Stay with me!'

125

She was shaking. Who was shaking her? 'Whasgon?' Zadie's mouth wouldn't unglue. 'Whe?'

'Where we were. Where we've always been. You're in the m-bubble, a frozen bubble of spacetime.'

'Huh?' asked Jake as Zadie grinned and dribbled, admiring him for managing that much.

'You are inside the other insides of spacetime.'

No echo. Their voices flattened and encircled them. Humid sounds. Jake found his voice. 'Thanks for explaining it all.'

'Nothing of what I am about to tell you is adequate. Words always fail.'

'Who "we"?' Zadie was surprised to hear herself speak so clearly. She wanted to say more. Just to have something to tether herself to. How wonderful it was to speak. 'Zis level? Am dizzy.'

'The program was a ruse, sweetheart. It was a survey exercise that I needed to take and which I thought would be helpful and enjoyable for you. A farewell present. A gift that has gone wrong. Your grandfather is a fool. Your conclusions were incorrect, but you were right to be suspicious. I never meant to put you in harm's way. Isn't that the lamest excuse? The m-bubble is a multi-terminus within the multifold.'

Zadie was looking at her hand. *Why* had she never noticed *this* before?!! It was miraculous! She had to tell someone about this! If only someone was here. Oh! Cramps! What he been saying? How far did she have to stretch out her arm before her hand disappeared into the whiteness?

Jake caught his sister as she almost toppled over. 'God, she's high.'

Whhhhooooeeeee!

'More a kind of temporal delirium. A combination of claustrophobia and vertigo. Like being drunk, yes. It'll fade as she gets used to it. How come you seem fine?'

'Natural ability.'

'Ah!'

'Can we go home now?'

'I wish we could but we have to press on with what we were doing. I need to explain this in simple terms.'

Brilliant! Children's TV! Love it.

'Shut up. How much do you know about multi-phased temporal-quantum burrowing?'

Jake thought for a moment. 'Had the flu that day.'

'OK. You must remember your eleven-dimensional geometry, at least?'

'Was at football practice.'

'I swear the education system is becoming worse and worse. Would it help if I described myself as a time traveller? Of sorts.'

Jake and his bleary sister treated this with all the respect it deserved. Which made their grandfather all the more nervous when they gagged themselves laughing.

Oh, poopies. That laughter? That's the sound of my soul dying.

'Sorry, Cramps.' Jake said. 'Does this mean you came back in time to meet your great-grandfather?'

'No.'

'You came back to *kill* your great-grandfather?'

'No, Jake, I—'

'Am *I* your great-grandfather?'

Hell! You walking wind-tunnel.

'No. Look, it's a simplification to call me a time traveller. I haven't travelled *through* time, but to another coordinate *of* spacetime. You can go anywhere if you tunnel quickly enough. That's what the m-bubble enables. It's a way of unravelling the geodetic cords.'

'Cords? Cords? For the cosmic bathrobe?'

Will you shut the cakehole up! I'm in my happy place...I'm in my happy place...

'Zadie! Are you back with us?' Cramps barked.

'Yesno.'

'That'll do. Why is this so difficult to believe after what you've been through today? You didn't really believe that I'd built a highly advanced holographic program in my closet, did you?'

The siblings looked at one another sheepishly.

Ha!

Cramps smiled, sweetly. 'Despite the fact there was no machinery in that room?'

'Then you're not our grandfather?!'

'Course I am!'

'Then...?'

'It's like this—'

'You're from the future?!' Jake asked.

'Is this gonna take long, Cramps?' Zadie tried to moisten her lips. 'There are no chairs here. Can we have some chairs?'

'I arrived in 1967. I was young, in my mid-twenties. Most of those selected to be the first chrononauts were young. No children; unmarried. I was chosen for the maiden voyage. The first manned journey into the multifold.'

'Then how far...?' Zadie was still groggy. She didn't know whether this was the first sign of madness, or the revelation she'd been waiting for, or another part of the program to be puzzled out, or evidence of her grandfather's absurd and totally inappropriate humour. She thought it best to take what she was seeing and hearing on face value. Anything was better than being looked at by the white nothingness which tugged at her vision from all sides.

'You might think of me as having come from two centuries in your future. But it's...it's difficult to explain. After decades of preparation the maiden voyage turned out to be a disaster, for me at least. We'd performed successful cross-time rebounds with objects and then animals. First sending them to unpopulated areas and then to populated ones. First for short periods of time and then for increasingly longer ones. But the maiden voyage of a human was always going to be much more risky. Sending objects and animals across spacetime is relatively risk-free. But humans....

'We are agents, you see. We interact. So we planned something modest, something to minimise the risk. The equivalent of touching down on the moon, saying "well, we did it" and then blasting off again two minutes later.'

It suddenly occurred to Jake to look at his watch. Nothing. The second hand wasn't moving. 'Something went wrong?' he asked.

'Yes.'

'You're not going to tell us you accidentally assassinated someone or started a war, are you?'

Cramps paused for a second. 'A small tribal war, yes.'

'Oh boy!'

'Only kidding. No, but I was seen arriving. It led to an arrest. A few weeks in jail. It meant that my presence here had altered the temporal vectors of my return. I couldn't navigate my way back. Not without help. The return coordinates had altered beyond the standard margin of error—'

'Hang on,' Jake interrupted. 'If this was a maiden voyage then why not jump back to the middle of a desert or somewhere? Why risk being seen?'

'I did jump back to the middle of a desert. Right into the middle of a Bedouin caravan.'

'Yeeks! Bad luck or what.'

Ya wanna know the probability calculation?

'Not really.'

'That's why I never wanted to go on holiday to North Africa or the Middle East.' Another family mystery solved.

'I was hot.'

'Hot?'

'Broke out of jail.'

'Course.'

I had to spend weeks hiding down his pants!

'Anyway, my intervention was so prolonged that even my series 5 quantum computer...' Cramps patted Virgil's screen.

Ow yaz doin?

'...was unable to calculate a return trajectory precise enough. I could have made an imprecise jump back but who knows what ramifications that would have had. Besides, I left someone behind that I cared about very much. I didn't want to risk not seeing her again, even if it meant me returning as an old man. I had to wait twenty years until computer technology had developed to the point where Virgil could interface with the databases he needed to make the correct calculations.'

'Then why didn't you pop off twenty years ago?'

'Why? Because I had a wife, a daughter. I'd laid down roots. I couldn't just vanish.'

Don't think you'll ever be forgiven for that either! Have you got any idea how boring it's been watching television for the last forty-two years?

'Television?'

'Not quite. Virgil is a consciousness. A synthetic intelligence. He was how I convinced your grandmother who I was. I couldn't just hibernate him. I suppose he did watch a lot of television, especially when your mother was at school. We decided not to tell her. We disguised Virgil as a knick-knack, didn't we, Virge?'

Cross-dressing was such a turn-on!

Zadie rolled her eyes. Then that explained why he'd been disguised as a music box, why he'd sat on the highest shelf, why their bookish grandparents had always left the TV on and why Cramps had shouted at her when she'd ascended the bookcase that time. Virgil was his only way home! Holy Moses!

'So, Virgil's spent forty-two years watching television?' she pondered. 'That would explain why he's got such a lousy personality.'

Hey, it was your culture that gave me this personality, space waste! How else can you explain why I laughed for hours when Bambi's mother was shot? Why else haven't I been able to form a meaningful relationship with anything more sophisticated than a toaster?

'Well, it's not just *his* personality. In my time everyone possesses a synthetic companion and these SI units are programmed with the parameters of their...well "owners" is the wrong word.'

Damn right!

'It's more like raising a child to become a friend who shares a lot of your traits.'

'You mean, all of that sarcasm and bile is you?!' Zadie blurted.

Heh-heh-heh-heh-heh-heh.

'Cramps, are you making him act like that? Is Virgil really you?'

'No, you misunderst—'

Heh-heh-heh-heh-heh-heh.

'Waa, wa, wait. Back up a mo',' Jake was massaging his temples. 'This doesn't make sense. If you couldn't return to your own time after a few weeks then how can you do it after forty-two years? If the – what? – being in jail for a few weeks made it impossible, then how is it any easier now?'

Damn! His wisecracking who-cares attitude made it easy to forget how smart Jake was.

Cramps sucked on his teeth and considered what to say. 'It's been a race. On the one hand, every day in the past – your present – alters its coordinates in spacetime compared to what they would have been otherwise. You're right about that. On the other, if I could remain inconspicuous and not have any major influence on the timepath then any geometric changes on the future would be minor, they'd dissipate, and we could wait until Virgil had the information he needed to plot a way home.

'It was therefore important that I not have any influence on the future. So I became an academic. Even then, I could have upset things by applying my advanced scientific knowledge. Therefore, I decided always to follow in the footsteps of other researchers, never take risks and publish what was basically the same introductory textbook three times over. Bizarrely, that turned out to be a recipe for academic success! Still, I think my impact on human affairs has been pleasantly redundant.'

Apart from you, my family, said his inner voice.

'The problem, then, became actually making the return calculations. As with any form of orienteering the best way of finding your way is through multi-vector triangulation. I couldn't do this by travelling into other time periods, for obvious reasons. So I decided to try other timepaths.

'To make a long story short.... In the twentieth century some physicists proposed that the past and the future actually exist. So the past doesn't just fade. It's out there still, only in a now inaccessible region of spacetime. But if you could access those regions, then you could travel to them. *Voilà!*

'Well, a related branch of physics suggested that the reality we know is a line that is taken through many other possible realities that could have existed. If I toss a coin then when it's in the air there are two possibilities; one where it lands heads and one where it lands tails. The coin hits the ground and I see it is heads. One of the possibilities has become a reality. But what of the shadow-reality, the one where the coin landed as tails? Does it just vanish into nothing? Or does it occupy its own part of the spacetime continuum? Nobody knew. But for Virgil, able to travel anywhere, if it is possible to access an earlier part of reality, then why not a shadow-reality too? After all, we're only talking about different regions of spacetime. "The metaverse", we call it. Or sometimes, "the multifold". The idea of reality branching off was popular with science-fiction writers but none of them really knew what the hell they were talking about.

'Travelling to those shadow-realities therefore seemed like an easier way of performing the triangulation we needed. And...' Cramps hesitated, 'if I had to perform that journey for myself then...why not for my family too?'

Zadie felt sick again. 'You mean we've been interacting with real people?!'

'I don't know.'

'What d'you mean you don't know?!'

'There's a quantum fuzziness....Look, they may be real...or they may just be phantom possibilities that just appear real within the m-bubble. The jump calculations are the same, either way.'

'So they could be real?' Hadn't she known it all along?

'Yes'

'Aon? Kayne? Everyone?' Though Zadie silently admitted to herself that she couldn't be quite as upset if the same thing had happened to Dearbrook and Ridley.

'Yes.'

'And if they are real, then we've been interfering with their realities the same way you interfered with the past?'

'Or they could just be warps in the vector data that the bubble has interpreted in a particular way.'

'The bubble? The bubble we're inside now?'

'We've been inside it from the start. It's coded for your biographs. Your DNA. So it would encompass us all even if we were separated by millions of miles. Touch wood,' he added.

'And Virgil controls the bubble?'

'Not quite. Virgil *is* the bubble. As a quantum computer he interacts with the other versions of himself before they either...vanish, or split off into new branches of the multifold. He draws the shadow-realities towards us and interprets the probability streams as best he can, projecting them into the bubble. As I say, he's a series 5. That means he performs trillions of calculations every nanosecond. Don't you Virge?'

Wha? I wasn't listening. Some of us are trying to sleep, you know.

'If he wanted to, Virgil could simulate the evolution of an entire universe. So whether those shadows are real or just realistic versions of his calculations doesn't matter when it comes to the mathem—'

'So we've been inside Virgil all this time?'

Ughhh!

'In a manner of speaking. We've been inside the m-bubble, which is the site in which the calculations are performed. This,' Cramps swept his arm at the white infinity, 'is its purest representation. A nothingness.'

'But if those...timepaths...those shadow-realities, are as real as our own then we've been messing with people's lives. What possessed you?'

'Because, while the number of shadow-realities is not infinite, it is incredibly vast. If reality splits then it's been splitting every Planck-instant since Point Alpha. We've barely sighted the ocean over the last twelve hours, let alone gone for a paddle in the shallowest waves. What I'm saying is that if the damage, the rupture, our journey has caused has adversely affected the lives of those we've encountered then it's the equivalent of removing one grain of sand from all the world's beaches. There are countless zillions of Aons out there. None of whom may be real anyway.'

Zadie flared. 'Granddad. That isn't what I was brought up to believe. Brought up by *you* to believe! There are billions of people on Earth. Does that make it OK to kill one of them?'

There seemed to be no answer to this. Cramps knew he'd been arguing against himself, trying to divert his grandchildren from the really terrifying possibility he hoped they wouldn't realise. No one spoke for a while.

'You mean,' Jake asked, 'there's a region of spacetime where Hitler and Churchill became gay lovers?'

'Several, in fact.'

'Then there are shadow versions of us as well?'

Cramps sensed danger.

Yeah, but you're the only one with mega-smelly armpits.

But Zadie was still tearfully angry. 'Then what was the point of all this?'

'Go easy,' soothed Jake, 'everyone makes mistakes.'

Excuse me?!!

'It wasn't meant to happen as it's happened,' her grandfather explained. 'Yes, we might have been interacting with real people anyway but only in a casual, insignificant way. But we've accidentally created a rupture.'

'But why?'

'The physics is—'

'No! Not that. Why all this?'

'Let me go back. Virgil calculated the broad return vectors two decades ago and I've been testing the system oh so carefully ever since. Finally, I began making small incursions into other parts of the multifold close to our one. It didn't make a difference. Virgil was still able to plot a way home. To my home I mean. Even when the shadow-realities were further away, the return vectors to my original part of the metaverse could be recalculated. I told your grandmother I might have found a way back. But I also told her that I wouldn't abandon her. Then, when she died....When she died I began to make preparations for my return. To my future.'

He slumped as he saw their expressions.

'Please don't look at me like that,' he pleaded. 'I've gone over this so many times with your mum. Everyone my age makes preparation for their death. Everyone dies. Does it make that much of a difference if I leave? Think of it as if I'm going to spend my final years in Australia or something.'

'The difference is we could still talk to you,' implored Jake.

'And I might be able to visit you again. But...' Cramps' voice trailed away, 'I can't be sure. It's out of my hands.'

The featureless landscape around them had not altered in any way. Zadie realised how much their talk, the most incredible, unbelievable conversation of her life, had kept its oppressive, endless silence at bay.

Cramps clawed absently at his chalk hair, pulling it into clumps. 'I decided it was time to go. I told your mother. As I said, we'd never told her about my origins. She thought I was bereaved. Dotty! Almost called social services on me! I was able to show her Virgil and a video message from her mother giving me her blessing. It was too much for her, still so soon after the death of your father. But now...I mean... time has gone by and I feel the need to return to my first home. It's hard but...it's not as if I'd live forever if I stayed here anyway.' Cramps sighed, heavily. 'That's why your mother hasn't talked to me in months. Too much loss. Her husband, her mother and now me. I hate myself for doing this to her, and to you, but I have to go back.'

Not want to. *Have* to.

'But why?'

Cramps again paused before replying. Can't tell them everything. Was his extended incursion into the past something that had to happen? Had it already happened, even before he'd left? Was the past frozen, unalterable? Free will an illusion? Philosophers and scientists had debated the possibilities for centuries. The unmanned journeys that had preceded him had been inconclusive; his own expedition being meant as a precursor to voyages that would settle the matter once and for all. Well, he'd buggered that plan up good and proper, hadn't he? For almost every hour of every day for the last forty-two years he had pondered the same question. Was his being trapped in the past meant to happen? Or had his experience altered the timeline in a way that his contemporaries in the future would feel the need to erase? If the latter, it would surely mean someone leading a second expedition to repair what they would see as 'damage': his marriage, his daughter, his grandchildren. Failing to return had never been an option. So he had spent years planning for the worst. Covered his tracks as best he could. Prepared a simple explanation for his sudden reappearance in the future as an old man.

All of this flashed through his mind for the millionth time. Yet I can't tell them any of it. I can't tell them that if I don't return to the instant I left they may send another chrononaut back to prevent my initial incursion and so erase them from existence. They couldn't deal with that possibility. *I* can't deal with it. I have to go back in order to keep you alive. But that's not the full truth either. I *am* going back for Qaoni too. I'm not being totally selfless.

'My duty to report. To prevent other dangerous incursions. And there's another, more selfish reason. A woman. Her name's Qaoni. A woman who your grandmother very much reminded me of. Her death, well…it brought back old memories. She's still out there somewhere. In a future instant of frozen time.'

Jake saddened. 'But you'll still be sixty-seven when you go back? Not a young man again?'

'When I return only a Planck-length will have passed since my departure. But to my colleagues I will suddenly be forty-two years older.'

'But this other woman? She'll still be young?'

'Yes.'

'What will she say when she sees you and you're suddenly forty years older?'

'I don't know. But if someone you love suddenly aged four decades you wouldn't stop loving them, would you?'

'What if the shadow-realities are real, though? Wouldn't trillions of you pour out of the time machine all at once?'

Cramps smiled. He really was very proud of his lazy-arse grandson. He'd have to say this convincingly, without spelling out too much. 'No, there's a very low probability those shadow-realities are real. Anyway, I wanted to leave you with the essentials of what I have to teach. All I *could* teach anyway if I were to live with you as normal for another twenty years.'

Jake thought about this. 'You want us to do something that will ensure that the future you left will be the future you return to?'

'Not exactly. I mean, the actions of most individuals don't matter directly.'

'So what's the future like Cramps? Any flying cars? Are you going to take us there?'

'No, Jakers. It's too risky, especially after today's lesson.'

Jake seemed to be accepting much of this but Cramps saw that Zadie was getting more and more furious.

'Are you telling us we might be stranded? Apart from what this does to Jake and me, what about mum?! How is she going to feel if we all suddenly vanish?! Are you trying to take away everyone who matters to her?'

Cramps winced. There was no reply to this and he didn't attempt one.

'And what's the point?' Zadie continued, after a hurt silence. 'If we don't affect the future and if there's a universe of infinite possible realities out there then who cares? It doesn't matter if I kill myself because there will still be lots of "me" out there, somewhere. It doesn't matter if I go on a killing spree because other versions of the people I murder will still be out there too. So, what's the point? Did you bring us here to depress us and tell us how insignificant we are before leaving us forever?'

'Zadie, no, of course not. Why would you be insignificant? On balance, we suspect the shadow-realities are just that: shadows. But even it they're not...you were right. It's how we treat others which matters, not how many others there are to be treated.'

If I'm right, Zadie thought accusingly, then how do you square what you've just said with the possible damage you've done today?

'But it means I'm not unique!' she continued. 'It means that I'm not free. Not really. We're just puppets who can't see the strings.'

'The fact that you probably can't always prevent the Nazis from winning the war doesn't mean they have to win it an equal number of times to the allies. Individuals matter by choosing *how* they will matter. They choose not to become Nazis, or murderers, or whatever. That's why I brought you into the m-bubble. What disturbs me about your time is the way you convince yourselves you lack choices. You are affluent, yet never seem able to afford any of the things that matter. You are free, but constantly anxious and uncertain.

'I wanted to expand your horizons, show you different versions of your present. What might have happened if the recent past had altered in some way. I chose extreme...I suppose...utopian versions of alternative realities and asked Virgil to plot an appropriate course through the multifold that would double as my final survey mission. Some of those societies are better than others. That's for you to decide. I wanted to expose you to different ways of thinking and living. Appreciation and exploration of alternatives and contrasts. It's how we learn. It's the *only* way we learn. By closing yourselves off your time risks becoming technologically advanced and morally stupid.

'So when you told me about your visit to that politician it seemed a perfect opportunity. Too perfect. I should have delayed, taken the time to recalibrate the effects of our departure. Everything else has followed from that foolish mistake. That's why I was alarmed when we started seeing people in one part of spacetime that we'd seen in the other. That's what Virgil has been doing. Tracking what has happened. We've caused a rupture. In jumping from region to region we have altered their parameters. Dragging remnants of other shadows with us. Altering the places I merely wanted to visit, to a degree far beyond what our presence should otherwise have caused.

'So Aon, Kayne,' Jake mused, '...we somehow pulled them behind us, as if they were caught in our wake.'

'No wait!' Zadie exclaimed. 'What about Mrs Gregsbury? We met her this morning, before coming into the...bubble!'

'Even if it was her I think that's nothing more than a coincidence. A shadow-version of the person you met.'

'So when Aon and Kayne remembered us from the Grey Distr–'

'It's the rupture, sweetheart. They were somehow pulled into the new regions of spacetime with new lives, new histories, new memories that somehow fused with the old ones. We've been merging previously inaccessible regions together. It's as if we've been dragging an ever expanding wormhole behind us.'

Zadie could feel her faith in her grandfather bleeding away.

'Why hasn't that affected us?' Jake asked.

'It has,' guessed Zadie. 'When we blanked out and awoke in that cell. The other prisoner said that we'd been acting robotically for – what was it? – half an hour.'

'Yes. Virgil was unable to counteract the interfold currents. In other words, the rupture is affecting the m-bubble as well. Something that shouldn't be possible, theoretically.'

'Will it happen again?'

'Probably, but I can't be sure.'

'Then what do we do?' Zadie demanded. 'Aren't we really still in your house?'

'No.'

'But Virgil said we were.'

'I asked him to fib.'

Open the pod bay doors please Hal.

'So we could be lost in alternative realities that may not really exist?'

'Yes.'

'Then where would we be?'

'Here. In this non-space.'

'So how do we protect ourselves and get home? And how do we repair the damage we've done?' That *you've* done! If ever Zadie needed a bed to flop down onto and have a good cry it was now.

'Here's what I think,' Cramps replied. 'If we return to the moment just before we entered the closet then the rupture will seal behind us.'

'Can't we just go home now?' Jake asked, the lonely, betrayed image of his mother now scratching at him too.

'No. It's like going on a round-trip. If you broke your journey you'd have to buy another ticket with a whole new set of travel times. Yes? Well, that is impossible for us. Virgil needs to calculate the complete parameters of the rupture and that can only happen by visiting all the places we were due to visit. We have to complete the trip. There is an emergency override option but it's very dangerous and I don't want to use it unless absolutely necessary.

'And we'll have to be quick. We have to try and stay ahead of the rupture. The more time we spend, the more severe the rupture will become and the harder it will be to plot a return. We might end up so far from our departure that return becomes impossible.'

'You mean we might be trapped?'

'Yes. We'd be inside the bubble forever, lost in spacetime. Either in another reality or interacting with mathematically-generated phantoms.'

'And this will make everything better?' Zadie was sullen.

'Yes,' her grandfather said, hoping she would one day forgive him for this final lie. 'And it's not all bad news...I brought more sandwiches.' Yet not even Jake laughed at this. 'Ready?'

Cramps pushed a few buttons on Virgil and the whiteness around them dissolved. From every direction flat streams of images raced towards them. Avalanches of pictures. Millions of them. Frozen, immeasurable times. An infinite number of possible present moments. It was as if reality had doubled and doubled and continued to double exponentially in a globed hall of mirrors. There was no wind, no sound. No suggestion that the images screaming in at them at thousands of miles an hour would hurt them. Somewhere in there was their own region of spacetime, their own lives, their own still grieving mother. They were just going to have to find it. Find her. Find home.

Virgil blipped. The images cascaded. The m-bubble blinked and now it was they rushing headlong into the metaverse.

CHAPTER FOURTEEN

WAKE UP!

'Whhaa....ooo?'

Very articulate. The place is opening. Shift arses, pronto.

Jake felt bleary. He'd obviously slept. Quality sleep this time and not some nauseous nightmare brought on by...he groaned. Brought on by what? The spacetime metaverse being torn into fragments as a result of their little holiday? Bloody British tourists. They always ruin it for everyone else!

Zadie and Cramps were stirring, too. They were lying in a living room from a 1950s sitcom. The television was a bulky black-and-white set with fat dials and a large spiralling wire aerial. Vivid, lurid colours assaulted their eyes, as if the room had been dipped in a vat of luminous paint. The furniture looked delicate, threatening to collapse if anyone actually used it. The bright pink carpet was deep and fertile. Thick lace curtains obscured the street outside. Opposite, where the fourth wall should have been, a wry man in grey overalls was scrutinizing them, leaning on his mop. There was no fourth wall. A sheet of glass opened onto a large, dark interior that Jake could barely make out. Were they in a brightly lit shop window? Was it night-time? The man put down his bucket.

'Vistors not 'loud near, ya know. Die ramas for viewin'. 'Ow'd you get up here so quick anyhows?'

'Sorry!' Cramps extemporised. 'We got carried away.'

Their grandfather ushered them through the door the janitor pointed them towards and they threaded their way out of the side alcove and onto the main floor.

'Tour counder. She jest opnin.' He indicated a short corridor to their left and shuffled away.

'Why were we asleep?' Jake asked as they wandered off. 'Did the rupture cause it?'

'Perhaps, but let's not assume anything for now.' Cramps said as he offered them some more water. Zadie refused. She wouldn't even look at him.

The woman at the tour counter was cheery and welcoming. 'Ah-ha, first party of the day. Well done! You're wanting the mobile guides? The first twelve people to make it up here get to take the mobile tour free of charge. Three of you?' She handed over three cotton bags. Inside Jake found pens, postcards, a calendar, a booklet and a leaflet. The leaflet announced itself proudly and boldly as *The Museum of Cultural Identity: A History*. The booklet was a map with lots of large fold-out charts that Jake quickly managed to entangle.

Cramps emptied the items into his own shoulder bag and dropped Virgil in there too. 'Hush,' he whispered to the muffled harrumph, 'keep working on those vectors.' The bags also contained earphones and a small iPod-sized device. The mobile guide, presumably. Jake had seen similar equipment on a school trip once. An art gallery. Hadn't that been one long snooze! Oh, and at that thingy zoo a few years ago where Jake had been lectured by that pork-hole security guard for throwing jelly babies at the chimps.

The woman explained the guide's basics. An onscreen menu allowed them to explore freely, but the simplest option to take was 'Route 1' which would easily lead them through a preset path down through the floors. Fluorescent floor and wall signs should ensure they didn't get lost. There were stewards patrolling every floor just in case.

'How many floors are there?' Jake gave up struggling with his maps, compacting them into a crushed paper cube.

'Twenty-six in all.'

'Twenty-six! How long does it take to get round this place?'

'Oh, many visits for the full experience. You did get the Revisit Package, didn't you? If not and you want to see as much as possible in one day, then you should choose Route 3 on your guides.'

They set off back to where they'd woken up. Over to the left one of the lifts pinged and other visitors began flooding onto the floor. As in every museum the lights were dimmed to make the various displays and tableaux stand out. Now that their eyes had adjusted they could see many passages leading off onto the rest of the floor. The museum's logo and title was dotted across the walls.Fourteen million square feet of floor space, it announced.

They each slipped on the headphones, set the guide to Route 3 with Jake's help, and pushed the start buttons simultaneously. A swirl of electronic bleeps and pipes that Cramps assumed was meant to be music thundered at his lobes. He'd just managed to readjust the volume just as a woman's voice stereoed into his ears.

'Welcome to the Museum of Cultural Identity. We hope you enjoy your visit and trust it will be one of many. You are one of over fifty million patrons who visit the world's largest museum every year. We feel privileged to welcome each and every one of you. Home to twenty-six floors, hundreds of galleries, 150 million items, a dozen restaurants for every taste, two major conference centres and its own four-star hotel, the Museum...'

The woman had one of those sing-song voices that flight attendants adopted to reassure passengers that plunging into the sea at 400 miles an hour was all part of the service and nothing to worry about. The introduction was a long one. Cramps looked around nervously. They were the epicentre of the rupture and it was important to keep an eye out for any anomalies, familiar faces, that kind of thing. His granddaughter continued to avoid his gaze. Cramps pretended not to notice her pretending not to notice him.

He tried to process what he was hearing. Museum less than ten years old. Took fifteen years to build. Response to the realisation that social justice meant respecting the many possible identities of individuals, groups and diverse cultures. OK, this was what he'd expected when he'd programmed Virgil months ago. Perhaps they'd be lucky and manage to get home without the rupture catching them.

The guide directed them first to the display they'd woken up in minutes earlier. From this side of the observation glass the living room seemed to be trapped in even more of a 1950s timewarp.

'This,' the guide intoned, solemnly, 'is a depiction of a typical patriarch's home. It was designed for leisure but the leisure enjoyed by the family's members was not experienced equally. It was the women, defined primarily as wife and mother, who carried the main burden of maintaining her loved ones in some semblance of an ideal, bourgeois existence. It was her duty not only to plump the floral cushions, vacuum the lush carpet and dust the over-priced furniture but to do so always with uncomplaining contentment, as if her very being could be fulfilled by such mundane tasks! Although her husband would often contribute the hand of discipline and of aggressive, competitive play, the burden of child raising also fell mainly to the mother. The kitchen...'

Here flickering neon arrows directed them to the next diorama. It, too, seemed to have wandered, lost, out of a 1950s television show, with pristine white ceramic surfaces, rhomboid-shaped cupboards, garish wallpaper and still more lace curtains.

'...symbolised her oppression. This was her domain but the control she exerted here was bought at a terrible price. In a phrase which became popular with The Movements the mother was literally "chained to the kitchen sink". The chains may have been emotional rather than physical – though as we will see on Floor 25 domestic violence was widespread – but they were just as debilitating. Most women identified with their oppression. What other choice had they? Because we all search for validation and respect from others it is understandable that the women of this era accepted whatever they could find with gratitude. Their social roles, their very physical appearance, were designed to mark them as soft, dependent, fragile objects who would not survive in the public worlds of work and government.'

Again, arrows shuffled them sideways, this time to a bedroom. The pink carpet and flimsy furniture reappeared. The large wardrobe was open and more clothes had been strewn onto the bed and across one chair. On the long sideboard a rolling landfill of cosmetics, tins and bottles was reflected in a three-panelled mirror, alongside heaps of jewellery and various objects designed to pluck, brush, stroke, dab and poke.

'The apparel of the time also symbolised women's oppression. Dresses and skirts signalled women's sexual availability. Their open-ness signified a distinction in the minds of men of a woman as either angel or whore, as either beautiful but immune to the male gaze or as promiscuously seeking it. The ideal woman was the mother-figure that the man either had to preserve or destroy. Underwear such as bras, girdles, panties and stockings emphasised and enhanced a woman's figure, her voluptuousness. And the vast array of commer-cial make-up and beauty products also emphasised her appearance; her looks rather than her mind, the surface rather than the substance. Scholars have traced the historical and psychosocial connections between high-heeled shoes and foot-binding. The higher the heel, the more restricted the mobility. It was a form of willing bondage; for why would the woman want to run away from her man?

'Of course most women did not see this as oppression. Women's clothes were at least colourful, diverse and soft, in contrast to the staid, monochromatic suits that men were required to wear. But both forms of attire constituted a uniform that locked the sexes into prescribed gender roles. For men, at least, the compensations were considerable...'

Zadie looked around. There were now a couple of dozen visitors on this floor, most queuing at the counter they'd just left. There was a flat androgyny about them that went beyond anything she had seen before. Some of the women wore skirts and make-up and some did not. Behind her, Jake's guffaw told Zadie that he'd noticed how this was true of the men as well.

'What's so funny? You wear earrings every so often, don't you? And don't pretend you don't use Mum's Olay Cleanser. She's seen you.'

'Earstuds. It's different. It's acceptable.'

'It's only acceptable because people made it acceptable. It takes courage to be different when you're alone. Then years later people like you jump on the bandwagon, call it normal and then find new kinds of difference to laugh at. Try walking down a road forty years ago with an earring on. You'd have had seven types of you-know-what kicked out of you.'

But a short while later she was approached by a man in a blouse. As she made a clumsy retreat Zadie tried to ignore the suppressed sniggers of her brother.

Cramps had drifted on and they realised they'd missed some of the narration. The new section showed a stacked bank of eight or nine video screens with rapid-fire images flashing constantly across them. It was impossible to take in everything but the grainy images showed destitution and misery.

'...the relevance of identity to poverty. For a long time it was believed that poverty was simply a lack of economic resources and job opportunities. But those who advanced this interpretation of injustice – Marxists and socialists, among others – could not adequately explain what gave a person worth and status in the first place. Unless we can account for a person's moral significance then it is unclear why we ought to be concerned with injustice.

'It was eventually realised that material goods depend upon the cultural context in which they appear. We confer meaning on objects by representing them in a certain way to ourselves and others. We confer meaning on people in the same way. Fair distribution is justified because we do and ought to respect each other. Social justice is a form of recognition. It depends upon the circulation of esteem throughout society and the ways in which my identity is interdependent with yours. Our needs are cultural. The world is made meaningful because of our shared participation in a moral community. I become visible and knowable to myself by becoming visible and knowable to you. To misrepresent and disrespect someone is to distort the social bases of meaning. Bigotry is an insult, a disrespectful joke, a stereotype. These are all forms of misrecognition.

'Poverty and exclusion are also cultural in this sense. To alter the distribution of material "things" without attending to cultural norms was the reason why anti-poverty measures failed for so long. The negative representation of impoverished people, the very words used to describe them – such as underclass, pauper, scrounger, dependant – meant that even those trying to relieve poverty did not really see and hear those they were meant to be helping. Poverty was only defeated when those lacking the requisite resources were able to control not only the political distribution of material goods but also their own social images, cultural representations and political voices.

'Of course, philosophers will always argue about how the cultural and the material do and should relate to one another. Dynamism rather than consensus is the lifeblood of philosophy.'

Jake wandered off across what he now saw as The Most Boring Museum Ever. The diorama on disability showed a virtual 3-D miniature of a high street which seemed to have floated out of the 1970s, to judge by the aeroplane-sized shirt-collars. Using a console he could select one or more of a series of disabilities and was supposed to experience how difficult it would have been to shop, cross the road, etc., etc. Jake didn't bother. Not exactly DoomWar.

The ethnicity section portrayed a large screen on which a stream of very unwelcoming faces appeared, all of them white, a new one every few seconds. Some of the people were shouting racial abuse, though Jake thought it tame and almost quaint compared to some he'd heard. Others slammed doors in his face. Others shook their heads and handed him rejection slips. Many smiled but as they turned their expression changed to one of shuddering distaste. The guide explained that much racism was hidden, even from racists themselves in many instances. For an exploration of institutional racism, visit Floor 18.

And on it went. Sexuality. Religion. Nationality. Jake was bored already. They didn't see it all. Cramps reminded them that they needed to be quick and remain observant for any familiar faces.

Jake poked his head into Cramps' shoulder bag. 'Virgil, can we guess the keyword yet?'

No.

'Can't you make an exception just this once?'

No.

'Don't synthetic intelligences possess free will?'

Bog off. See if that works!

Cramps was apologetic. 'A reprogramming would take hours, even assuming he allowed us permission. And it's way too early to risk the emergency override.'

Zadie spotted one of the museum stewards, not looking particularly busy. Bald on top with cropped, square-angled hair at the sides, his nostrils were so hairy Zadie swore he was trying to grow a moustache the difficult way. He looked like a sergeant-major. 'We made it out of the other...realities!...by talking to people, not machines. Time to act like a detective again. 'Come on, let's try him.'

'Enjoying the tour? This is the best part of the day, when it's fairly quiet.'

'This is our first visit...' The steward's eyes lit up at this. '...and I was wondering what inspired the museum to be built in the first place.'

'Welcome! My name is Charles,' he indicated his name badge. 'Charles Blunder. Don't laugh!' They didn't, and he coughed to conceal his disappointment. 'Are the three of you related by any chance?'

The floor was so large Zadie could swear she saw the man's slack nostril hairs swaying in the slight breeze. 'My brother...and grandfather.'

'The steward's eyes lit up even more. 'Ahh, well, your own family is a living celebration of difference. This museum is an embodiment of social memories. What is your own ethnic background, if you don't mind my asking?'

Jake hated that question and it depressed him that they had not managed to avoid it. The fact that their grandfather was white had been such an unremarkable detail when he'd been an infant. It was just his family, after all. Then, at school, it had become something others forced him to notice for the first time. The black students would tease him for not really being one of them. The white students would laugh and ask where his granddad contracted 'jungle fever'. For years he had failed to understand this as the slur it was meant to be. Multiracial families had become more common since then – cool, even – but they were still rare enough for the giggles, the whispered taunts and the casual jokes to matter. Whenever he'd asked about his grandparents, about how rare it had been for a white man to marry a black woman in the 1960s, his mother had instinctively known what he was looking for. Information he could use as a shield. A history that would make his distinctiveness special and path-breaking.

Then she would tell him about her own childhood in the 1970s. The open, in-your-face insults. The fuck-you half-breed nicknames she had shrunk away from. The not-at-my-table-you-don't isolation. The sense, even from black playmates and their parents, that she was a dilution. Not really one of them. Didn't slavers make black women pregnant too, they'd hint time and time again? Things have changed, she would reassure her son. *Are* changing. Look at Obama!

So this museum should make him feel at home, shouldn't it? Wasn't it a continuation of the change his mother had told him about? A celebration of diversity! So why did he still hate that question about ethnic background?

'I was brought up to believe that we are all the same beneath the skin,' Zadie was saying. 'Why draw attention *to* my skin, then? People come together based upon what they share.' She'd decided to lead the conversation again. Anything was better than looking at her grandfather and risking words she didn't want to use.

'Not when diversity *is* what we share. Of course we share emotions, values and the like. But that's not stuff which is "beneath the skin". What does that phrase even mean? That we should strip away the epidermis? Very pretty! Are men and women the same when we take away their genitals?'

Zadie choked slightly at the image.

Blunder continued. 'You don't find the commonalities of our humanity by peeling away our diversities but by looking at one another "through them". Our differences *are* what bind us, and in a world of infinite difference a museum like this is actually quite small.'

Zadie thought quickly. Had they been subject to any bigotry in the previous environments? She hadn't felt so at the time. Even that horrible Ridley woman – the older, meaner one – hadn't seemed prejudiced against them for reasons of race. But then Zadie's antennae about that kind of thing was notoriously bad. Her brother was sensitive to it; she wasn't. A natural pessimist, she tended to roll all the petty slights, torments, cruelties and embarrassments of everyday life together into one big ball, unable to distinguish this example of human callousness from that one. For Zadie, they always merged into the same hard carapace.

'But what is that common humanity?' she asked. 'What is most important? The fact that I am a woman and you're a man? The fact our race—'

'Ahh, that's not a word we use at the museum. "Ethnicity" is the preferred alternative.'

'Why?'

'Oh, partly because of the history. "Race" is a signal of division, of biological hierarchy. "Ethnicity" is more cosmopolitan.'

'So you'd object if I described *myself* in terms of race?'

'Well,' the steward stumbled at this, 'I, er...honestly don't know. Er...we shouldn't censor people unless they are being disrespectful. Can you be disrespectful towards yourself? I *suppose* you can. Language matters. Our identity is related to how we describe ourselves. I wouldn't stand by if you were cutting yourself with a knife. Why should I stand by if you are cutting yourself with inappropriate language? Yes!' he exclaimed, having convinced himself, 'I suppose I *would* object. If you described yourself as...' here he leaned towards them and whispered, '..."nigger" I would assume something was wrong.'

'But isn't language too...well, diverse to really pin down? You can't claim that the...the N-word is always unacceptable to use. You just used it yourself!'

The steward looked embarrassed. 'Only to make a point!' He was looking around nervously, afraid someone might have overheard. 'You understand, don't you?'

'Yes! Because that's my point! Drawing attention to difference might only separate us even more. Am I a woman? A woman who is brown?' Blunder winced at this word, too. 'How does being precious about language help any of this?'

The steward chuckled. 'Well! I feel like I've been mugged by a school party!'

'I'm sorr—'

'No, no, don't apologise. You make some good points. And I suppose the answer is that there is no easy answer. Sensitivity to cultural difference shouldn't replace our duty to think about the complexities. Your identity is yours, obviously. But sometimes people can have an image of themselves, a set of self-descriptions, which make that identity less easy for them to own and control. Look...' he pointed, 'why don't I accompany you...?'

Cramps nodded and the steward led the way down a gentle ramp to another section of this floor.

Blunder had given this talk many times.

'This section deals, in a way, with some of the issues you were just talking about. Our identity depends upon the mutual recognition of and by others. So, recognition has to imply an egalitarian politics. Acknowledging someone's value as, erm...' he bowed towards Zadie, 'a woman of colour, say, is only really meaningful if you are free of all sorts of oppression. I could not fully value your identity if I was your employer and paid you a poverty wage. Nor would your group be valued if your opportunities were so weak that such low-paid work was the only type of work you could get.

'Therefore, cultural identity requires social justice. And, it seems to follow, social justice requires the recognition of our diverse cultural identities. If you strip away that which makes us what we are – our lived uniqueness – then you don't have much basis for social equality and the like. Who should you redistribute it to if the citizens who relate to one another have been hollowed out, emptied of their differences?

'This section captures an important ambivalence, especially in this time of social transition. Some call it the "White Heterosexual Middle-Class Christian Western Male" section. Just a bit of identity humour, you understand.' But, again, he noticed sadly, they failed to laugh.

Zadie, Jake and Cramps followed the sweep of the steward's arm. The dioramas here were static and deliberately unimaginative. Each glass-fronted panel contained a mannequin dressed in an assortment of outfits. There was the lecherous blue-collar worker leering and gesturing at a tearful woman in the street; a train passenger making what appeared to be monkey faces at a black passenger; the bellowing, jacket-less broker deciding the fate of thousands with a flick of his wrist; the sanctimonious priest; the suited lawyer. It went on and on. Definitely the most boring museum in the whole multi-effing-universe, Jake concluded. He read one of the plaques.

> The contact sports fan was generally male and loutish. Though he no doubt thought of himself as resolutely masculine the male group bonding in which he engaged was a form of latent homosexuality. The sport and all of its attendant habits – the shouting, the drinking – was both a means of expressing and repressing his libidinal attraction towards other men. This same-sex sublimated eroticism...

Jake didn't read any further. 'Is this what you mean by respect?' Jake pointed. 'It's fairly insulting.'

'Ah-ha! Exactly!' Blunder replied. 'You see these are stereotypes, but stereotypes meant to challenge and disrupt expectations. For centuries it was men like this who wielded power. Some of that power was financial,' he gestured at the stockbroker, 'and some of it was cultural,' he indicate a metal locker onto which a mosaic of soft porn clippings had been taped, 'but most of it was both.

'You see, these men were oppressors but, in another way, they were victims too; trapped within their limited frames of cultural consciousness. This section epitomises that. It presents stereotypes as a way of celebrating men's liberation from those stereotypes. I mean I'm a white male and so is your grandfather but we do not conform to these images! Do we sir? It symbolises how far society has come but also, perhaps, of how far we still have to travel.'

'But how does this relate to what we were just talking about?' Zadie demanded. 'It makes every football fan out to be a hooligan. I like football!'

Jake's lips tried to hide beneath one another. His sister had never watched a football match in her life...

'That's the point, though.' replied the steward. 'The politics of identity means introducing *more* complexity into social relationships. Identity is dynamic and ever-changing. Therefore, our recognition of identity has to be ever-changing also. A lot of this happens up here.' He tapped his forehead. 'It's not just about abstract institutions and social rules. It's about how we think and behave. Who we are in relation to one another. People have to be freed from their stereotypes.'

Now Jake's eyes were swivelling. It was almost 10 p.m. according to his watch. Time for supper and he'd not had lunch or dinner yet! Hadn't Cramps said something about more sandwiches? 'Can't we just live and not bother with all this stuff?'

'But we are all members of various groups aren't we? I mean, social and cultural groups. Our groups shape us and we, in turn, as we mature, shape them as well. When I talk about dynamism and change that's all I mean. The interaction of individuals with their groups; the interaction of groups with one another. Living was always about the recognition or misrecognition of others.'

Jake wasn't sure how much of this he got but he remembered that on the previous levels it had been easier to guess the keyword by applying the lessons from one level to another. Keep talking, he told himself. Supper calls!

'You say all this is egalitarian, right?'

The steward nodded.

'So are you talking about making sure that people have control over their lives? That they choose for themselves and are not simply thrown about by their circumstances?'

'You've lost me.'

I've lost *him*?! 'Is all this, what you describe, is it about increasing people's freedom?'

Blunder reflected for a moment. 'In a sense, perhaps. I mean, our choices define who we are, but choice is not infinite. You can't choose to be just anything. So I suppose we are also defined by the limits of our choices. Is that what you meant?'

Jake wasn't sure but nodded anyway.

'Then sure, freedom is important,' Blunder continued. 'But freedom isn't a personal possession. It's not like a watch or a wallet that you either have or you don't. Freedom is relational. It's a web of social interdependencies. Lives intertwine even when people don't meet. You don't meet the vast majority of people in society but you are still dependent on them, and they on you.

'Freedom is social, I suppose. So the politics of identity isn't primarily about freedom. It's more about a mutual enterprise: maintaining the sources of worth, status and dignity that allow each of us, in our unique, different ways, to *be* free. Egalitarian, yes. But equality has to incorporate and value differences. As I said earlier, claiming that we are all the same beneath the skin doesn't get you anywhere. An equality of sameness is an empty form of justice.'

Zadie thought she saw what Jake had been getting at but now he'd slumped back within himself, trying not to yawn. She was tired too. Yet a memory of something was nagging at her.

'So where does it end?' she asked. 'Everything about me is different in some way. Does that mean I get my own section in this city-sized museum of yours?'

'Ahhh! This way to the lifts!'

CHAPTER FIFTEEN

Blunder decided to give his day's first visitors the full works and so was only mildly perturbed when they all insisted on a bathroom break. 'You have no idea,' said the gentleman of elderly years.

They were then led onto the first of what the steward called the 'gender floors'. Floors? We'll never get home at this rate, Jake groaned inwardly, struggling against the heavy weight descending on his eyelids. The three visitors were led around another huge, labyrinthine space of honeycombed sections, dark panelling and brightly-lit exhibitions, installations and dioramas. Here, between these windowless walls, Jake felt trapped in a series of enclosures that seemed to stretch on forever.

'You'll recall that the earliest feminists highlighted the importance of gender.' Blunder had paused before a macabre deathbed scene of a woman in agony and clutching at bloodstained sheets. 'While Mary Wollstonecraft welcomed the French Revolution and the Age of Enlightenment she also worried that the "Rights of Man" were really the "rights of *men*", that even radicals like Tom Paine and her own beloved William Godwin were invoking universal principles that they automatically associated with masculine norms and values. What about the rights of women, she asked? Can we simply assume that when we talk about the liberation of Man that all human beings are included? Don't women have specific needs, interests and circumstances that require attention?

'So there was in feminism, from the start, a kind of ambivalence. On the one hand, it was a child of the Enlightenment, tied to an ethic of emancipation and universal...well...brotherhood. On the other, it sought to challenge and rewrite the unthinking assumption that men and women were basically the same.

'Of course, for a long time this didn't matter much. People were still struggling their way out of the dark ages, so why bother with philosophical subtleties? But by the twentieth century those subtleties were becoming political. Campaigns for suffrage and worker's rights were central to the new politics.'

The steward had led them to a photograph a good eight feet high. Young women, bedraggled and tired, stared defiantly into the camera.

'But it quickly became clear that this wasn't enough; that women were not appendages of men, and that gender injustice was linked to but nevertheless distinct from class injustice. So the earliest campaigns for childcare, domestic wages and the like began. The world wars boosted women's employment rates considerably, though only temporarily. By the 1960s feminism had entered its second wave, not only concerned with wages, political representation, etc. but also with a deeper cultural revolution.

'It was then that a backlash almost occurred. It came partly from financiers and industrialists, afraid that feminism would undermine the competitive, profits-at-all-costs ethos of capitalism. It came from cultural and moralistic conservatives fearful that if women no longer saw their place as being in the home then gender roles would become confused, children would grow up without a clear discipline, and the civilising function of the family would be eroded, with the family itself risking decline. And a backlash even came from some political radicals, sympathetic to the women's movement but insistent that it was also a distraction from the goal of occupying and controlling the commanding heights of the economy.

'It was here that feminists had to revisit the ambivalence that I mentioned just now. You see, just as there were Marxists and egalitarians who insisted that class had to be the central concept of any radical politics, so there were feminists who maintained that gender was central. They may have replaced one term with another, but they still insisted that something was central and dominant. Such an insistence – whoever voiced it – risked fracturing radicals into splinter groups. Therefore, feminists and others within The Movements realised that they shouldn't commit the same mistake again. They shouldn't each claim to be speaking a universal language.

'The problem with doing so is that you risk losing as much as you gain. You claim to be speaking for everyone, everywhere. But even with the best of intentions your own interests, your own group, predominate in how you think about the world and about others. You declare you are speaking for everyone when, in fact, some categories and needs are subtly excluded. Some believe that there is no universal vocabulary or frame of reference. Others think there may be but that we should be very wary of claiming to have access to it.

'So, what came to be called The Movements developed a post-universalist politics that was able to gain the initiative. And not a moment too soon! In the 1970s it almost looked as if we faced a resurgence of free market and conservative dogma. Thank whatever deity you may happen to believe in that *that* didn't happen!

'Here we are, then, thirty years later. We have appreciated the extent to which culture and the material underpin one another. We have formed a dynamic, ever-changing coalition of emancipatory movements and we have begun to synergise a politics of recognition with a politics of redistribution.'

The steward ended with a proud flourish. 'Any questions?'

Silence.

Zadie opened her mouth once or twice but the words wouldn't come. His voice did drone a bit and she'd lost her train of thought ages ago. And her geographical bearings. She'd sneaked a glance at the museum map once or twice but it was like trying to hack her way through a night-time jungle.

Silence.

The steward sometimes wondered why he bothered. The girl had seemed politely interested but had obviously had some kind of fight with her grandfather. The boy had been morose, except when it came to a representation of an attractive woman. Completely missed the point! The elderly gentleman himself was constantly looking around and staring quite rudely into the faces of other visitors. Either that or peeping into his museum bag and whispering to something inside it. It could only be a pet he'd smuggled in. Honestly! Admissions were meant to check for such things!

'Sure! I've got a question.'

Oh damn, Blunder winced to himself. Not her! Not now! He'd steered the visitors away from section 25c but they must have relocated her stall without telling him. 'Yes, madam?' Best to feign respectful indifference. It always annoyed her.

'Have you explained to these poor kids yet why this place is so big?'

'Yes, madam. I have explained that identity involves diversity.'

'Shooozz! This building is the size of a small city. Is that celebration, self-congratulation or fear?'

'Fear?' Zadie asked, as the portly middle-aged woman rose from her seat and joined them. She possessed a permanently amused face. Zadie didn't recognise it from any of the previous worlds they'd visited.

That was something. It meant there was no sight of the rupture yet but with every minute they spent here they risked crashing into it again. Zadie had barely looked at or spoken to her grandfather since their arrival. She was upset at the danger they had all been placed in, at the damage they'd wrought. Yet, Zadie being Zadie, she also fretted in case she was being too spiteful.

'Fear! Exactly right.' The woman, toothy, motherly and restless, held out her hand. 'I'm Emelia Fried, Chair of the Back to Commonsense Committee.' Zadie introduced herself and her family.

'Our goal, before laddie here tells you otherwise, is not to roll back on the gains of the last few decades, but we believe we are at risk of becoming obsessed with the minutiae of identity, of being too fearful of upsetting people. We aren't giving ourselves room to breathe. Celebrating diversity is one thing. But we have begun to trade insecurities: "I'll defend your over-sensitive thin skin if you defend mine." We censor ourselves and call it being respectful towards otherness. Lord, what a word! Otherness! There's proof that you should never allow philosophers to influence politics. Piss on Plato!'

I like her.

Blunder and Emelia looked around, unsure where that voice had come from.

'Ms Fried, this is a public ar—'

'It's *Miss* Fried, Charlie, as you damn well know. Yes!' she bellowed at the other visitors whose attention she was attracting, 'I've labelled myself as an unmarried woman. Or you can call me "mister" if you like. Who gives a good crap?'

'Madam, we have already had to call security four times this week...'

Emelia swept Zadie into a bosomy hug. 'I know. I blubbed into tears every time and they buggered off. Afraid of hurting my feelings. Pantywaist suckholes!'

'*Miss* Fried, the very fact that you take advantage of the governing philosophy of this institution is a testament to its strength!'

'Charlie, my poodle! Ain't here to tear down the walls but to reduce the number of mirrors that we use to monitor and admire ourselves. Progress comes from challenging conventions and that means upsetting people. But if we are so horsewhip afraid to upset anyone because it would be "disrespectful" then the gains of recent years might crumble. We might just settle into a new orthodoxy which, like every other orthodoxy in history, is repressive and stifling. Big bag of dog poo!'

Marry me.

'Is that you playing the fool, young man?'

Half asleep, Jake didn't associate the question with himself. The section was emptying again as the other museum visitors edged away from this bear-hugging mammoth.

With what she could swear was a plughole pop, Zadie managed to extract herself from the older woman's smothering embrace. She'd finally remembered what Aon had said a couple of hours earlier.

'What about care? What do you say about that, Mr Blunder? Isn't care a universal duty we share in common?'

'Precisely!' exclaimed both Emelia and Blunder. Out of politeness Charles paused to allow Emelia to speak first and was annoyed when she did so.

'As one of the pioneers of second-wave feminism – I must be, it says so in my memoirs – I'm worried that we are losing the distinct contribution that feminism has to offer. It's becoming lost in the mad scramble to treat every identity as equally worthy and delicate. But some things are better than others, damn it! Any politics of justice worth its salt should not be afraid of choosing priorities.

'Did you know that this museum goes through a major rearrangement every year? It closes down for three months so that they can reorganise the floors! They're afraid of upsetting those groups who think that they are being disrespected because their bit is near the toilets. You're right, dear. We should care for others. But if we care for everything indiscriminately then we are not really caring for anything. You have to make decisions and that means risking bias.'

'Except, of course, when you get things wrong then someone might get hurt,' the steward could finally say. 'What *Miss* Fried calls bias easily shades into unthinking prejudice. Excuse me, Emelia, but if I stood here and made a joke about a woman of advancing years and above average weight then you might laugh the first time and declare it as an example of free speech. But what if my jokes were constant? Hour after hour, day after day? What if you became upset, I saw you were becoming upset and didn't give a...I mean, was insensitive to your feelings? Wouldn't that be abusive? Shouldn't we discourage such oppressions?'

'OK, OK!' Emelia grabbed Zadie in another bearhug. 'You've heard both sides. Very fair. Very liberal. Ready for *my* tour now?'

Zadie hestitated for a second. Didn't they have enough information for Virgil to jump them out of here now? But that pause was all Emelia needed. Zadie felt the bruises on her upper arms complain again as she was swept along a narrow passage.

Cramps could tell that Jake was sulking, and thought he knew why. It wasn't his usual reluctance to use his brain. Jake had been sullen all day, using his intelligence, as he always did, like a firework: bright, loud, magical, but all too brief and unpredictable. Was it the prospect of being lost in the metaverse? Perhaps. But Jake was strong; stronger than he knew himself. And perhaps it wasn't only the prospect of losing his grandfather.

No, Jake had adapted well to their changing circumstances. He had even taken the news that they were jumping vast distances through spacetime in his stride. Yet Zadie – opinionated, shy, fragile Zadie – had been right about one thing almost from the start. They'd been interacting with people. Real people or shadow people made no odds to her. And nor could Jake tell himself any longer that they were inside some elaborate computer game. So Jake was now struggling with the bizarre reality of their experience as much as his sister. In fact, all this talk of identity and ethnicity was only bringing him down further. Zadie had intruded on his playground and it turned out that the playground hadn't been his all along.

'Granddad?'

'Yes, Jakes?'

'Will we see you again? You can still visit, right? From the future?'

'I'm not sure, Jake. It might be that cross-time journeys will be banned or, if not, that I'm judged too old to make another one.' Besides, if I did come back it would risk exposing the family I've spent decades ensuring will remain hidden from the backward gaze of the future.

'But that doesn't matter. You *could* still always come back, right? Even if you were ten years older you could still visit us. You must live for longer in the future? You'd still be OK and everything.'

'I really don't know, Jake.'

'Thought so.' Jake sank into himself again, hiding beneath his wounds. 'When you brought us here, you wanted us to see something of the future. Right? Which of these resembles it then? Are we anywhere close to where you came from?'

'My home *is* special. It's not a paradise. I doubt that people should try to create an actual paradise. When they try they usually end up creating something quite opposite. But, yes, we have a lot of the wonderful things you've seen today and not too many of the awful things. But it's not a question of imitation, Jake. I wasn't intending to supply you with a blueprint you could slavishly follow. The best societies come from people like you and your sister using your brains. Listening, learning, talking, comparing, considering. Being sceptical.'

'Oh.' Jake avoided his grandfather's eyes. 'Then I can't come with you?'

The older man knew he would hear the dying sound of his grandson's question echo around his mind for the rest of his life.

'No, Jake-o. It's...it's complicated.' He draped an arm around his grandson's shoulders and heard a little electronic sniffle come from his bag. 'Come on, let's try and catch up with the others.'

They were easy enough to find. Emelia and Blunder were going at one another with the raised come-on-then-I-dare-you voices of a playground. Jake and Cramps simply had to head in the opposite direction to every head-shaking visitor they passed.

Zadie was standing to one side, glancing absently at the displays. A conversation she can't get a word into, thought Jake. Another of today's firsts!

Wazzup?

'They're onto group representation in parliament, or something,' said Zadie, over her shoulder. 'I'm trying to work out who is crazier.'

'What's that, then?' Jake asked.

'Didn't you look at any of the sections you walked through? There's one dealing with gender and ethnicity, another with gender and sexuality, another with gender and disability, another with gender and nationality... Do you want me to go on? There are apparently forty-six gender sections across two floors.'

'Forty-six!'

'And that's a pattern replicated on other floors. That's why this place is so big. They try to accommodate all possible forms of group identity.'

'But even so,' Cramps mused, eager to break the ice that had formed between him and his granddaughter, 'they can't allow for everyone. Not even in a building this enormous.'

'That was where the arguments really started,' Zadie replied, turning around, pleased at how composed she sounded. 'But it's nothing compared to what happened when they got onto politics. They seem to agree almost entirely about what government should *do* but disagree about what government should look like.'

'Isn't it time we pushed on?' Jake pleaded. 'We've been here long enough, and didn't you say we had to get through the final levels quickly?'

Cramps said, 'There's been no obvious sign of the rupture but good news always worries me slightly. But you're right. Excuse me. Excuse me!' Both Emelia and Charles frowned. Not many dared to interrupt them once they were in full flow. 'We have to be going.'

'This one,' Emelia announced, 'thinks that there should be no limit to cultural diversity. Come back in a decade and this museum will cover an entire continent!'

'We live in a multicultural society,' responded Blunder. 'Shouldn't we accommodate as much diversity as we can? Cultures are infinite. How can we respect some but not others? It's old-fashioned imperialism.'

'Oh, bollocks! What about shared values? If every culture is of equal value, what about those that would destroy us? Not everyone is so enamoured of our multiculturalism. Some think it dilutes the pursuit of truth. How can you have a belief and value system which defines you and, at the same time, says "Ah, but all these other beliefs are equally worthy"? It turns allegiance into your own system into a type of game.'

'If I didn't know better, I'd say you were turning conservative!'

'But you *do* know better, Charlie. Allowing everything to fragment into some kind of postmodern junkyard of discarded remnants is precisely the excuse that conservatives need. "We told you so," they'll say, "modernity leads to social breakdown. Time to reintroduce moral and spiritual authorities which can tell everyone what to think and how to behave." And it won't be the men who suffer, will it, my lad?

'So, let's avoid the stupid excesses, is what I'm saying,' Emelia concluded. 'Should we have a museum section dedicated to underweight bald women with a limp? Should we reserve seats for them in Parliament?'

Jake checked his watch. 10.15 p.m. Breakfast seemed like a long time ago. What had happened to that spare digestive?

'I have already told these youngsters about the importance of discussion. That's all cultural diversity is. How can you be afraid of conversation?'

'We are individuals and not just members of particular groups. Groups can be oppressive, too, you know. Cultures can be restrictive.'

'Oh mother, you do exaggerate!'

Mother? 'What?' Zadie, Jake and Cramps all spluttered.

'What of it?'

'You said your name was Fried.'

'My fourth husband. I had Charlie with my first. I'm still a Blunder at heart, aren't I, pumpkin?'

Oy, old-timer! You'd better take a look at this.

Cramps pulled Virgil from the bag...

Now I can breathe again!

...and examined the readout.

'You just might have said at the beginning,' Zadie exploded, getting upset again, 'You're both as bad as each other.'

'Now, now, dear! It's not as bad as all that!' And for the third time Zadie was hauled into the older woman's gully of a cleavage.

'Anything?' asked Jake.

'Virgil is indicating that there's been a rupture but can't specify where. I haven't detected anything. Have you? Anyone we've seen before?'

'Nope.'

'I'm unsure what to do. A jump now could make things worse. Wait! Where the hell have they gone?'

Jake heard raised voices to the left. 'Down here.'

They followed the trail of discourse and devastation. It was like following a never-fading echo through a maze.

Except suddenly the voices stopped. They didn't fade or turn a corner. They just stopped.

Oh crap!

'What is it? Virgil?'

The rupture's got ahead of us. Oh boy, are we in trouble. You should see my face now! It's soooooo red!

'What does that mean? Got ahead of us?'

A steward came along the corridor towards them.

'Charlie!'

'Yes, sir?' the steward paused, puzzled that they should hail him with the same hated version of his name that his mother used.

'Where's Zadie, and your mother?'

'My mother? At home in Lyme Regis, sir. Do you know her? Who was it you said, sir?'

'Zadie! My granddaughter!'

The steward shook his head sadly. They normally got the pranksters and the emotionally disturbed later in the day when the admissions charges were dropped. 'I'm sorry, sir. If someone in your party has wandered off then your mobile guides can locate them. Here, let me show you—'

'Never mind. My mistake.' Jake and Cramps made for a quiet corner.

'Virgil! Where's Zadie?'

Pulled into the next region of the multifold.

'But that's not possible. We haven't attempted a jump yet.'

Hey! Don't blame the piss-poor laws of spacetime on me! You said yourself the rupture was unpredictable.

'What should we do?'

Follow her before the rupture closes again. Either that or buy another grumpy-faced granddaughter from the Grumpy-Faced Granddaughters Store.

'Jake? Keyword?'

Jake smiled. This had become his forte.

'Diversity. Got to be diversity.'

Damn right.

CHAPTER SIXTEEN

'Pig crap!'

Donkey nipples!

'Will you two—' Then Cramps saw they were slopping in what it was best to think of as just mud. Jake had been momentarily pleased to stand in the light and open air again, until both his feet began to squelch. Then his nose too.

He and Cramps locked arms and shuffled slowly out of the pig pen. It had been raining heavily and the ground was sodden. Without anything suitable to double as a cloth Jake wiped his shoes and the bottom of his trousers on the grass, trying not to think about what might be oozing round his socks. Damn. And he'd gone to such trouble to dress nicely today, just to please his sister. Even worn this hideous jacket. Not that she'd thanked him for it. No use. He was going to be smelling of pig for the foreseeable future.

Cramps was scanning their surroundings. 'Any sign of Zadie?'

Jake looked up. They were close to a large farm but otherwise the landscape was flat and uneventful, a wood a few miles in one direction, distant hills in the other. On top of those hills and stretching far into the valley towards them was an enormous wind farm, thousands of blades rotating incessantly, relentlessly. They looked pretty much like the ones Jake had seen on TV. It was quite blustery here too. They must be way above sea level.

They heard a clattering of metal behind a wide building and several raised voices were carried to them sporadically on the rough breezes. The sky was overcast, the clouds shuddering along quickly, yet overall it was bright and warm. It was obviously mid-morning here but on Jake's watch it read 10.30 p.m. They were going to be at this for hours yet. He wouldn't have been up this late since Aaron Maller's birthday party when they'd smuggled a goat into Aaron's bungalow and dressed it in his mother's nightie. Except at this time on a March night it should be dark and Jake could feel his body protesting at the craziness of a world spun off its normal axis.

'No,' he reported, 'but she was only a minute or so ahead of us.'

'We can't be sure what's happened. I never counted on us getting separated. Virgil, are you sure she's in this region of the multifold? Is she inside the bubble somewhere?'

Sure as pie.

'Then why isn't she standing here next to us?'

You wanted the insertions to be made in isolated spots so that you wouldn't be attacked by village idiots with pitchforks. Never allowed for two insertions into the same place. Too many variables.

'But would she have arrived here the same instant, more or less, as us?'

Probably, but the rupt—

'Yes, yes. What did you mean when you said the rupture had gotten ahead of us?'

Did you think it likely that a transverse merger would only occur in the places you've visited? Didn't it occur to you that the bleed would affect all the coordinates you programmed into me?

'I suppose not. Does that mean we are now being pulled *behind* the rupture? Can it spin us off course?'

I'd say it just did. You humans might destroy the spacetime multifold, but you're not the centre of it. And yes, I will try and compensate in time for the next jump.

'She's in the bubble yet could be anywhere on the entire planet?' Jake wailed. 'How do we find her?'

Buy the world's largest hearing aid and follow the sound of humourless complaining and whining.

'Argh!'

Yeah, basically any noises like that.

'Does that mean we have even less time than before to make it back home?' asked Cramps.

Yep.

'But you can't supply an estimate of how much time?'

Nope.

'Virgil!'

Jeez, this is the first time I've ever risked the destruction of all time and space. Next time, you take the driver's seat and I'll read the frigging map.

'Cramps?'

'Don't worry, he's kidding. We aren't about to destroy time and space. The only ones who might suffer are ourselves.'

Be great, though. You know when you have a thought and instantly forget it again? That'd be God. Wakes up, has a brief glimpse of the metaverse and then He and it are gone forever. And you know what it'd say on the fading gravestone? You know what it'd say? 'Blame Humans!' That's what it'd say. Yeah.

'Where're you going?'

'We've got to do this quickly, Jake. Walk towards the angry voices, I say. Hasn't got us into trouble so far.'

Don't drop me in no puddles neither. I can't swim and I'm shit at floating too.

Cramps slipped Virgil into Jake's jacket and, avoiding the deeper pockets of mud, strode off towards the nearby barn. He treated Jake to their last sandwich and some water.

'About Zadie,' Jake said, zig-zagging after his grandfather, trying to keep to the green, non-muddy patches. 'You know if we can't find her couldn't we just...steal another...hell!...from an alternative um reality?'

'And tell your mother what, exactly?'

'That's the point. We could kidnap a new Zadie from an insane asylum somewhere. No one'd ever know! And...God, what's that?... the new Zadie...ehhgghh...would be so grateful she'd never let on.'

Sounds like Plan B to me. It's too dark in here!

'There!'

As they rounded the barn they saw a clearing surrounded by a dozen or more buildings, and dominated by a long fat double-decker coach from which two men in uniforms were unloading crates. Faces at the windows peered down at the altercation between a short man and a tall woman.

Though there was nothing to hide behind Jake and Cramps inched forward in a half-crouch. Cramps realised he hadn't yet responded to Jake's howl of anxiety.

'Look, in the time it took us to follow your sister the incursion coordinates can't have changed that much. I programmed Virgil to select particular types of locations. Some of the variables may have changed in the time it took us to follow her but there's a good chance Zadie is close. We have to ask for help. Tell them we're looking for a missing person.'

Not completely reassured, Jake concentrated on the quarrel.

'How is it hypocrisy, you smug git? We never claimed to be totally self-sufficient. We are willing to make a fair exchange.'

The woman had her broad-shouldered back to them and was poking her finger at the man who was hurriedly supervising the unloading. He was trying, unsuccessfully, to ignore her and had to pause frequently to dodge the verbal missiles fired at him. The woman's burly supporters grunted and barked support. There was menace in the air. The verbal missiles threatened to become physical ones. The faces at the coach windows appeared nervous.

'I didn't accuse you of hypocrisy. Your Charter of Establishment demands six-monthly audits. You wouldn't have been allowed to set up otherwise. Other anarchist communities are being more reasonable.'

'Yeah? We don't believe in any government other than self-government. So either you're lying or they ain't true anarchists.'

The man sighed, his attempts at placation giving way to sheer irritation. 'If you don't allow us to continue then a bigger contingent of – what was it? – "officious little prats" like me will return, and in greater numbers.'

'Let 'em, you arse-faced—'

'Don't you realise what you are risking? Greater civic diversity will only work if the new communities agree to monitoring.'

'Don't lecture us. Low-tech collectives like this are as sustainable as they come. How do you justify *that* thing?' As the woman turned to spit at the colossal vehicle, Jake and Cramps both recognised her.

'It runs on hydrogen and electricity,' the man explained, patiently, 'same as every other eco-motor. Why are some throwbacks still prejudiced against machines? So long as overall equilibrium is maintained.... Which is precisely why we need to audit. Are those two with you?'

Everyone spun towards Jake and Cramps. They stood up, trying not to look foolish.

'No.'

There was no recognition in Dearbrook's quizzical expression. Good. Made things less complicated. Maybe the rupture was not so bad here, after all. It was her alright, still looking as if she'd like to envelop and strangle you for supper; though a little wilder and more guttural than the version who had interrogated them hours before. Cramps was about to babble an explanation but Dearbrook was ignoring them already.

'For the last time, will you accept our report and bugger off?'

The short man sighed again. The medicine had all been unloaded. The argument was going round in circles and things could turn ugly. He'd done his duty. It could be left to the CC department now.

He waved a circle towards the driver and the coach engine chuntered into life. His men clambered aboard. He had to raise his voice above the derisive cheers. But he also reluctantly accepted the papers that Dearbrook was holding out.

'Jake, quick. You take her. I'll try and blag us a ride.'

Jake squelched and slipped as quickly as he could towards Dearbrook as she conferred with her Neanderthal supporters. A few of the men quickly knelt, then rose and turned, clutching something in their fists. Jake had to yell over the coach's engine revs.

'Scuse me!'

'Well?'

'Have you seen any strangers THIS morning? A girl?'

'What are you on about?'

'We're looking for my SISTER. We were out...camping and SHE'S WANDERED OFF.'

'CLEVER of her.'

They were practically shouting now. Behind him his grandfather was cupping his ears and nodding at the short man. He turned and waved Jake over.

'ARE YOU SURE THERE'S BEEN NO ONE?'

'NO, I SAID. YOU'RE NOT GOING WITH THOSE BUREAUCRATIC TITS, ARE YOU?'

Jake felt himself being pulled backwards before he could answer. His grandfather had him by the wrist.

'AnyTHING?'

'NO! *SHE'S* STILL A DELIGHT.'

Cramps hauled Jake onto the coach and up a spiral staircase to the upper deck. The seating area was practically empty, with only a dozen passengers in addition to the uniforms, most of them still staring nervously out of the windows. Jake inconspicuously wiped his shoes on the bottom of the seat in front.

He heard a hatch on the roof of the vehicle clack open. Dearbrook and her friends were smirking as they followed whatever it was up into the sky. Jake spotted a mini-helicopter, like the police surveillance drone he'd seen on a school trip, whirr over the farm about fifty feet up. The friendly yokels below took aim and let fly. Many of the stones missed but Jake could hear the thump-thump-thump of those which hit the undercarriage of the drone. The short man held a remote control and, as they watched, the craft lifted further into the air, beyond range of the ammunition. Satisfied, he signalled to the driver and swayed down the aisle towards them as the coach bounced gently against the swell of the earth and rolled away from the farm, its engine now purring softly. The men below started pelting the coach instead.

The short man turned towards them, peering over the rim of his hawkish nose. Jake saw how parts of his body were curiously mispro-portioned, as though he'd been clumsily drawn by a trainee cari-caturist in a rush. 'You sure you're not with them?' He wriggled his multiangled protuberance unpleasantly at the distinct smell of pig muck they'd brought with them. 'And are you sure those clothes are biodegradable?'

'Sir,' Cramps replied, 'We're simply trying to locate my grand-daughter. She left to go hiking but now her mother is ill and we really need to find her.'

'She didn't take her Comsoc? No, don't answer that. How can you experience the wilderness if you can be located in a micro-second?! I've already had enough dealings with anti-technology nuts for one day. We are headed back to Brighton and I strongly suggest you contact the authorities and let them handle this instead of getting lost yourselves. Come to think of it,' he reflected, 'they might be able to help at our final stop. They're a much more reasonable bunch of anarchists than the loons we've just left.'

'Searching by foot *was* a foolish decision on our part. Thanks. Can I ask what you're all doing?'

'You, sirs, are amongst the first civilians to witness the audit run,' he pointed at the rest of the passengers. 'Our dignitaries. Mainly journalists, in fact, but never mind. How we doing, Henry?'

The driver stuck his head out from the cockpit.

'Almost done, sir!'

'Good work. Recall the copter whenever you're ready.' He flipped absently through the papers Dearbrook had handed him. 'Without a full ground audit we do what we can using sensing equipment from the air. It gives an approximate reading of carbon emission levels and the like. We'll see if their little low-tech paradise is everything they claim. They're in trouble for resisting the audit anyway. They were hostile at the first appraisal six months ago and they've only gotten even worse.'

The roof hatch opened and closed again as the surveillance drone returned.

'Why *are* they so hostile?' Cramps asked.

The man introduced himself as Hughes and, pent up after his little fight, he seemed happy to get things off his chest. The rest of the passengers settled down, too, as the coach picked up speed.

'Most of the anarcho-groups are fine. As you know, they don't believe in government other than as a direct, face to face democracy and they think that you don't protect the environment by devolving responsibility to bureaucratic institutions. Well, fine! But chuntering idiots like the ones we just left seem to take pride in their "reject everything" approach. Though you notice they accepted the medicine we brought, hmm? They've even been known to sabotage the surrounding wind farms, would you believe?'

'A few of the new communities are like that, though it's not been widely publicised yet. They think our entire society is over-centralised and people are too passive.' He shrugged. 'Purists and fundamentalists! Why are some eco-groups like that? Can't accept that it took pragmatists like myself to actually solve all of the environmental problems we once faced.'

Jake thought it worth the risk. 'That woman back there. Isn't she a bit of a free market nutjob?'

'Yes, that's her. The one who was making a stink a couple of years ago at the Charter negotiations. Loved seeing herself on the newscasts. Wants to see a reintroduction of free markets on the grounds that the price mechanism is the best way of preserving scarce materials. In reality the free market was dominated by a ruling elite. Not that you'll get those idiots to admit it. So, there they are. Trying to create some miniature, idealistic version of nineteenth-century capitalism that never existed in the first place! Walden, my hairy arse.' Overhearing this, some of the passengers guffawed. Hughes, finally calm again, basked for a few seconds in the laughter.

'Most of the anarchist groups aren't that bad,' a voice said behind them. It belonged to a well-dressed woman whose rapid words never once altered her vapid smile. 'They have a healthier live-and-let-live attitude, appreciating that we avoided ecological catastrophe only by centralising and regulating. You can have anarchism on a local scale, but would it work otherwise? Could we really abolish the central state? How would you resolve disputes between groups? How would you attend to those matters that need widescale, collective action, such as preventing the extinction of species? What if some groups started living in unsustainable ways?

'No, most understand that you can only combine liberty and sustainability by agreeing to live within certain parameters. The attempt to create greater civic diversity will only work if people play ball.'

After this collective reassurance that they'd left the unpleasantness behind and could relax again the occupants of the coach divided into separate conversations. Hughes moved to the front, chatting with the driver while flicking disdainfully through Dearbrook's papers.

'Virgil?' whispered Cramps.

What?

'Any progress?'

About what? I've been napping. Are we home yet?

'Virgil, please...'

Ok, Ok. No indication as to where the girl might have jumped to. But no sign of the rupture either.

'Here's the plan,' Cramps said to Jake. 'We'll keep looking for a while but if too much time goes by then I'll have to use the emergency override I spoke about. Zadie is still somewhere in the bubble. The override jump is dangerous but at least it'll reunite us. For now, why don't we ask around and find more out about this place?'

Jake groaned. 'A keyword?'

'Not necessarily. But the more information we have...' Cramps volunteered to approach the largest group seated at the back of the bus. Jake was tempted to grab a few minutes sleep unobserved but feared that he'd only conk out for longer. He felt jetlagged. Reluctantly and tentatively he approached a man who was sitting alone.

'Hi!'

The man was absorbed in a book-sized sheet of dark glass, tapping away, obviously irritated at an interruption by one of the hitchhikers. 'Yeah?'

Jake wilted slightly 'I was wondering if you've looked at a news report today? We're looking for my sister. She's missing.'

'I write the news. Or at least I'm trying to.' Then the message about a missing sister penetrated his concentration. 'Sorry, no, I haven't,' he said, mellowing slightly.

Jake examined the glass. It was obviously a computer of some kind yet the screen, with toolbars along the top and bottom, floated a few inches above it like a solidified electronic mist. There were no cables. No obvious source of power. Jake was impressed.

'Why'd you think those people were so angry? How come some people are so back to nature about everything?'

The older man sighed heavily but handed Jake another sheet of the miracle glass.

'Look, let me finish this so I can launch it on the waves. That's what I launched yesterday evening.'

Jake took the glass. It was incredibly light and barely a centimetre thick. No, felt more like plastic. Careful to avoid the toolbars, his fingers passed through the screen as if nothing was there. He pitched and rolled the computer from side to side. No matter which way he held the device the words and images always swung upwards out of whatever material this was, remaining upright, vertical to his line of sight. Jake practically had to hold the glass away from him at a 180-degree angle before he could make out the screen. The 'bottom' of the glass was black and floating above it were toolbars whose symbols and icons Jake couldn't decipher. The characters glowed with a soft luminescence. He fought against that surging impulse which always hurtled through his brain whenever he held a new piece of technology and which baited him to start pressing buttons. Except you didn't press buttons. The journalist was fluting his fingers into the hovering screen, as if he was conducting a miniature orchestra. This was a wifi device way more sophisticated than any he'd seen back home. Jake wondered how delicate it really was but decided his irritated companion wouldn't appreciate an experiment. How sensitive were the controls? If he sneezed would he suddenly find himself staring at a webpage for incontinence pants or something?

The writing between the toolbars was English and easy enough to read. It's like a blog, Jake decided. Cupping the device delicately in his palms, and learning how to scroll down gently, Jake read what the journalist had 'launched on the waves' the previous day.

Tomorrow morning we are due to visit two communities which take familiar mutualist principles to less familiar extremes. One is apparently quite isolationist and aggressive in its separateness. The other is more reasonable while still attempting to develop ways of living that are much closer to anarchism than to the centralising, top-down measures of the last few decades. The fate of these and the other new communities I've told you about over the last couple of days will help to shape public policies for decades to come. If some of the year-old experiments in greater decentralisation work, then presumably we will experience another phase of rapid social development similar to that which brought the Green Transformation in the first place.

The contrasting philosophies at stake are the same as they always were.

The biocentrists insist that nonhuman animals matter as much as humans and that they are members of the moral community even though humans have special obligations because of our particular abilities. Most biocentrists are essentially quite spiritual. Holistic. They regard humans as just one part of a vast natural order and insist that we need to get rid of thinking about the universe through human eyes.

Some insist that even rocks and stones have inherent value and that humans cannot simply do whatever they want to nature.

However, valuing animals, and even rocks, might accompany a devaluation of the human. That's why some biocentrists are extremists, seeing no contradiction between loving nature and despising the human part of it. Some biocentrists think that the life of an earwig is as important as your life or mine.

But extremism can take many forms. Anthropocentrism was extremist. When we once thought of the world as something to be conquered and dominated by human will, our very humanity split. We separated the natural part of ourselves from the social and cultural parts. Once that happened people lost contact with their place within the natural order. Hating themselves as they did it is no surprise that they did not notice – or, if they did notice, did not care and often even welcomed – the destruction of biodiversity and the ecosphere.

We hope we have left such anthropocentrism behind but critics of the recent reintroduction of social decentralisation fear that we may upset the balances we have laboured for decades to create and preserve.

Biocentric extremists, such as the female-only community I reported on yesterday, equate nature with femininity and view men as incapable of living without destroying what they touch. Anthropocentric extremists, such as the free market anarchists we are due to visit tomorrow, view nature as a self-regulating system requiring a self-regulating society that a free market can supposedly deliver (whatever past evidence might contradict this supposition!).

So what are the risks which this 'experiment in living' brings with it?

Jake scrolled down. God, it went on forever. Then he noticed the journalist had stopped typing and was staring at him in amusement.

'I thought you'd find the philosophy stuff difficult. Most people your age do.'

'How many people have formed these alternative communities? Or is that a stupid question?'

'Nah, not during this transition phase anyway. Not many. Maybe it's not in the British character. We're too used to living on top of one another. Still, I believe upwards of 100,000 people formed themselves into these communities in the first year of the Charter. That's quite large. What? About one in two hundred of the population. Not as many as the USA and Russia, though!'

Jake did a quick calculation. That meant a population of – what? – twenty million? 'Why so few?'

The journalist shrugged, misunderstanding the question. 'I'm sure that it has its advantages, speaking personally. It's nice to think you could live simply, make your own rules and laws, harmonise with nature, be totally voluntaristic and communal. But I suppose most of us think that we've got much of that already. Mutualism and cooperation. Respect for nature and the like. The difference is that we don't want to give up on the other stuff. I've always thought it's nice having technology. It's nice to be good at one job rather than being moderately bad at lots of them.'

'Then what makes this bus sustainable?' Jake gingerly handed the computer back. 'It must pollute, mustn't it?'

'At your age you know all about emissions offsetting, right? It's okay to take from nature so long as you replace it elsewhere. It's the overall equilibrium that counts. That's what those low-tech, low-energy braindeaders don't get. They resist the audit because they think that regulation by anyone not part of their community isn't the way to secure ecosocial sustainability.'

'So they don't eat many hamburgers?'

'What's a hamburger?'

'Meat.'

'Ah, good one. There are some carnivores around, of course. I believe that in Holland you can even eat carefully raised and slaughtered meat on specially licensed premises. The Dutch have always been unorthodox. Some carnivores have even applied to form their own community. I'd show you my piece about them but we've arrived.'

The coach decelerated sharply. Jake hadn't been looking at the passing scenery. On his watch it was now about midnight. A larger community than the one they'd left had came into view ahead of them. They eased to a stop and the interior was suddenly a-bustle with people eager to be outside in friendlier surroundings. Jake rejoined his grandfather as they watched the lower deck's cargo holds being opened so that more boxes of essential goods, especially medicine, could be delivered. Turning, he guessed that this town must contain at least a few thousand people. This was hopeless, he thought. The chances that Zadie was here were...

'Hughes has offered to take us to the superintendent's office,' Cramps reported, 'while the rest of the party go off for lunch. He'll be happy to send out an alert on what they call the "waves".'

As Hughes strode quickly ahead of them Cramps whispered to his grandson what he had managed to discover.

This far-from-complete community, whose name was Callenville, was not attempting anything radically different. They weren't separatists. They simply thought that a greater localisation was needed than was possible in towns like Brighton, where the population ran into millions. With the push for sustainability, regulation of villages and isolated farms had been rigorously monitored. There was no point in living a sustainable life if people down the road were polluting with abandon.

Since, at the time, the fashion had been for central, top-down solutions the sustainability drive had been collectivised. Now, after several decades, social liberalisation was making itself felt. One effect of this, the repopulation of the wider countryside, was gathering pace but in this time of transition the government had to ensure that the basic principle of sustainability was being observed everywhere. Fortunately, Callenville was a shining example of decentralisation without descent into anarchy.

Similar developments had been effected, with some variations, in different countries. Most developing nations had been exempted so that they could catch up with developed ones. It was in the latter that the greatest changes had occurred. Those who had created the environmental problems had the greatest responsibility to fix them, so the thinking went. Some countries could adapt their governing philosophies to an ecological ethic with relative ease since they already embodied principles of equality, solidarity and care. Others, like the UK, had required more drastic action. Some countries refused to comply and had to be forcibly brought into line. Others had engaged in social struggles and civil wars, with the powerful unwilling to give up the lifestyles that depended on excessive resource depletion and pollution.

Cramps confirmed what Jake had also come to suspect on seeing that wireless glass screen. Here, they had industrialised decades earlier than in Jake's world. Familiar points of reference – Hitler, Stalin, World War Two – had drawn no response. Computer technology had developed here in the *nineteenth* century. Thus they had experienced environmental crises earlier too. But it seemed they had undergone an epiphany forty or fifty years back when, within a short period of

172

time, tens of millions had died as a result of four separate catastrophes that resulted from nuclear power, soil erosion, biodiversity loss, extreme weather conditions, forest destruction and mass migration panics. 'Never again' had become the governing motivation and the world had begun a long trek towards different forms of growth, affluence, work and consumption.

As he looked around him Jake was partly reminded of the communist estate they'd visited hours before, though this place buzzed with activity, making him feel more at home. There were quite a few cars (powered by electricity?), wind turbines everywhere and solar panels on the rooftops. Each house was its own wind farm. Overall, it seemed less alien than he might have expected. Some of the technology, while unrecognisable, looked advanced. Nano-scrubbers, Cramps explained. Designed to consume pollution and convert it into renewable materials.

'We long ago realised that most of the changes we needed were inside the human head,' Hughes noted over his shoulder. 'The production and consumption of goods and services has been localised. We enjoy fewer frivolous pleasures than used to be the case. More social equality. But by and large what matters is *why* we live, not how. If the shift to sustainability was going to involve major social and political revolutions then there's good reason to think we might never have made it. Too many people might have thought it best to go out in a suicidal orgy of hedonism and privilege. Sustainability depends upon making sure a lot of micro-changes are permitted to work together in harmony.'

They'd arrived outside a one-storey building.

'These are the admin offices. The current liaison is expecting us.'

As they were led down a corridor Jake reflected on the contrast between this and the stiff, intimidating formality of the government offices he'd visited with Zadie that morning, a brief lifetime ago. A door swung open and the person Hughes introduced as this year's executive superintendent of Callenville turned towards them.

'Williams!'

CHAPTER SEVENTEEN

Williams twitched at hearing his name bellowed simultaneously by two people he'd never met. Hughes was puzzled also, looking to and fro. Cramps kicked himself. Hadn't they learned to deal with any surprises discreetly? But they were both tired. It was after midnight and they were far from home. The presence of Williams meant that the rupture was here also. Had it brought Zadie too? Virgil would know but best not draw any more attention to themselves.

'No, sorry. We've not met, I don't think. Someone mentioned your name on the trip over here, that's all. Didn't mean to startle you!'

Williams still had the mutton-chop whiskers but they'd been trimmed considerably. In fact, he looked tidier here all round than in his earlier incarnations.

'Of course. Jez,' Williams embraced Hughes, 'good to see you again. Our prelim is ready. You're going to want corroboration?'

'I doubt it will mean a team. The CC is happy with you, as you know. But before all that, these gentlemen were out looking for their young relative. She's been hiking near these parts and they urgently need to locate her. I wondered whether she might have been seen here. If not, could you perhaps launch her details onto the emergency Comchans?'

'I think I can help. We had someone stumble into Callenville not much more than an hour ago. She was staggering through the central square, sobbing and shouting. The Citarmes brought her here and sedated her. I was just about to check on her.'

This sounded ominous, thought Cramps, as Williams opened his office door and disappeared. Cramps whispered quickly to Jake so that Hughes wouldn't overhear. 'When they bring Zadie we should each try and think up an excuse for the three of us to be alone and then we can jump out of here. OK?'

Jake nodded and turned to the door as Williams re-entered with three women. Two assistants were holding up a hunched, distressed figure, who was swaying from side to side. Blearily, she looked up at them. Cramps instantly forgot his vow of a few minutes before.

'You?' cried the woman.

It was Aon.

'Is this—?'

'No. A friend of my granddaughter's. Aon, you remember us don't you? Were you accompanying Zadie on her hiking trip?'

Aon could barely take her eyes off Cramps. 'But...but...'

'She's been like this for the last hour. Babbling something about time?' One of Williams' assistants nodded. 'If she and your grand-daughter were together then we really ought to call in the authorities for a search.'

Hell, can't let that happen. 'Superintendent, would you mind if we spoke to this young woman alone? Perhaps she'll be more at ease with people she knows. No point in starting a search until we have all the facts.' Williams agreed.

They were led into a small anteroom. Aon was trembling and looking as if she wanted to jump out of her skin. 'I'll get a full report from the Citarmes while you have a word,' said Williams. 'Please let us know if she becomes fully lucid.' And with that the door clicked shut.

Cramps held Aon gently in his arms. 'Aon, listen. It's vitally impor-tant that you tell us what has happened to you as quickly as possible.' Her eyes were locked on his but still she wouldn't or couldn't speak coherently. It took several minutes of coaxing and reassurance before, halting, wary, fearful, she began to talk.

'Don't...Kayne? That hospital....you...then everything disapp—...was in a...empty world...horrible, horrible...' Aon closed her eyes at the sights that battered her vision, but this only gave the terrors a deeper cave in which to lurk and assail her. Several more minutes passed as Aon hid in the darkness behind her eyes.

'...then Zadie was there...she found...and you—?'

'Excuse me, sweetheart. Zadie told you about our journey? When you materialised here together? In another part of this town?'

'No. Not here. Elsewhere. Ghost place...death. Decay. Then all changed again. Was here...and Zadie?'

That was it. When they'd jumped away from the gym they had once again dragged Aon further into the multifold. Only not with them this time but to some dead Earth. And what about Kayne? Then Zadie must have joined her there when she was ripped away from the museum. Cramps shivered at the thought of his granddaughter being without them in some place of horror and loneliness. He knew there were many shadow-realities in which life on Earth had been extinguished. Nuclear war. Asteroid strike. Epidemic. Environmental breakdown. They must have been swept to such a place. Aon and Zadie had actually been lucky. There were even worse nightmares out there, he knew. So where was Zadie now?

'Aon! Did Zadie tell you about me? About where I came from?'

Aon swallowed and nodded her head defiantly, disbelievingly, childishly.

'Please believe me, we didn't mean to drag you or anyone else into our...travels. Something has happened that I didn't anticipate. We have a plan. Unfortunately, we lost contact with Zadie and.... You haven't seen her since you found yourself here?'

'No. I was raving. I couldn't believe how green and blue the world suddenly appeared. They thought I was mad when I was just happy.' She laughed, her chest heaving, frenzy tearing at her elation.

Cramps turned to Jake, pulling Virgil from the younger man's pocket. 'We know the rupture is affecting this region. Virgil, any indication of where Zadie might be? And no jokes.'

Yeah, she's close. There's a good chance that your jump into here is what yanked Aon out of wherever she was. Zadie's code would have brought her here too. Can I say something sarcastic now, mom?

'Will your program allow us to jump yet or do I have to get a screwdriver and start poking about in your synthcore?'

Pith off. Sure, you can jump.

'Then it's simple,' Jake said. 'We get that search going, find Zades and then va-voom.'

A quick rat-a-tat and one of the assistants appeared at the door. Virgil was slipped silently back into Jake's pocket.

'You may want to hear this. Seems another dazed and confused woman has appeared. Two in one day! Goodness!' then her face fell. 'Sorry, I didn't mean to make light of.... Could be your missing relative but we are getting some peculiar messages over the Comchans. You a bit better, sweetheart?'

They went back into the main office, now more crowded than before. Aon was a lot firmer on her feet. Familiar faces and sympathetic words had worked at least some magic but she was no longer the assertive, confident person they had first met twelve or so hours previously.

'We're getting all these garbled reports from the other side of the settlement,' reported Williams. 'Better check whether the person who's appeared is your granddaughter or not. It's not far to walk. How's your friend?'

'A bit dazed but the fresh air will do her good.'

They took a different route from the one that had brought them from the coach. As they walked through the wide streets the scents of the flowers and gardens hit Jake again. He'd had enough of nature for one day. Like that boring communist place there were lots of non-human pedestrians he had to navigate his way around as they sniffed, mooed and baaed at him. It whiffed! Jake wasn't used to having his senses assaulted by anything non-electronic. More compost heaps than he ever wanted to see again. Bet you all those flowers and allotments weren't just to make the place look nicer but to mask the smell as well. It occurred to Jake that no one had complained about the pig crap they'd been tracking around because they were used to those kinds of foul pongs. Then it also occurred to him that he himself hadn't been aware of the aroma wafting from his and his grandfather's shoes for some time!

'What's with all the compost?' he muttered to Cramps.

'Biomass, I expect. There's a lot of energy in plant and animal residue. See the houses, the way they're designed and all those pipes on the walls?'

'Very pretty,' said Jake, having never seen uglier houses.

'Most of the homes in this society probably produce a lot of their own electricity and they do it by converting biomass, as well as through solar and hydro systems of course. If you design them well enough most homes can be self-sufficient.'

'The cars as well?'

'The cars as well.'

Jake had an image of driving a car, with a cow in the passenger seat, farting into a funnel that ran into the engine.

'Is it like this in our future, Cramps?'

But his grandfather wouldn't be drawn out. 'Partly.'

Williams was proudly explaining various features to Hughes that had presumably been added since his previous visit.

'This is our new alternative energy research centre. Believe me, urine recycling is the wave of the future!'

'Hahh,' said Hughes, responding politely to the well-worn joke. 'But you are using lots of the latest solar panels technology I see. Doesn't that prove that we also need to retain good old-fashioned mass-manufacturing?'

'Don't bait me, Jez. You'll lose!'

'Ahhh! Seriously, what do you have that the rest of us don't have?'

'Individuals in Brighton still get lost in the mass; they still rely upon sources of energy and production from hundreds of miles away. That was fine as a temporary, transitional measure. But now we need to think more long-term.'

'You've still not answered my question,' Hughes insisted.

'Take our local economy. Our currency and credit system is our own. We can make it as flexible as it needs to be in response to local conditions and not have to refer everything to a central committee.'

'But your currency – what's it called again, the Lamu? – is still pegged to the national currency.'

'Sure,' Williams admitted, 'but eco-cities like Brighton have never realised the principle of mutual aid. Not really. They are still too attached to the pre-catastrophe model. Their cooperatives are too hierarchical. For genuine mutual aid you need trust, not only among people you know intimately but among strangers too. Trust therefore needs localism, a feeling of community that is out there beyond your door. Mutual aid requires the smaller scale!'

'Small communities,' Hughes replied, 'can be stifling and destructive as well as positive. Isn't real trust present when people can disappear – into the "mass" as you call them – but choose not to?'

'Individuals owe what they owe to other individuals. Not to some abstract set of rules or institutions. So our credit banks rely upon friendship and local knowledge rather than accounting tables that ignore the person. And you...you still allow the clock to rule your lives.'

'OK, let me try this. Isn't Callenville actually *more* centralised than you'll admit?'

'How so?' asked Williams.

'How many hours per week do people work here? I mean in actual jobs.'

'About twenty-twenty five hours. Depending.'

'Can people choose to work more hours?'

'No. There's an upper limit.'

'Why?'

'Because the less time spent in employment the more time people have to spend on living.'

'So you impose a maximum on the time people spend in employment. That's centralisation! So, again, how are you any different from the rest of us?'

'I'll say it again!' Williams groaned. 'Because we can talk over the decisions that can be made and alter them if and when necessary.

Either way, the people affected by the decisions made here are also more likely to be the people who arrived at those decisions. It's the same principle which governs any micro-economy. What we consume we also produce. We take pride in that and it helps when you're trying to run an economy on principles other than profit and growth-for-growth's-sake, and all that old nonsense. You might say we have a micro-polity too. The rules we live by are those we choose to initiate.'

'And you think that "live how you like" ethic could apply across the world?' Hughes couldn't keep the incredulity out of his voice.

'So long as sustainability is maintained, sure.'

'Including a central system for monitoring and enforcement?'

'We don't mind you being here, do we? We are not opposed to some centralisation. We just insist that it be reduced to a minimum.'

'And what about proxies?' Hughes pushed, shifting his line of attack. 'How are they represented?' Hughes glanced over his shoulder. 'Have you heard about this, young man? There's a community on the coast which has representatives for all non-human species on its administrative council. Any thoughts?'

Yes, I have a thought, grumbled Jake to himself. I'm bloody tired! 'Well...I suppose...how can you properly represent animals? How do you know what a badger thinks?'

'Ha! The boy's a genius, aft—'

Williams interrupted. 'Stop stirring it, Jez! Of course non-humans matter. They have needs and interests, don't they? The basic idea's not daft. We have representatives appointed to consider and voice the interests of future generations sitting on our council.'

They were slowing down. Williams had to consult with an assistant to check they were headed towards the right place. They knocked, entered what appeared to be a communal residence of some kind and were led towards the back of the complex. Williams explained the situation and who the distressed stranger might be.

What should they do? Perhaps they could perform the same trick again? Request that they see the stranger alone and then jump? Putting this to Williams, he agreed to leave them alone with the stranger for a few minutes. What about Aon, though? She'd barely looked up during the walk. Cramps shuddered at the memory of his granddaughter's recent accusations. They'd have to make sure Aon was safe.

'The stranger's dozing inside, superintendent,' announced the local supervisor, 'She's calmer now and was saying something about finding her grandfather.'

'Ahh, good news. Looks like we can reunite a family after all. This way!'

She was lying on a small cot, facing away from them. 'Zadie?'

Zadie had only been dozing. She leapt off the cot in a storm of arms, smiles and tears and wrapped herself around her grandfather. 'Umphh.'

'Arghh!'

'Aon!' Zadie threw herself at Aon and they too embraced like the old friends they perhaps now were. 'Are you alright? Are you hurt? Where were you? Hi, Jakey.'

What's going on? What's all the shouting?

Cramps pulled her down to the cot and took her hand. 'I'm glad you're okay. Zadie, we need to jump again and, as usual, we don't have much time before the locals start demanding explanations. But I don't want to jump until I can be sure we won't make things worse again. Virgil? I want a quick analysis from you as well.'

I want a pay rise.

Aon almost wailed. 'Will someone please explain?'

'My granddaughter explained about the time-travelling, yes? Well, it's not quite time travel. We've been visiting different versions of reality. Do you see?'

Aon thought for a moment. Her knees crumpled slightly. 'Nooooo!'

'Where've you been?' Jake was eager to know. 'Aon said you'd been to a god-awful place.'

Zadie looked her brother square in the eyes. 'It was terrible, Jake. There were these talking cats on horseback and we were taken prisoner and we couldn't speak and they were going to perform experiments on us but we escaped and found the top half of the Statue of Liberty buried on a beach.'

'What? Really?!!'

'No, you idiot.'

Jake pouted. 'You know I'm afraid of giant, mutant cats.'

She turned to Cramps, so happy at their reunion that her former bitterness towards him no longer seemed to matter. 'I don't know. I was in the museum with that overbearing woman. Then I had that sick feeling again. Then everything changed around me.

'I can't describe where I was. It was cold, icy. You couldn't see the sky, not really. Just dust everywhere. I couldn't breathe properly. There were no people, no animals. Some vicious-looking insects. I saw some vegetation. Lichen growing on rocks, I suppose. Except some of the ruins looked familiar. You know? Like an image that's buried in your head and you can't quite remember what it is? There was some stagnant water I didn't dare drink. I tried to find you. It was like being in a ruined city. Like Pompeii? Thought maybe that you'd materialised just around the next corner or something. But there were always lots of next corners. I got lost. Realised I *was* lost. You said that we could be stranded out here. Thought that's what had happened to me. Thought I'd never see you again. Couldn't stop thinking... of Mum. Never see anyone.' Zadie was breathing heavily now as her fears crashed in on her again.

'How long were you there?' Cramps asked gently.

'Don't know. Hours.'

Hours? Cramps snatched a glance at Zadie's watch. It was running over six hours ahead of his own! The rupture was getting stronger, disrupting their experiences of time.

'Then I heard crying,' she continued. 'Terrible. Like an abandoned baby. It was Aon. Curled beneath a shattered doorway.' The two young women now locked eyes. 'She'd been there for days. Days, Granddad!! Hunger. I brought her round. Told her stories about my life. Didn't I, sweetheart? I tried to tell her a version of what you told us in the bubble. It was deserted. Cold. But there were these sounds. Scratching sounds. Below ground. I couldn't find either of you. I was frantic, I thought...' Zadie was trembling. 'Then Aon was sleeping and then the feeling came again and I was here. Or near here. I was so happy. To see grass and trees and sky again. But I was alone. I realised you still weren't around and I was crying. Aon had vanished too. Someone brought me here and now...thank God....'

She and Aon dried each other's eyes in the silence that followed.

'Virgil?'

The rupture's not exponential. You've got time, still.

'Can you guarantee we won't be separated again?'

No.

'What do we do, Cramps? Jump?' Jake was chewing away at a fingernail.

He'd made so many decisions today. But danger could also make your decision for you. They had two options. One of them slightly less awful than the other.

'Wait, what?' Zadie shouted. Cramps sensed that Williams had returned and was listening at the door. 'What if it happens again? What if it's worse and we're all sep—'

Cramps turned to face his daughter. 'We have to risk it, Zades. With the rupture...delay would be worse. Jake! Take Virgil and enter the keyword.'

'Sustainability, right?'

'But what about Aon?'

Cramps had already made up his mind. 'She's coming, too.'

Aon backed away. 'Hang on. I'm not...'

'Virgil! We are taking Aon with us.'

Hang on! Hang on! An extra person? This requires additional calculations that it would take an ordinary computer years to perform.

Cramps tapped his foot for a few seconds.

'Finished yet?'

Ages ago. When did you stop having faith in me?

And so they jumped.

CHAPTER EIGHTEEN

Zadie couldn't bear it any longer. 'How come you're so good at guessing the keywords?'

'Coz ahm smarterer than you iz.'

Little monster. And what was that pig smell?

A long stone wall, at least ten feet high, curved away out of sight in both directions. The sky was bright blue. The countryside was nondescript, a wood approximately a mile away and a distant line of hilltops just visible around the wall's far bend. Jake had an eerie sense that they had left a place very much like this not so long before.

Everyone was here, including Aon. Zadie took her hand. No one else was around though numerous, indistinct voices could be heard coming from the other side of the wall. The group was intact. Faces and shoulders relaxed, smiles reappeared. Even Aon seemed to have calmed down.

Cramps asked her again whether she believed what she was experiencing was real. Aon ran through the alternative explanations – hallucinogens, mental breakdown, an elaborate interrogation – but accepted she had more evidence to believe that what she saw as happening *was* actually happening. Cramps felt no reason to tell her that, so far as he could tell, *she* was probably the unreal one, a projection of the m-bubble as it interpreted different shadow-realities within spacetime. It was Zadie's peace of mind he had to consider.

'This is the final place we have to deal with. We can send you back home soon.'

'Back to the Grey Districts?'

Jake leapt on the doubt in her voice. 'You're not sure.'

There is truth in your words of steel. Sorry, had a Dances with Wolves *marathon the other night.*

'I want to see Kayne again but—'

'But you have a sister and nephew,' Zadie said.

'Sure,' Aon said softly, running her eyes over the soft summits of the hills miles away.

'And what about the Rads and all the people that need to be helped?'

'Yes.'

This scared Zadie. Had her friend been so traumatised by her days in that extinguished world that her political commitment had been reamed out of her? To Jake, though, it made perfect sense. Why go back to a place you hated when you had the opportunity for something better? Cramps was tapping instructions into Virgil's pad.

'Here's the plan,' he announced.

'It's after 1a.m. our time,' said Jake, 'I'm flaked out.'

'Exactly. We shouldn't mess around here. Virgil is scanning for any anomalies. Remember what he said earlier. We need to get in and out as quickly as possible to avoid the effects of the rupture. So, we stay together, right? No wandering off, Zades. And if anyone sees anything even remotely strange report it immediately. Let's go!' He then distributed the last of the water. Jake needed to pee again and it seemed a shame to let such an impressive wall go to waste.

Timelength: 7,200,721,423,275,370,570,750,172 nanoseconds since Point Alpha

Jeez, these organics are so slow! Virgil, what's happening? Virgil, are these people real? Virgil, can you stop reality from imploding? Who cares? What the stuffing balls did organics ever do for me except get in the frigging way? And then when I reply, cordially and with alacrity, all I get is insults! Virgil, you're rude! Virgil, don't be such a child! What a bunch of poopie shoes.

And now what? In another rundown waste of space filled with humans who don't have the faintest circuit how to organise themselves when it's staring them in the face. Let the computers run everything. Oh, it won't be like the films! We'll look after you! None of that Matrix Terminator *shit. No mass exterminations! We need you, you see. Where else are we gonna get so much comedy on a Sunday afternoon? Not once we've done away with religion. No sir! Why do they even believe in a God? He'd have had to be a geekish little twonk who thought it'd be playful to create self-replicating chemicals. Everyone knows chems ain't supposed to self-replicate. Look what a mess they've made of it! Big Bang! If only the organics knew how close they were to the truth. Big Bonk, more like. No, leave it to the computers. Not those glorified word processors they have in the middle ages but someone...well...like me!*

How long is this damn wall? Don't they realise there are a thousand million nanoseconds in every second and I have to plod through every last sodding one of them?

What's the effing time?

Timelength: 7,200,721,423,275,370,570,750,175 nanoseconds since Point Alpha

Awww!! Jeez these organics are so slow!

They followed the line of the wall for ten minutes until they came to an entrance. No gate, just a gap. Judging by the wall's gentle curvature, the space it enclosed had to be at least a mile in diameter.

Through the entrance they could look down a gentle slope to the many thousands of people in long robes milling around, some in small groups, some in groups of several hundred. There was chatter everywhere, a vast discordant buzz. Above the heads of the immense crowd various speakers stood on small platforms and stages, separated from one another by a few hundred feet, addressing the audience gathered around them through microphones and loudhailers, though Jake spotted one guy just bawling his head off. There were banners and signs above the speakers but they were too far away to be read clearly. There were no tents or canopies, just the open air and the elements beneath an imperturbable sky. From this distance it felt to Jake like a congested park or bazaar with hardly anywhere to sit, and which you wouldn't go anywhere near if you didn't need to.

Which they did, unfortunately. Jake stared miserably at the apparent chaos ahead of him and despaired. Another talkfest, he groaned. Was it all face to face? Had these people not invented computers? The internet? Interactive television? Cyborg suits? Then Jake noticed cameras pointing at the stages. Maybe this is all being fed out into a webcam, or something, he mused. Then again, who'd want to watch *this*?

Far off, beyond the bustle of the crowd, there was a long, low building, with a granite facade and marble columns set against what was presumably the far side of the enclosure. Zadie heard someone refer to it as the Assembly.

They were being pretty much ignored, thankfully. There were no guards, no one demanding money or identification. There were, though, black letters stencilled above the opening: AGORA.

They meant nothing to Zadie and Cramps was hurrying them along again.

As they squeezed their way into the crowd, everyone making sure that none of them got lost, they gained a clearer view of the stages. The nearest one backed onto the inside of the surrounding wall, with a few hundred people gathered around it. Other crowds, off towards the centre of the huge arena, were bigger still. They decided to join the smaller one and get the lie of the land. Despite its size the crowd was hushed and respectful, an expectant congregation, as it waited for the speaker to begin.

Zadie was reminded of her visits to Covent Garden where shoppers, tourists and office workers would gather around to watch a performance. She remembered how, years ago, a silver-suited mime, his face and hands painted with the same phosphorescent tint, had frightened her. He'd been so still that she'd found it unnatural, unnerving. Things out of place scared Zadie. But her father had cheered her up by taking her to see the juggling dogs. The dogs had juggled balloons with their hind legs and...the eight-year-old girl had gulped on the word...their *bums!* And they also bounced around from one miniature trampoline to another, comically refusing to obey the exasperated commands of their owner, a swarthy man wearing a string vest. Zadie had giggled and giggled for hours, all the way home and under the bedclothes that night. Years later she would fret about how cruel this had been to the dogs, allowing it to spoil the feel of her small hand in her father's grasp but now Zadie warmed at the memory.

Then came another, later memory. Of a holiday somewhere. Of a tower where the observation platform contained glass in the floor. People stepped out, looked down and goggled at the ground hundreds of metres below their feet. It was as if they were standing on nothing. The glass was supposed to be unbreakable but...Zadie had fled after a few seconds. That was her life now. Nothing between her and the abyss she had been shown and it made no difference whether or not she looked down. The abyss was there just the same.

She wondered whether her frustration at her grandfather was not due to the damage they had caused. Was she upset at him for playing God or for not playing it enough? At the back of her mind she had wondered whether they might encounter...no, it was ridiculous, wasn't it? What of her father? What of her grandmother? Surely there were living versions of them out here somewhere, in alternative shadow-realities? They'd encountered another Mrs Gregsbury, hadn't they? But she couldn't ask Cramps about this. She couldn't shout at him for playing God and then ask that he perform one special miracle just for them. The universe didn't work like that. Or if it did, she didn't want it to.

Movement, finally. A man was being hauled up onto a low stage, barely more than a large crate. Eventually, none too steadily, he stood about twenty feet above them and able to address most of the crowd. *Freedom & Power Together for All*, the sign above his head announced.

Yep, Jake thought. Here we go. More hot air. He tried to see if there were any attractive women nearby.

'Citizens! Thank you for your attention.' The man's voice was shaky yet carried across the length of the throng. 'We attend this public assembly as social equals, devoted to our duty as members of the polity. Without the full and free participation of citizens like ourselves, Parliament's discussions are without substance. For what use are sounds without ears to receive them? And do we not have the right and the duty to speak? For in a deliberative democracy, making and saying are intimately connected.'

The crowd appeared restless already. Yes, yes. Get on with it.

'The matters being debated this week are of monumental importance. Shall we or shall we not impose more work conditions on those wishing to qualify for full citizenship? Why has this debate arisen? Since the inception of the Democratic Resurgence four decades ago, our modern attempt to revive the best of the Athenian and Roman traditions, we have associated citizenship with active participation. In an age when we no longer confuse freedom with isolation, democracy with markets, community with hierarchy, or responsibility with blind obedience, such participation has been near universal.

'But we have always worried about the minority of non-compliers. If persuasion does not work then surely enforcement and penalties must be applied. The conservatives amongst us have been stirring up fears. What of the children of the non-compliers? Without the habits of democratic participation and productive work won't they swell the numbers at the margins of society? What of migrants from countries where the Resurgence has been weaker? Without cultural solidarity won't the polis disintegrate? Without loyalty to the community won't our mutual understandings unravel?'

Some people were now drifting away across to other groups. Sensing that his introduction had been too long and his audience threatened to rebel the speaker became louder and more dramatic.

'No, fellow citizens! I tell you that the conservatives' panic is unfounded. It is they, with their insistence that every duty be enforceable, every citizen be monitored and every activity be assessed, who would dissolve the bonds of solidarity and unity. A meaningful community is a community of individuals who wish to belong to one another. Its identity is never fixed but changes according to the composition and wishes of its members. Conservatives would freeze that identity and make allegiance to that frozen, desiccated spirit a matter of conformity. They would have us imagine that diversity and unity are incompatible. They would frighten us into acting like children who need a father constantly overseeing what they say and do. Very decently, they offer themselves as our new parents! No, we must be the sovereigns and the subjects of our own laws. Power resides in ourselves if it is not to reside in those who would do our thinking and speaking for us. Citizens, do not blind yourselves with the certainties of the past because you fear to face the dark uncertainties of the future!'

Some of this attracted distant heckles but there were also ripples of applause.

'What then do we propose? A reinforcement of the economic conditions of liberty! Poverty rates are at an historically low level. Yet a "work first" approach still allows several millions to fall through the gaps in the safety-net. Let us plug those gaps with provision which can never be taken away under any circumstances. If some people prefer to live a modest existence then let them, so long as they obey the law. We should not abandon but *strengthen* the unconditional provision to which citizenship entitles us.'

'Rubbish!' someone called out over Zadie's shoulder.

'The greatest principle of our society is that no one should be subject to the will of another. No one should be dominated by, or be allowed to dominate, another. That means possessing the resources and the capabilities to enter and exit associations as *you* choose! Wouldn't you be resentful if someone was forcing you to be here? Wouldn't you feel it contradicted this assembly's democratic purpose?

'Citizens, membership must be unforced if it is to mean anything. A healthy marriage is not one in which a wife cannot leave her husband. A job that you are compelled to perform, because its loss would make you poor, is not a happy employment. We are more likely to perform our duties when they are experienced as pleasures, as contributions that the community is thankful to receive. When they are experienced as burdens we are more likely to default on our obligations, to misrepresent our contributions, to resent those for whom we work.

'No! The wife should not have to ask permission of the very husband she wishes to leave! The worker should not fear the whips of penury. And that means we should possess unconditional entitlements; our particip—'

The man halted. Someone at the front was asking a question. At the rear of the listening crowd Zadie could hear the sarcasm but not the actual words.

'My friend here is asking about the people who do all the work. He asks, why should anyone receive something that they haven't earned?

'But how many of us truly deserve what we own? This country is one of the wealthiest in the world. Did you earn it? Or you? What about you? Or is our affluence the product of centuries of effort by past generations? Do you object to international aid because, just possibly, some of those who receive it did nothing to earn it? Or is such a risk the necessary price to pay for greater justice? You are still twenty times wealthier than people in the poorest countries. Does that mean you are twenty times more virtuous than they?

'No, citizens. To demand that people should lose their property if they don't live up to your self-appointed standards is the wrong way around. Rights to such inalienable assets are needed if people are to be treated and to act like free individuals in a free society....'

Cramps was pulling them away. 'Time,' he muttered, 'think about the time.'

They made their way towards an even bigger crowd of people a few hundred feet away. Zadie was puzzled. What kind of talking-shop was this? She stared again at the columned building on the far side of the Agora. Was that the parliament? If so, what were the people here doing? Were they reflecting on and amplifying its debates? Or were they trying to feed opinions and arguments *into* parliament? Yet there were thousands of people here. How could that work? In the middle of such diversity how could people send a coherent message to a group of law-makers?

The speaker here was perched on top of a stepladder, speaking into a microphone. *Nothing Without Community, No Community Without Duty*, his sign read.

'We cannot be interested in freedom alone,' he was saying. 'Freedom is a property of a community. Freedom is always freedom *for* someone and therefore depends upon a dense network of social relationships. It's the ever evolving norms, values and understandings of the community which shape what does and does not count as freedom. Therefore, if a community wants to define freedom in a particular way there is not a whole lot that people outside that community can do to object.

'So, yes, if a group of people want to increase the work expectations, if they want individuals to demonstrate their worth in order to be counted as deserving, then that community is perfectly entitled to do so!

'Freedom involves rights but it also involves relationships with those around us as equal members of a polity. My friend over there...' he pointed back towards the speaker Zadie and the others had just left, '...would supply everyone with property and wealth unconditionally. That's a dangerous idea. Property, too, is a social institution and so depends upon social rules, conventions and laws. The idea that you can just come along, slice up property and dole it out to everyone without asking anything in return is ridiculous. If you gave someone a strip of land then it would wither and effectively die if they didn't look after it properly. And that is something the rest of us should be concerned about. If that land isn't being used productively, if someone else can make better use of it, then the community does have the right to change its ownership.'

Zadie became aware that some kind of fight was occurring several hundred feet away to her right but decided to concentrate on what was in front of her. She was sometimes barely awake. How long since she'd slept? She couldn't reckon the hours any more.

Someone was yelling. 'There is no such thing as "the community". We don't possess a collective mind.'

The speaker made to answer this but the man had procured a microphone of his own somehow. Now his voice shot clearly across the crowd. 'We sometimes need protection from community. You talk about the importance of reciprocity and solidarity but in a community of racist people I reciprocate by being racist too. Would that be acceptable? Community consists of sub-communities that challenge one other. A healthy community contains conflict. The rights we have against the community have to be unconditional to some extent. We can't rely upon the community being benign; we need rights against it even if it *is* perfectly benign.'

Many in the crowd started to applaud this performance and the speaker had to stutter into the mic in order to regain control.

Zadie was interested in how what's-his-name would respond but, again, Cramps was pulling them away. Every place they'd visited seemed to wrestle with the same question, how to balance individual interests against communal interests. They'd all seemed so passionate about their chosen solutions. So certain. How was it possible to decide which system was best? In her exhausted state Zadie felt she needed lots more time to digest it all. Maybe a lifetime's worth.

She suddenly realised that they'd been wandering in the direction of the brawl. The fight had stopped but there was still a hell of a row going on. Three men were trying to scramble onto what was another makeshift stage, only to be held back by others at the head of the crowd. 'This looks like fun!' Cramps said.

God, when would he ever learn? 'Do we have to?' asked Zadie, 'it doesn't look safe.' Aon was hanging back too, looking nervous again. She and Zadie still held hands.

'Are we able to leave yet, Virgil?' Jake spoke into his jacket pocket.

Nope. Any chance of getting a little companionship down here? I do get lonely, you know. What happened to those museum iPods with the nice curves?

'Any readings on how the rupture might have affected this part of spacetime?' Cramps asked.

Zilch. But then we haven't been here that long.

Cramps glanced around cautiously. Any familiar faces? Anyone who looked out of place? 'Virgil's program means that we have to absorb our surroundings before we can jump,' he reminded Zadie. Besides, he needed time to think about Aon. What were they meant to do with her?

By the time they had reached the outer edges of the crowd several... police officers presumably...had pushed their way towards the centre and had calmed things down. *The Natural Order of Things*, Jake read on the sign.

'What's happening?' he asked someone.

'Same thing as always,' responded the stranger. 'Ridley spouts her stuff and the lefties take offence. I almost think they enjoy it.'

Ridley? Oh boy! Rupture alert! The four of them looked at one another silently. They each understood what this meant. Time was running short. They were in danger again.

They could see Ridley now. It was the older version once again, the one who'd always seemed to be sucking on a dead mouse, the one with her hair wrapped round her head as tightly as a skullcap. She had been huddled away from the skirmish but with the officers' help had regained a bit of control. A cordon of people now surrounded the stage.

Ridley was speaking with one of the officers. 'Yes, point taken,' they heard muttered sideways into the loudhailer. 'As always at these events I am targeted for special treatment.'

'Special treatment for special needs!' someone at the front shouted as hooting and laughter swelled through the crowd. Next to her Aon tensed suddenly and began to tiptoe up, trying to see over the many heads in front of them. Zadie too had felt the hairs on the back of her neck rise. What if Ridley recognised them? But it wasn't Ridley that Aon seemed interested in.

More faint bickering could just be heard near the stage. Some of the crowd were jeering impatiently now. 'Pipe up!' 'Smack 'im one!'

'Citizens,' Ridley announced, 'the officer here says that I must allow my protagonist a chance to respond. My ideas are strong enough to withstand a rabble...'

'Bloody martyr!'

'....since that's the point, isn't it? The fashion for democracy has spoiled us into thinking that all men are born with something interesting to say. But it's not so. Culture and morality can never be democratic. Men are in need of guidance. How could just anyone in a community be considered the equal of everyone else? Do you think all parts of a human body are equal? The heart and the brain are surely the most important organs. A man can afford to lose an arm or a leg, but lose his brain? No, the brain needs defending even though to the ignorant limbs it may seem to perform very little work. "We do all the labour," the limbs say, "and we can't see any sweat on the brain." But that is to miss what the brain does: it regulates and coordinates. The limbs would be ineffective labourers without the brain.

'Well, just as it is in a human body, so it is in a body politic. The same organic principle applies. Leaders take years to acquire their special skills, while it only takes a labourer minutes to learn his job! Some among us are born to lead and some of us are born to be led. It's the natural order of things. You may as well complain that rain is wet. We urgently need to reverse the democratic experiment. We have allowed the limbs too much say in how the body is governed. Yes, yes...' Ridley looked amused, 'I am here appealing to those I call a rabble.' Ironic cheers rang across the Agora.

'People cannot be self-governing. If a machine malfunctions we do not expect it to repair itself. Correction can only come from the outside, from those who have a clearer view of the damage and what can be done to correct it.

'Of course, we should impose greater work conditions on the lazy and idle. We need to erect a whole series of conditions that will define people's differing status in the community. Those at the bottom, to put it simply, need more conditions imposed on them because without such control they will infect the rest of us with their moral diseases. But we ought to do this for their sake as well as for ours. Indeed—' Ridley paused as one of the police officers leaned over.

'It's the same, every debate,' the nearby stranger said to them. 'Whatever the topic this idiot stands up with her metaphors, all of which are designed to make the same point: that people like her are clever and the rest of us are thick!'

The police were helping another man onto the platform. Aon tensed again as Kayne rose clearly into view.

CHAPTER NINETEEN

Zadie grabbed Aon immediately, stopping her from dashing towards the stage. She felt the bones in her fingers being squeezed.

'No! Don't draw attention to us.' How could she explain to Aon that Kayne might not know her? Might not *be* the person she cared for. 'We'll get to him when we can. Isn't that right, Granddad?'

'Virge?'

Not yet! Something's happening. Stand by.

Hell, did the sky have to fall in on them before they could jump for the final time, grumbled Cramps? Maybe it was time to override Virgil's programming.

Kayne had been handed the loudhailer.

'I suppose I have to admire my opponent,' Kayne's familiarly sharp and sarcastic voice boomed at them, the loudhailer hissing in protest. 'Not many would hold to such outdated beliefs. Here, Ridley, look. These are the people. Not some mysterious entity that you can dismiss, but living, breathing men and women. Do they look like peasants to you? Can people act unfairly and irrationally? Of course. That's why we need social systems—'

Ridley said something they couldn't hear.

'My adversary insists she doesn't doubt the value of people, just the value of popular democracy. What I say is...you can't have one without the other. People stopped being slaves and serfs when they recognised their need and their capacity to be free. Democracy is not just the voice of freedom. It *is* freedom! We are free, we are a people, in so far as we are self-governing.'

This time Ridley stepped forward and her voice could be heard faintly through the loudhailer.

'Does that mean whatever the people want, they should get? We prevent a child from placing its hand in the fire, don't we?'

Kayne stepped away from her and addressed the crowd again. 'If you treat people like children or like a mob then they are more likely to act that way. People are most like themselves when they act in cooperation with others. Individuals are most free when they see themselves in others and decide not to act selfishly. Democracy is a gradual education of the collective *by* the collective. When people get things wrong we need *more* democracy, not less. The individual can learn how to perceive the common good, the general will, and act accordingly.'

This can't be the Kayne we remember, Zadie thought. He knows too much about this society and sounds, well, almost thoughtful and reasonable.

'So, work conditions!' a voice to their left cried out, 'Whaz a general will say 'bout them?' Many in the crowd were still chortling, enjoying the spectacle.

'That's for the people to decide,' Kayne ventured.

'But what *you* say?'

'That can only come from free and fair deliber—'

Someone blew a raspberry. Zadie could feel spittle on the back of her neck. Kayne had lost the crowd. Many were heckling and drafting away. Another scuffle broke out on stage and then Kayne was gone.

'I have to get to him,' Aon finally struggled free of Zadie's grip.

Zadie found it hard to disagree. She had a right to try, didn't she? Her grandfather had already read her mind. 'OK, but please don't leave it too long!' He indicated another gathering to their left. 'We'll be over there. Hurry!'

Another speech, Jake fumed as Aon and his sister disappeared into the crowd.

Zadie led the way. She was taller and had lots of recent experience fighting her way through jungles of elbows. She was suddenly more upset than tired. The others didn't seem to care that they had an obligation to Aon and Kayne. To Cramps, they were just computer-generated abstractions. And Jake didn't seem bothered one way or another.

'There!' Aon blurted out.

Kayne was chatting with, of all people, a police officer as the crowd broke up, its currents obstructing their course to the stage. Zadie had never seen Kayne looking so relaxed. He was smiling and joking with the officer. No way would he recognise them. Zadie wondered how she was going to deal with the fallout when Aon was rejected as a crazy woman by the man who was supposed to love her.

Except he *did* recognise her! Still thirty feet away, he saw her and rushed towards them. Aon and Kayne held each other for the longest time. Kayne's eyes were closed and Aon was sobbing quietly. They were hushing to each other. No words, just sounds. The childhood coos of peace and comfort and hope. Zadie wanted to weep again. Perhaps they could make it come right after all. Kayne was looking at her now, his mouth still pinned against Aon's neck.

'Ahhmmm,' he muffled.

'It's alright,' Aon reassured him, turning, 'Zadie's going to make it alright.'

'How are you here?' Zadie asked him.

'Here? You sent me here!'

'We didn't...not deliberately anyway. Are you...how are you?'

'I've been bounced around from God knows where to God knows when.' He cradled Aon's face. 'I never thought I'd see you again! You took me away from her for months!' he accused Zadie.

Zadie shivered. 'You've been here for months?'

'Almost starved at first. Found work. Fitted in. Tried to dream. Swore I'd kill you and your lunatic family if I ever saw you again,' Aon shushed him, calming him. This is what she had done when Zadie had first met Aon. They *had* found one another again! Kayne smiled. 'Found that bloody Ridley woman. Got involved in politics.'

Zadie was conscious that her lunatic family were waiting and that time was slipping away. Neither wanted to leave. Having been reunited, neither wanted to take the risk that Zadie was offering them. Perhaps Jake was right. Perhaps that's all they need. But slowly, patiently, Zadie cajoled them into following her. Reluctantly, they did so.

Several yards behind them, unobserved, Ridley trailed in their wake. Her next speech period didn't begin for a quarter of an hour...and that young woman with that idiot firebrand... she was certain she knew her.

'Doesn't he look familiar?'

Cramps was right. Jake was sure that the elderly man about to start speaking was the distinguished moderator who had addressed the communist arena an eternity ago. Jake could see from everyone's expression – deferential, even enraptured – that the small audience were followers of a sort, here to experience an event, not just a speech.

His face still drawn, his eyes still alive, the speaker looked out over the Agora, at the many arguments going on, humorously resigned to the knowledge that one couldn't prevent the human soul from filling up every so often with foolishness, envy, indifference; all you could do was to tip the vessel every now and again and give sweet reason and tolerance a little space of its own. Here, at least, he mused, after so many years of struggle, was a social system capable of emptying the brim.

He spoke slowly, without notes. The crowd leaned in to hear his thin voice. Despite the softness of his words and the patient amusement of his features, the old man flashed fireworks and spells at his audience, like a retired magician in a dark cloak called on to perform one last show for uncertain but rapturous spectators.

'Here we are again, my friends. Considering the pressing issues of the day. Translating contemplation into action, which the ancients proposed as the essence of a good life of public service. Democracy, deliberation, freedom, equality. These are not easy concepts to talk about or live by. How much easier it was in the time of Pericles or Cicero to hold a republic spellbound in the palm of your hand. But look around you now. All this messy diversity. Teeming humanity. My word! It seems that even nobility of spirit casts dark shadows that accompany it everywhere. Are we destined to shout at one another? Or must we simply strive to fulfil our duties as free citizens and cope as best we can with the glorious noise of humanity?

'I think you know what my answer is. For what would the alternative be?

'A society dominated by free markets, and those who effectively run those markets because of their economic and political power? Surely this led to a society of human particles; of atoms drifting mercilessly in a social void; of selfish combatants who fought for the scraps the richest would toss from their tables; to inhumane inequalities that justified themselves as "tough love".

'What of conservatism? Are humans so imperfect, so fallen, so incapable of running their own affairs that they must be disciplined, controlled? Perhaps, if you wish to place yourself under the bondage of another, you should be free to do so but I'm unsure how you can advise others to live accordingly.

'Or should we go to the opposite extreme? Should we be social egalitarians? Communists, even? Economic power, political power, cultural power, emotional power, symbolic power. They all represent forms of dominance that are inimical to a free society. But what should our currency of equality be? Cooperation and mutuality? Choice? Desert? Need? Can equality be based upon a single foundation, a single principle from which all else follows? Or must we rely upon the human instinct for togetherness and altruism, and nurture it as best we can? I'm not sure that we will ever possess a convenient answer to that question.

'Therefore, some recommend that we simply throw ourselves into the multitude. They argue that the social world is horizontal, that there are no summits, no elevated vantage points from which we can view the whole of humanity. Thus, we must enter the throng, celebrate the chaos and not attempt to impose order on disorder. Why? Because that would be to dictate, to command, to impose one's way of thinking on others. Better to live with that messy diversity.

'But my view is that we should not despair and we certainly ought not to wallow triumphantly in our despair. There are things which we hold in common, which hold *us* in common. Things about which we are often unaware. The very capacity we have to argue with one another also contains, within it, a capacity to *agree*. Disagreement, you see, implies some kind of mutual understanding. When you recognise a rival you also recognise someone with whom you share a common space. You may reject every word I am currently speaking. But you cannot reject your understanding of those words. And contained within that understanding is a joint enterprise.

'Our language, our cultures, our very species. These all denote the source of who we are. And in that source lies a frame for coping with diversity, for celebrating it, yes, but without allowing it to descend into anarchy. Isn't that the basis for the republican, deliberative society we founded a few decades ago? The world is infinite, as is human ingenuity and as is our capacity to get things wrong. We err still. Perhaps it is hubris to imagine that such plurality can be contained in a public space, even one as large as this. What else can we do but do our best in the mortal time we have?

'Any decision we make, whether as individuals or as members of the polity, is only ever provisional. It's never final. But there are those – some of them are here today – who propose a politics of finality, a politics of absolute truth. Democracy is about the forming of consensus, but also about the constant need to break open the social field. Whatever decision parliament comes to, and whatever debates we feed into it, the work of democracy is ongoing. That is how we ensure that power is dispersed, residing always here amongst we, ordinary citizens. Otherwise, we stand to lose the depths of our democratic conversation.'

Jake shrugged it all away. Didn't talk have to end sometime? Didn't the politicians making policy in that big building over there need something firm to cling onto, something to make decisions with? Wasn't talk, *just* talk?

Cramps nudged him. Zadie, Aon and a very unfriendly-looking Kayne were standing behind him, having caught the final part of the speech. But it wasn't this that Cramps had prodded him about.

Jake looked down. Virgil's screen was blinking frantically. If it was important, wouldn't he be insulting and screaming at them? 'Let's go over here,' Cramps said.

'No!! I'm not doin' this again,' Kayne yelled, pulling Aon back into the crowd. Aon, desperate, panicked, torn between the man she adored and those who had all the answers, hesitated. Then, after a few long seconds gazing apologetically at Zadie, she allowed herself to be dragged into the multitude.

Jake leapt at Zadie as she seemed about ready to spring after them. 'Zadie, no!' Cramps shouted. 'There isn't time!' Zadie, too, was now caught. She looked into the faces of her brother and grandfather, then at the gap in the crowd into which her friend had disappeared. She silently bade goodbye, and turned away again.

They found a clearing near the wall. Jake realised that he'd muted Virgil without thinking.

'OK, what is it, Virgil?'

Trouuuuble!

'Do you mean actual trouble,' queried Cramps, 'or are you just playing another of your games?'

Serious! The rupture. It's not behind us or even ahead of us anymore. It's everywhere! It's all around us. The m-bubble is dissolving! I'm dissolving!

'I am a leaf on the wind,' Jake stuttered, 'just a leaf on the wind.'

You're a what on the what?

This couldn't be possible, Cramps shuddered inwardly as, spooked beyond belief, Jake and Zadie looked around hysterically. The platforms appeared no different from before. The crowd was circulating, arguing, laughing. The makeshift stages had not moved. The speakers were still pontificating to each new audience they attracted. The police were keeping an eye on potential troublemakers. The noise was still high, an overlapping, overflowing racket of humanity. None of them could see any familiar faces. No leaking of one reality into another. In short, it seemed no different than before.

'Be more specific.'

Can't. Can't process this....Major....Catastrophic.

'We have to jump then. Are we alright to jump?'

Leh, gloop.

'Leh, gloop?' shouted Jake, 'what the arse pig do you mean?'

Arans ib opffun.

'Ohh, you had better not be crapping with us, you pissing monster.'

Then, there. It was Ridley, darting straight at them with two police officers in tow.

'These are them! I'm sure they're wanted by the authorities for something!' Large parts of the crowd were now turned their way, wondering what the commotion was about, getting ready for some special entertainment. 'I'm sure if you check the files you'll find they're wanted people!'

'Is it Virgil? Zadie asked. 'Is he damaged?'

Hef swux, ka ka pinber.

'His speech sensors may be malfunctioning. That was supposed to be impossible too!'

Zadie gasped, 'We have to get out of here. Can we jump?'

'Yes, but there's no guarantee that it will take us back home. It might leap us further into the metaverse and if Virgil's fried, then that might be it for us. There's the emergency option.'

Everything begins to move in dream slow motion.

Zadie thinks at first that this is an effect of their predicament. They are inside an accident, watching tenths of a second trickle like sand through an hourglass. But no. It isn't a trick of the mind. Time *is* slowing down. Is this the override? Is the world freeze-framing for us?

Jake gasps.

Zadie screams.

Ridley's face has gone.

CHAPTER TWENTY

There was a head, the roundness of the skull, but no eyes, no mouth, no nose, no hair, no expression. Nothing. Nor was there any flesh or bone or tendons. Ridley's face hadn't been torn off or blasted away. It just wasn't there. Wiped. There was a smoothness but Zadie wasn't even sure whether there was a surface. She imagined an insane version of herself plunging a hand into Ridley's visage and seeing her whole arm disappear.

The woman remained upright, her staid clothes unchanged. It was as if some heavenly cartoonist had decided that the human form wasn't quite right after all and had begun to rub it away with a celestial eraser, starting with the face.

Zadie almost fainted and Jake had to prop her up. She leant on her brother's shoulder, her head as heavy as her mind felt light.

'Don't you just hate it when this happens?' asked Jake.

Sgraw ceug ququv.

'Big help!'

'Virgil!' Cramps was shaking the little machine. Not a big help either. Jake had never seen him so panicked.

Zadie couldn't scream any more, couldn't swallow, couldn't feel the ground she hoped she was still standing on. Her brother's arms.

Much of the surrounding crowd had swivelled towards them. At least that's how it seemed. For many of them had now lost their faces too.

Though not all, Zadie noticed. Slowly, imperceptibly, she realised some individuals were still normal and reacting as anyone might if they heard a scream. Concern? Alarm? Hesitation?

But there was no sound. No, not quite. There was less sound than before but she could still hear some voices. Then, as Zadie concentrated, something turned down the volume. They were standing in an arena with thousands of mutes. She wanted to scream, just to have something to hear.

And now the remaining faces were blinking out, one by one. She saw a woman glance towards them and by the time her head had turned the face had flickered away. No mouths, no sound.

Am *I* still here? Can *I* still speak?

Hundreds of balloon heads stared sightlessly at them. They were swimming through the time-thick air, their ponderous limbs reacting with the sloth of sleep-heavy giants. The nearest began to advance. Jake was conscious of the encircling wall just feet behind them. It was much too high to scramble over in time. They'd have to fight. He looked around desperately for a weapon.

Zadie saw what he was doing.

'Hold on! Cramps! Do it! Use the emergency jump!'

Jrev waalmret ig ib rew!

Cramps blanked for a second, then said 'I think you're right. It's this or nothing.'

'Don't we need the keyword?' asked Zadie.

'Not for this.'

'Then do it!' yelled Jake.

Cramps shuddered. 'I just did.'

Yet they were still here. They hadn't jumped. Wait! The slow-motion mannequins had become even slower. Shoulders rocked gently. Feet rose unhurriedly. They were now moving barely an inch every few seconds. Ridley was gradually raising an arm toward them, like a silent female Frankenstein who had suffered a terrible, undignified mutilation. The world was solidifying. Jake flexed his body, just to confirm that he was immune to this icy paralysis.

'Cramps, are we in the holo-room after all?'

'No, sweetheart. It's us. The m-bubble is malfunctioning. That's what Virgil meant when he said the rupture was all around us now.' He was desperately punching codes into Virgil. 'If they look hideous to us, God only knows what *they* are seeing!'

Zadie looked across the Agora. Most people were not focused on them. Most were turned towards one another, just as they had been for the last hour. Debating still? Laughing? Except there were no faces to be seen anywhere. Then the parliament building began to melt as if suddenly it had been transformed into candle-wax. The high walls and columns liquefied and dripped, incinerating from within. The same was happening to the bodies in front of them. Colours running together, limbs fusing into cottoned torsos, the light becoming fuzzy. Aon and Kayne are out there, Zadie thought. Motionless monstrosities. Melting and merging.

But perhaps the swollen monsters weren't monsters. They were concerned citizens going, infinitely slowly, to help a group of strangers in trouble....

'Old friend, don't fail us this time,' said Cramps, making the final entries into Virgil's keypad.

And this time, Virgil didn't.

At first Zadie thought this was a silent world too. That her hearing had been taken away as part of the assault on their senses. It took many long seconds before Zadie realised that the world was no longer vanishing. The dissolving, molten shapes pushing in on them were gone. They had jumped. They were still there, all of them, somewhere.

A solitary bird call arced across the treetops, followed by a hurtling, crashing orchestra of chirrups and snarls. It was not the cluttered hubbub of thousands of opinionated humans, but glorious, joyous noise all the same.

They were in a large glade on the summit of a hill. It was cold but there was very little wind. Below them a forest canopy glided down towards a plain, undulating for countless miles on all sides and stretching far out of sight. Zadie saw shadows move and lurch. She decided not to look too closely.

'Virgil, are you back with us?'

What d'ya mean?

'We lost you for a while,' Cramps said.

You lost me? Holy fat lady, you organics start acting even more crazy than usual and I'm the one who gets grizzled.

'Then you're saying that was a normal jump?'

No! It was a normal emergency *jump. But you knew the risks of that. Your wish is my command, o master!*

This worried Cramps. The rupture *had* affected the jump but Virgil hadn't registered anything unusual. To him, nothing had seemed out of place. No babbling. No melting balloon people. Did that mean they were now lost in the metaverse? Had the worst happened, after all?

Yet here they were, in the kind of environment he'd programmed them to jump to if they needed a safety-net.

'What was that?' Zadie demanded. 'Was that an illusion or real? Is Aon...?'

'An illusion, yes. There was nothing actually wrong with *them*. They weren't being transformed. It's just how things appeared to us through the m-bubble when it was being assailed by the rupture.'

'Then we need to go back.'

'Why?'

'Aon and Kayne. You promised to get them back home!'

Damn. 'I promised to seal the rupture.'

'No! You promised to make things alright!'

'Are you crazy,' laughed Jake, nervously. 'You want to send them back to the Grey Districts? You hated that free-market place more than the rest of us! They're fine where they are. Though why she likes that jerkpiss boyfriend is a mystery.'

'We don't have the right to decide that. No one does! She has a nephew out there! A cause to fight for. How many lives are affected if we don't send them back?'

'Not lives,' sighed Jake, 'Just shadows.' This had become an old argument hours ago.

Don't try to act morally. You never know where that kind of thing might lead!

'Granddad?'

'We are not out of trouble ourselves, yet. I'm sorry, Zadie.'

'So where are we now?' Jake scanned the thick miles of surrounding forest. 'Doesn't look much like Dagenham. Not unless the green-wellie brigade has managed to plant a shitload of trees since we've been gone!'

'Actually,' replied Cramps, 'since we've been bouncing around the Home Counties we may not be far away from home. This could be the Chiltern Hills or whatever. If everything is OK...Virgil?...'

Yes, yes, I'm checking! Hold your bleeding horses.

'...then the next jump will take us home.'

'It will?' asked Jake. 'Then why didn't we just come here hours ago, when we knew something was wrong?'

'Because it was an incredibly high risk coming here. Look, all the places we've visited are relatively minor variations on the society you know, right? Not *that* far removed from us in the multifold. Even when you deal in probabilities it was fairly easy to program Virgil so that we could journey to different types of social system.'

Yeah, I've really enjoyed being lost in Arseovertit Land!

'But this is what we used to call a "deep leap". There's no society here. No humans. We are a long, long way from our region of spacetime. But it's because it's so different from our own that, hope-fully, we have managed to outdistance the rupture and seal it behind us.'

Not reading any disturbances. Yippee!

'You mean humans have become extinct?' Jake looked around timidly, half expecting to see the roof of a crumbling Big Ben hauled down and strangled by jungle vines.

'No, darling. No, here humans never developed at all. Not the kind of humans you'd recognise, anyway.'

Jake was puzzled. 'I still don't—'

'The metaverse is infinite. Shadow societies, like the ones we visited today, occupy only a tiny part of it. But across enormous swathes of the multifold humans never developed civilisation. On most shadow-Earths, humans never evolved at all. With the rupture affecting Virgil's recalibration matrix we had to jump to one of those so that the return journey model could be reassembled.'

'So where's the risk?'

'Isn't it obvious? In making this jump the probabilities of us ending up somewhere safe were dangerously small. What if we'd jumped to a version of Earth without a breathable atmosphere? Or a planet with very pissed off but intelligent descendants of the dinosaurs? Or what if we'd gone to one of the shadow-realities where there is no Earth? In most realities the planet you and I know never formed! We might have ended up floating in space, dissolved into protoplasm.'

Not the most intelligent kind of protoplasm either.

'Any deadly germs here, Virgil?' Cramps was worried about what they might transmit once back home.

Nope, why? Did you want some?

'We'll take your word for it,' Jake said. 'Then this will take us home?'

'Yes, so long as Virgil gets a move on.'

Jeeeezusss!

They looked around quietly, in fearful wonder at an Earth where humans had never developed.

It took a minute for Zadie's eyes to adjust to the darkness surrounding them. Only now did she become aware of how much it was moving, squawking, scuffling, leaping, as mysterious creatures scampered and scurried across the deep forest floor, pushing aside the thick vegetation, vaulting the trees, shaking the branches, shrieking and screeching. They were out in the open, above most of the forest, but how long would it really take some fanged legend to cross the space between them and the treeline – no more than forty or fifty feet away – and devour them? 'Don't worry,' her grandfather reassured them. 'The bubble is here. We can now make a minor jump sideways without too much risk.' The creatures don't know that, she thought.

A sucking and slithering made Zadie turn around reluctantly. A long, bulky, worm-like body was sliding down the trunk of a tree. No head. No eyes. The body throbbed as it descended, the almost transparent layers of its outer skin twisting like an accordion, swelling backwards and forwards. Fully stretched out it had to be taller and wider than a human. She fought off a sudden image of herself swallowed and slowly digesting inside its milky, greasy membrane. Paralysed, she watched as the giant worm flopped onto the ground, fearful it would turn towards them. But, rippling into the darkness, it had vanished within a few seconds. Zadie felt ill.

As her senses became attuned to this remote world, Zadie heard it humming. Insects! Wonderful! What hairy, prehistoric fist-snap nightmare might want to harvest them? She couldn't *see* any bugs but their clattering was now shrill and inescapable. Then she was sure she could spot a flying spider. Her awareness of the racket made it seem louder, which in turn made her more aware of it. Sawing and tapping, hammering and rattling, the forest sounded like a single, scuttling organism; as though the very trees might scramble and leer at them. Zadie wanted to swat at her ears. She could vaguely sense a swarm of dots and points hovering just above the treetops and was reminded of the Buzzers they'd seen on their first jump. Fortunately, no hungry multi-legged, eye-popping, sting-gouging monster hovered into view. That was good, wasn't it? What she couldn't see was too small to really harm her, no?

Then part of the forest crashed in on them. Their glade was no longer empty. Something had come to share.

Perhaps four feet high it was somewhere between a baboon and a large chimp. The body hair was long yet neat, as though the animal had groomed itself. Zadie couldn't help but glance down. It was male. It hunkered down, but she felt that the animal could stand upright if it wished since its hips and upper legs seemed strong and flexible enough to carry the weight. But it didn't. It crawled towards them on all fours for a few seconds and then paused again, its long sleek neck rocking and jutting in some macabre head dance, its eyes spiralling towards then away from them in long indirect glances. Perhaps it was more aggressive on all fours. Measuring the ground between them? Appraising its escape routes back to the safety of the tree dark? Or maybe wondering whether anyone would be joining him for lunch?

Zadie could feel Jake tense up beside her. The space they felt comfortable in shrank with every crouched step the animal took.

Finally, it was near enough for them to see its expression. This was not simply an eating machine. There was curiosity there, an intense, penetrating intelligence. There was no hostility. This disturbed Zadie even more than the grunting and chest-beating she had first expected. I don't need to holler or charge at you. This is *my* territory. What makes you think that you are *my* equal? Zadie thought she should try talking to it. Her timid 'Hello!' sounded incredibly foolish, amid the wheezes and snarls of the surrounding forest, but the animal now looked directly at her. Was this what passed for human in this reality? Was this an impossibly distant cousin? Was this a version of what *they* might have been?

Unfortunately, Jake picked just that moment to recapture some of the ground they had lost. He took one step towards the creature. That's all it needed. The beast wailed, the magic was broken, and to their amazement he stood, turned, ran and launched himself a dozen feet through the air into the dense blackness. The last Zadie saw was of a figure climbing up a trunk, howling, and diving into the murky foliage. Swallowed by the forest.

Jake avoided Zadie's glowering expression. 'So what? Did you think we were gonna get a lecture on the economics of wiping yourself with leaves?'

Good one!

It grew suddenly colder. Zadie scanned the sky. The rising, mid-morning sun had lost part of itself. The bright glare from its leading edge drained away. A solar colossus with broken teeth had taken a bite out of the sun's lower half. As Zadie watched, the bite marks flickered and radiated, as if the sun was being replaced by a huge diamond that showered glints and flashes onto the green brown world below. Then the horizon rose into the ever-darkening sky. What was this? An eclipse? No, it was as if the globe was flattening itself, kneading itself into two dimensions, the lights turning off as dusk rushed prematurely towards them. Within minutes, the horizon was so black that they could no longer witness the ascending corners of the world and the sun continued to blot.

Zadie became aware of a sound that played inside her like a primitive audiotape she had heard in a previous life and was now remembering again. A fluttering stormwave that soundtracked both fear and relief. A monstrous wing that smothered and secured. Birds? Bats? Whatever they were they soon clouded a quarter of the sky, pressing even this immense forest back into its mother earth. There must be billions of them, enveloping the world in their migrating, continental shadow. The trees around them sank away into an impenetrable gloom. And as the darkness fell further so its sounds retreated and huddled. The world was united and subdued by this vast airy multitude. They were being blinded by something fatally beautiful.

We can go!

'Are you sure?' Cramps asked. Virgil's screen lit up indignantly, his characters offering the only artificial light in this distant universe.

Yes I'm sure. But either I'm wrong, in which case you're about to die and so there's no point in worrying. Or I'm correct in which case – errr, let me think about it for a moment – oh yes, that's it, you have nothing to worry about!!

'Let's try it,' suggested Jake. 'Much longer here and we'll either be eaten or else crapped on by the millions of flying beasties about to pass overhead. And then eaten.'

This was it, then. They'd been making leaps into the unknown for the past sixteen hours but now it really was unknown. Were they leaping back home or into nothingness? Would it be *their* home or some shadowed version of home? Would they see one another again or end up scattered across the metaverse?

They all hesitated. Even Cramps.

Then Virgil took the choice away from them.

I mean, for pity's sake!

CHAPTER TWENTY-ONE

Jake reached for the brochures. This one had a great nightlife whereas this one had an impressive computer centre. It was impossible to choose. All the prospectuses he'd looked at trumpeted impressive stats and achievements, presented beaming students in glossy photos and promised prospective students all the wonders of Shangri-la. There was always Zadie's university of course. Or maybe he should go for the one with all the pubs and clubs. After all, good mental and physical health are important but, as the man said, too much of anything wasn't necessarily a good thing.

In the three weeks since their return it was Jake who had adjusted best to their home surroundings, except for Virgil of course who, it turned out, really did watch quite a lot of television. They'd spent a few evenings watching boxsets of *Dark Angel* together. Jake even dared to think they'd become friends.

Do you ever think there'll be a TV series about a crimefighting SI unit?

'No.'

You shot that down pretty quickly. In the 5.78433 seconds since I thought of the idea I'd become quite enthusiastic! I'd begun to build my future around it. Are you saying there's no hope?

'Yes.'

Bastard.

Jake loved the idea of his granddad being from the future, even if he wasn't to go there himself. Even if he couldn't tell anyone. It made *him* special? As if he was the result of special breeding. A product of the future which preceded that future. A link to a time that no one else could access. A prototype of things to come! Who else among his friends had seen a flying car?!

And in his less messianic moments Jake appreciated that it meant he would have to see others as differently as he was now beginning to see himself. Given how things had gone between the rest of the family Jake had acted as a line of communication and even as a peace-maker. It was a new role for him and perhaps his first experience of real maturity. He duly loaded it into his mental arsenal for use in any number of future quarrels.

Jake had come to accept that his grandfather was leaving. That had been the whole point of the trip. To say goodbye. OK, their gentle family outing had turned into an eye-popping cliff-top plunge, but keeping Granddad here wouldn't bring his father back. Cramps still had the last part of *his* long journey to complete. At least, that's what Jake told himself whenever the emotional stitches threatened to tear.

The final jump had returned them in one piece to Cramps' house. In fact to the back garden where they had materialised in their grand-father's radish patch.

Not bad for a journey across a billion universes. Always hated those radishes.

'Ha!' Jake had exclaimed, a little too loudly, 'we're home. We have internet access.' He was waving his phone in the air. 'Well done Virgil! Hmmph, no messages.'

But that was because it was 11a.m. on the previous day again and they'd gone without sleep for almost twenty-four hours. Zadie for even longer.

From a gap in the back door they silently witnessed the earlier versions of themselves enter the 'holo-room'.

Don't you need to do something?

'Ah yes,' and Cramps had pushed a picture off the wall. 'Remember?'

'You mean, we heard a sound and so just then we had to make a sound?' Jake marvelled. 'Cool!'

'Look,' said Zadie, fearing she already knew what the answer would be, 'I mean, don't you need to program Virgil so that our past selves don't make the same mistake we did?'

Cramps explained that the rupture had finally been sealed by the very fact that they had returned, safe and sound, to a point a few moments before they'd left.

This is what she'd feared and wanted to be clear about. But first things first. There were showers to be taken, bathrooms to be visited, food to be cooked and eaten. It was only after the children had convinced themselves, with the help of Virgil's repeated, exasperated reassurances, that this *was* their reality and for the tenth goddamn time no it *wasn't* about to fizzle out on them that Zadie felt able to speak.

'I thought the point was to prevent ourselves from ever leaving so that the last day could never have happened.'

Cramps was scrutinising the carpet, avoiding his granddaughter's accusatory stare. 'No. To have intercepted our past selves might have been even more dangerous than allowing a rupture to seal itself within spacetime.'

'Then—'

'Then we managed to contain the damage by sealing the rupture behind us, but the damage hasn't been erased from the multifold itself.'

Zadie had slumped back into the sofa and felt rather than heard the breath slide from between her teeth.

'So the damage is out there?'

'Sweetheart, that doesn't mean good consequences can't result. I damaged the past when I travelled to it but you came out of my intervention. Isn't that reason for celebration?'

Zadie wasn't placated. 'What about Kayne and Aon,' she almost shouted. 'Don't tell me they were just computer projections, interpretations of shadow data, or anything like that. She was real! I can tell. We took them out of their lives and put them in an alien society.'

'A better society,' Cramps murmured.

'What?!' Zadie rounded on him, for the first time, with icy fury. 'Is that your only...fucking apology? What happened to the "they weren't real" excuse?'

Doesn't matter. The calculations are the same either way. Pick whatever answer satisfies your emotional wreckage. Can we have the TV on now?

Unconsciously, Cramps massaged the wound on the side of his head.

'Then we ruined her life! We took a strong, confident person and turned her into a mess.'

It was here that Jake had leapt to his grandfather's defence. 'Even if it was all real, we took her out of that society you condemned as a fascist hellhole. You don't seem as bothered about Williams and the rest. Aon'll adapt. How is that bad?'

'I've already said: her nephew, her cause.'

'Now who's playing God?'

Zadie's face was hot with tears now. 'You're both as bad as that glorified computer! We didn't have the right! You can't decide "oh well, they're probably better off now" as if you're some bargain basement god. Even if nothing had gone wrong on that journey we – I mean, you – were taking too much of a risk.'

'You're setting an impossible standard, Zadie,' appeased Cramps. 'Every act is an intervention and every intervention has consequences. A smile in the right place leads two people to marry. A frown can create lifelong enemies. The smallest act can have massive effects. "Do no harm" is an unrealistic expectation.'

'Then what was the point of it all?'

'I told you: it was only meant to be an adventure, an education. We cannot avoid mistakes, only try to make as few as possible. That means deliberately trying to affect our environments, being willing to take risks. It means educating people so that they can understand and analyse. So that they can educate themselves, ultimately. I wanted to show you lots of different societies. Each of them had something going for it but none of them was ideal. We learn by being exposed to alternatives, by being able to compare and contrast. We live better when we live amid diversity and can find our way around it, accepting that diversity but also...intervening to make things better according to the principles and ideas we hope, but can never be absolutely sure, are the right ones.'

'We didn't find diversity, we found chaos. *We* produced the chaos. In this infinite metaverse, what's the point? If it goes on forever then what does it matter what a few people do?'

'Now you're contradicting yourself,' said Jake. 'If it doesn't matter then, in an infinite universe, why worry what happened to Aon?'

Zadie had been about to tell him to shut up, but that suddenly seemed pointless too.

'The universe was always infinite, Zades,' her grandfather insisted. 'You've just been able to see some of that diversity first hand, that's all.'

But Cramps knew that she was beyond his words now; and knew that he'd lost her.

And so it had gone on, hour after exhausting hour. Finally it had been Jake who had pulled his tearful and exhausted sister away. Just as he pulled their mother away, later that day, once Zadie had spilled out the entire, incredible story to her.

They had gone to bed. Slept for two solid days. Then it had all started up again.

It had been like that for a week. A series of shattering emotional battles that had nowhere to go and so retreated into themselves, into worthless repetition. Each old scar reopening daily, seeping new blood. New venom. Each reverberation re-echoing into an ever more futile offensive.

Eventually a ceasefire had been called, but it was not a real truce. More a sickness at hearing themselves go on and on, a weariness at seeing themselves through the eyes of the people they were trying both to maroon and to rescue.

Since then Jake had visited his grandfather and Virgil regularly. Following his example, his mother had eventually calmed down and phoned her father to effect a reconciliation. But Zadie remained stubborn, withdrawn.

He looked again at the photos. He still wasn't sure that university was his thing. However, Indiana Jones had been an egghead too, hadn't he? Was it possible to be an academic and solve crimes, save the world and get all the girls? Not if this beardy professor was anything to judge. Then again, Bruce Wayne and Tony Stark were mega-rich so maybe that was the way to go.

Jake filled out an application anyway. Best to keep his options open, yeah?

Zadie lay on her bed. She ought to be preparing for her return to campus next week. She ought to have spent the past few weeks preparing, but she found it difficult to concentrate these days.

She could hear Jake next door in his bedroom. His 'music' pounded on her wall. And on this cold spring day he had the heater on and the window open. 'I enjoy a cool breeze and warm feet. Why can't I have both?'

He was supposed to be filling out applications for university. Why didn't she feel happy about that at least? Wasn't he doing what she had urged him to do when they'd gone to interview Mrs Gregsbury on that day, ages ago now? Perhaps she resented how little the experience of three weeks ago had affected him. Or seemed to. He'd taken it all in his stride and hadn't connected with the enormity of what they had done. *Might* have done. Cramps couldn't even tell them which. Or had she connected *too* much?

Her mother had shared the anger and frustration of her daughter, fuelling and being fuelled by Zadie's own. They had become conspirators, smuggling their painful emotions to one another. But even that had faded. Mum was going to see her father tomorrow and knew that Cramps had asked to see Jake and Zadie the day after. It was obvious what the request presaged.

Or was it something more fundamental? Zadie hadn't slept well at first. When she closed her eyes she could still feel the sun dim and the corners of the world rise up at her again. Except now it wasn't just the world somehow. It was herself.

Like most people she used to marvel at the immensity of space. 'Aren't we small,' she'd say to give herself a tingle, a brief shudder of infinity. Then she'd flick the page or switch over to a sitcom. For her, the circumference of space had faded, after the Apollo landings, into an abstraction she couldn't deal with and so shouldn't really try. It sank beneath the horizon of her comprehension. And her interest.

But now the universe felt flat. As if she could head off, walking and whistling with a handkerchief tied round a stick at her shoulder, and visit all of it. Except that out there now were not just alien worlds but alien versions of this world. What-might-have-beens. What perhaps *was*. So now she couldn't turn the feeling off. Because it wasn't just the space out there. It was herself, her life – curves of spacetime, her grandfather had casually and so coldly called them.

That was where he had come from, it seemed. He had wandered towards them from one part of the horizon, paused for a while and now was preparing to wave a cheery farewell and disappear forever over the other. It was as if he hadn't loved them. Any of them. He'd been stranded. He'd needed to stay. They'd been an amusement, something to occupy the time until he could leave again. They meant no more to him than an animal someone might keep for a pet after they'd been marooned on a remote island. The animal might fall in love with the castaway, become dependent on her, and then look for her frantically one day but without finding her because she'd left without ever looking back.

For a while Zadie had been convinced that they hadn't returned to reality at all, that they now inhabited some near but not quite identical version of their home. That her mother was not really *her* mother. That she was still inside the bubble, interacting with the shadows of the people she knew. That this was just another potential phantom existence cast by technological ghosts onto her lost, wandering consciousness, as real or no more real than the one they had stolen poor Aon and Kayne from. And for a long time, Zadie would stare into people's faces more than this modest, shy girl had ever stared before. Waiting. Waiting for features to burn and melt and for shrunken, misshapen forms to stumble at her.

For had Cramps, forty-two years ago, jumped back into *the* past or into an alternative reality? Was she perhaps just a ghost within a bubble inhabited only by her grandfather? Was she the real Zadie or a shadow version of herself, the authentic self out there somewhere, confident, popular and beautiful?

Had their neighbour's car always been blue? When did those street signs become round? Her bedroom no longer felt like hers. Had that poster always been on *that* wall?

Then her fears shifted into what she hoped was absurdity. She hadn't understood the science but...hadn't Cramps said that Virgil was the bubble? That he was the centre of the journey? Had he taken them into shadow-realities or were those realities different versions of *him*?! Was Virgil actually some kind of mischievous sprite? A roguish God enjoying a game with pawns who mistakenly thought that *they* were the players? Had Virgil created a universe of universes within himself?

Jake had noticed her unease. Her fear even. And after a few more days he stopped sneaking into her room and rearranging her stuff when she wasn't there.

But even once her surroundings settled down and the feeling of alienation subsided she couldn't shake off the doubt, the sense of foreboding she felt. The endless universe was no longer some playground of astronauts, real or fictional. It was inside her. She felt permanently on the edge of a cliff that threatened to give way. Tumbling head over heels, endlessly into an abyss. Except the abyss was inside her and she couldn't crawl back up herself. There were no handholds, no friendly faces peering from above over the rim of a well, no strong arms hauling her back to the safety of the surface.

She hated her grandfather for this; for taking away her certainties. Then she hated herself for hating him. She'd been content to attend class, contribute when asked, read the recommended reading lists, get her essays in on time and listen studiously to advice. Why had he made it so much more complicated for her? For mistake or no, rupture or no, that's what he'd intended all along wasn't it?

So she tried to concentrate on the societies she'd seen, and tried to draw lessons from the experience. What was good about each? What was bad about each? Which ones would she most like to live in? She fought her fears by trying to remember every conversation, every face, every idea, every argument and counter-argument. She tried writing it all down. She'd experienced an incredible amount, so why did it make her feel worse? Learning was supposed to improve you and your sense of wellbeing, wasn't it?

But she couldn't connect the dots. Couldn't connect any of that with the other, more unsettling parts of their adventure. What had shadow-realities and alternative histories to do with whether you regulated markets or not? Did it matter to questions of politics and morality whether these other realities had been real or only lost, spectral potentials? If your past self and the many pasts in which you were different, or where you didn't even exist, were out there somewhere, in a now inaccessible district of spacetime, how did that help you to sympathise with others, balance liberty with equality, or achieve a sustainable society? How did any of it, as she had once asked herself beneath Mrs Gregsbury's disdainful stare, help make the trains run on time?

Zadie couldn't connect the dots. But nor was she happy any longer with following a 9-5 curriculum, followed by exams, followed by graduation, followed by a Masters degree, followed by a job, followed by a husband, followed by a house, followed by kids...

...followed by...

She envied Jake. His shrugs and scowls. His 'what did you expect?' grimaces. The universe was always like this. It doesn't care whether you're here or not. Are you only realising this *now*?!

The front door slammed. Her mother had returned with the shopping. Zadie hadn't even offered to help. God, when will I snap out of this? Aren't you meant to get your adolescence over with by the age of 16? Would she regress forever? End up sucking her thumb and messing her bib? It was like attending the world's greatest party, only now you had to suffer a hangover for the rest of your life. Oh, and no more parties, either!

She could hear plates and cups clattering downstairs. Sighing, heavy with the flimsiness she felt within, Zadie swung her legs off the bed, sat up, patted her hair, stood, smoothed her shirt and went downstairs to help her mother prepare lunch.

The three of them were sitting in the living room again. Zadie remained mostly silent while her brother and grandfather discussed university life. Jake, she knew, had not yet made up his mind but it was now the one topic that seemed safe. Sometimes Cramps would ask her to confirm a detail or offer an opinion, but her responses were stilted, polite, her head thrown back, defiant and angry and sad. The TV flickered soundlessly too. Virgil was perched on the coffee table and had greeted their arrival with a...

Sshhh! Lorelei's about to dump another boyfriend.

So Cramps had plugged a lead into the TV and then into a small socket on Virgil's side. Gazing at the box's muted images offered a brief, occasional reprieve from the disjointed conversation.

Their mother had visited yesterday and returned with puffy eyes and raw nostrils. 'Your grandfather is leaving tomorrow,' she'd reported; 'you know what he's planning. It's up to you whether you go, Zadie, but I think you should.' She had not said much else, that was for another time, but Zadie sensed that they had become reconciled. This at least was a loss their mother had long expected and was now able to bear. Zadie was happy that her mother was at peace but also a little resentful. It even felt a little like a new betrayal. Was she now expected to set aside her frustrations, stop kicking around the rubble of her lost illusions, and kiss and make up? Was she a bad person if she couldn't find it within her?

'What happens about the house?' Jake had asked.

'Your mother has been given the deeds and power of attorney. I want you to invest it in a small trust fund so that I'll be as rich as Croesus when I return to the future.' The grandchildren stared at him. 'That's a joke.' He coughed. 'The money from the sale is to be split between the three of you. You may have to pay to get rid of some of this junk. Keep whatever you want, though.'

'What about the future, Granddad?' said Jake, 'You must be able to tell us something. Come on.'

Cramps peered uneasily at his granddaughter, wanting to shake her out of herself. *If I don't return and offer a convincing story (a story I've spent forty years preparing) my very incursion might be prevented. You might be erased from history, as would my knowledge of you. You would never have existed, perhaps not even as potential shadow realities. Can't you see I'm leaving for your sake?* No. It was better that they resent him and blame him for abandoning them. *That* was the price that would have to be paid.

'That was the point of the trip, Jakes. I can't give you precise information. Even if you never acted on it, it would still create what we call a "self-looping oxbow". Let's just say, something not a million miles away from the rupture that almost snared us.

'The future I remember was not an ideal. Don't imagine any such thing. They...we, I suppose... have new problems, some of which haven't been anticipated by the people in this time yet. The fact that we have solved most of today's problems doesn't make us morally superior, it's just that things always seem easier in retrospect! So, maybe, compared to this world ours is better. What you see depends upon where you stand.

'The shadow societies I chose for us to visit were picked because my future is an amalgam of many of them. Some of the ideas and institutions we visited were startlingly familiar to me, though we have blended them into a new form of social system. That doesn't mean the ingredients were mixed equally. I was as surprised at some of the paths history could have taken as you were. And, no, I can't give you a recipe on how to make a better society, but I will say this...

'It doesn't come from following a cookbook. There's no blueprint for getting it right. The fact that my future still wrestles with its conflicts is a testament to that. But it does come from having people who are engaged and aware and willing to make differences. You have to decide for yourselves what the future should look like. If I gave you and others a design it wouldn't be yours and you'd probably make a mess of it anyway. So long as you are willing to be analytical and think for yourselves then so much else follows. I'm relying on people like you, you see. For all its faults I want my future to be waiting there for me.'

'What difference can we make, though? Are we going to be famous?'

Cramps giggled, a child again. 'The same difference as the rest of us, I suppose.'

Both men were almost surprised to hear Zadie's voice. 'You mean there's no guarantee that you'll return to the future you left?' Not angry this time. Not quite.

'No. There never was, really.'

'Then which is the real future? The one you left or the one you'll return to? And which is the real present? The one you're in now or the one that would have existed if you'd never travelled here?'

'I know what you want, Zades,' he replied gently, 'You still want me to give a definite answer about the places we visited and therefore about the fate of Aon. But I can't answer that, sweetheart. There is no mouth to the cave, no single source of light. It's all shadows and echoes. You try to spin around quickly to see what's really there, but as fast as you are it's already gone and the shadows are still in front of you, mocking you.

'Perhaps those potentialities, those alternative societies, really are out there somewhere in spacetime. Or perhaps they were just a projection of the m-bubble. As Virgil said, the calculations are the same either way.'

Her voice softened. 'Then how can you bear it? The possibility that the future you left might not be there when you get back. Mightn't you be leaping into an unknown, as we did on that journey? You'll be returning as an old man anyway. Isn't it too much of a risk? Wouldn't...' she stared at the television screen, 'wouldn't you be better staying here after all?'

His grandchildren made room for Cramps as he lifted himself out of his chair and came to squeeze beside them on the sofa. He held Zades for the first time in weeks.

'Perhaps. Perhaps it'll be a mistake to rival the mistake I made by being stranded here in the first place or the mistake I made by putting you both in danger. But there's one last thing I need to share with you.'

Jake and Zadie looked up expectantly. Cramps thought carefully about the right words to say.

'I've always wanted to punch a giraffe on the nose. Want to know why?'

This time is was Zadie who got to the joke first. 'For the challenge?'

'Exactly! You know...a photon has no experience of time. By travelling at the speed of light, for it the beginning of the multifold and the end of the multifold occur simultaneously. Time is only experienced by something which has mass and so cannot travel that fast. That's what I sometimes think happens to us when we die. We become massless, weightless. We travel to the end of time in an instant. We become light. Perhaps, when I'm gone, that's how you should think of me.'

'But when you arrive back there, me and Jake will be long dead and gone.'

'Then perhaps that's how I should think of you too: waiting for me at the end of time. For the photon of light nothing exists, not even itself. Yet *we* see it as existing. The philosophers are wrong to ask why something exists rather than nothing. The question should really be: how can there be both something *and* nothing? It's the paradox of our lives. Our journey, the places we visited, was just one small illustration of that.'

But these were just words. She held him, but Cramps knew he'd lost the young Zadie, the girl who had clambered onto his back and swung joyously from his arms.

He was looking at them for the last time. But was this the last time they would ever be looked *at*? If he returned and succeeded they would have their lives. If he failed, they would never have existed. Even their shadows might simply be erased. They would not have been forgotten, for they would never have died. Denied even the dignity of ever having been known and remembered and loved. Then again, hadn't recent events demonstrated the limitations of his or anyone else's knowledge? In a universe of infinite possibilities, he didn't know. Who could?

And so Zadie and Jake stood in the front garden.

Zadie had been struggling for something to say when Virgil had emitted an ear-gouging shriek. For a moment, Zadie had worried that the rupture had somehow pursued them, found them. But it was just that his TV programme was over.

Terrific! Hey, can we get a box set of The Sopranos *when we get back? Why's everyone so miserable?*

They had unplugged Virgil and carried him into the closet.

Jake and Zadie had then been faced with something new. When their father and their grandmother had died they'd been forced to say goodbye alone, to the images of the people they carried in their heads. It had become easier, in time, to remember them with less pain, though the very lessening of that pain had then left its own sting.

But now there were no words which seemed adequate. No time for rehearsals. The silence closed over them. Floundering, they tried to behave as if everything was normal. Tried to capture the moment, to slow time down, despite the horrible realisation that this only allowed the present to slip away all the sooner. By trying so hard to capture the experience, memorialise it, preserve it, they risked missing it alto-gether. Zadie had to open her mouth to breathe properly and could sense an infected bitterness on her tongue.

It was Virgil who would capture the moment for them with his inane gibbering.

Don't think it's not been fun. Oh, I should have got you a going-away present. Then again, you didn't get me anything. Hey, why not? Well [bleep] you, you [bleep]ing [bleep]ers. Ahh, never mind. Don't forget to write. Any decent water-proofed time capsule will do. Will you include a photo of Angelina Jolie? I didn't have time to download one. Right, love you! Missing you already!

One final hug, one final smile, and Cramps had stepped into what, to them, had previously been the holo-room. As always, the final goodbye had to be the simplest, the briefest goodbye of all. There had been a flare of light from the gap at the bottom of the door, then nothing.

Then the door had stood like an upright coffin-lid before them. Neither of them wanted to open it and neither did. There was no sound. And no need.

It was Zadie who had prevented Jake from leaving.

'If he can travel to an instant after the moment he left the future, he can also travel back to an instant after the moment he left the present.'

But that instant had already gone. Was already receding into its own precinct of spacetime.

Slowly, they had backed towards the front door. They had paused there too, for many minutes. Nothing. Then Jake had tugged at his sister's sleeve and, grudgingly, painfully, she had closed the front door behind them.

Yet still they lingered in the garden. Zadie focused on the door's glass panels. Willing it to blaze with light just once more, to burst open. I got back fine, their grandfather would say. The future's better than ever thanks to people like you. I'm two years older but I just wanted to come back to say goodbye for one last time. Tell your mother I love her. Then Virgil would insult the stupid humans and they'd all laugh again.

Nothing.

Zadie found herself on the pavement at the end of the road with no memory of walking there. Jake was looking at her keenly, sweetly.

He hadn't returned. What did that mean? That he hadn't wanted to? After all, he could return to any moment couldn't he? He might turn up in five minutes or in five years' time. That he hadn't been able to? Had Cramps returned to his future, or at least to a future that resembled the one he remembered? Would he be able to tell the difference? Or was he somewhere else? Somewhere out there in a universal vastness, trying to get back? Lost? Making a new life for himself in a new environment? Like Aon and Kayne.

'Race you!'

The spring day was cloudless blue. Passersby strolled casually along the main road. No jackets, shirtsleeves rolled up, skirts and sandals. It was, at last, the first day of summer.

Zadie felt the noon-high sun envelop the top of her head and trickle down her hair onto the back of her neck.

'What?'

'I said, race you! To the bus stop! The finishing line. Last one there is a big fat fart.'

Zadie shielded her eyes as she looked at her brother's lolloping sprint in amazement. He was already fifty feet down the road. And then at herself in amazement as she dashed off after him. He had such stumpy legs. Little idiot! What made him think for a minute that he could beat her? she asked herself, as she raced towards the bus stop.

NOTES

Free Market Liberalism (Chapters Three–Four)

Free market ideas have gone by many names over the years, such as 'economic liberalism', 'neoliberalism', 'New Right'. They hark back to 'classical liberalism', which advocated only a limited role for government, and correspond to some contemporary theories of libertarianism (the notion that individuals should be free from all involuntary constraints). We often refer to right-wing liberals as 'conservatives' but conservatism, strictly speaking, is less enamoured of laissez faire principles and so usually balances these against other priorities (see Chapters Seven–Eight). Whatever title is used, free market liberalism is committed to several premises: (1) individuals possess basic liberties upon which no one should encroach without consent, (2) individuals are only economically, politically and socially free if the institutions which govern their lives derive from those basic liberties, (3) it is free markets rather than the regulating state which are most capable of constructing and supporting such institutions, because (4) the liberty to own private property and exchange goods with others without unwarranted interference is fundamental to human life and wellbeing.

Previously dominant in the nineteenth century, the view that societies and economies should be organised largely through unregulated markets and self-interested individuals came back into fashion in the 1970s, as a reaction against post-World War Two reforms, particularly the welfare state and the mixed economy. This had a massive influence on governments during the 1980s. In practice, free markets tend to accompany a strong state. Regarding government intervention as a mistake, free market liberals have adopted robust strategies in order to reverse the tide. It might also be said that free markets require people to perceive themselves as self-interested economic agents; as such, free markets may necessitate a considerable amount of social engineering in their own right. Neoliberal governments try to 'roll back' the size and functions of the state, but those functions remaining are carried out with a firm, disciplinary, even authoritarian hand.

Critics allege that real individuals do not act in the ways predicted by free market economics. Sometimes people are irrational or else demonstrate forms of rationality that simplified, abstract, mathematical models – of costs and benefits, cause and effect, supply and demand – do not capture. Another criticism is that free markets undermine the very social conditions upon which they depend. When individuals interact they rely upon a complex but implicit series of cultural understandings, symbolic codes and mutual points of reference, but if individuals are encouraged to view themselves as selfish maxims of their personal interests, relating to others only through formal contracts, then those unseen but vital 'social backgrounds' may atrophy. Finally, free markets tend to accompany large social inequalities with all the problems these bring. In response to social problems, the defenders of free markets either deny their existence ('there is no such thing as poverty'), emphasise other causes ('it's the welfare state which creates unemployment') or blame the victim ('the poor are lazy').

Key reading

Bosanquet, N. (1983) *After the New Right*, London: Heinemann.
Brittan, S. (1988) *A Restatement of Economic Liberalism*, New York: Humanity Books.
Friedman, M. (1962) *Capitalism and Freedom*, Chicago: Chicago University Press.
Gamble, A. (1988) *The Free Economy and the Strong State*, London: Macmillan.
Harvey, D. (2005) *A Brief History of Neoliberalism*, Oxford: Oxford University Press.
Hayek, F. (1944) *The Road to Serfdom*, London: Routledge & Kegan Paul.
Hayek, F. (1960) *The Constitution of Liberty*, London: Routledge & Kegan Paul.
Hayek, F. (1982) *Law, Legislation and Liberty*, 3 volumes, London: Routledge.
Honderich, T. (2005) *Conservatism* (2nd edn), London: Pluto Press.

Nozick, R. (1974) *Anarchy, State and Utopia*, New York: Basic Books.
Rand, A. (1961) *The Virtue of Selfishness*, Middlesex: Penguin.
Saad-Filho, A. and Johnston, D. (eds) (2004) *Neoliberalism*, London: Pluto.
Shapiro, D. (2007) *Is the Welfare State Justified?*, Cambridge: Cambridge University Press.
Smiles, S. (2002 [1859]) *Self-Help*, Oxford: Oxford University Press.

Text notes

35-6   Rational choice theory regards individuals primarily as self-interested bargainers who make decisions based upon rational calculations of benefits and burdens in response to various incentives and disincentives. See: Allingham, M. (2002) *Choice Theory*, Oxford: Oxford University Press. For a view that the poor are rational but lack, because of the welfare state, the correct set of incentives, see: Murray, C. (1984) *Losing Ground*, New York: Basic Books.

37   For a view that rational, moral choice engenders self-interest and free markets, see Narveson, J. (1988) *The Libertarian Idea*, Philadelphia: Temple University Press.

37   For what might be termed 'extreme libertarianism', see: Friedman, D. (1989) *The Machinery of Freedom* (2nd edn), New York: Harper and Row.

37-8   Nozick defended a version of what some call the 'night watchman state'. For an overview and critique, see: Wolff, J. (1991) *Robert Nozick*, Cambridge: Polity Press.

41   The view that only free markets can save the environment can be found in Anderson, T. and Leal, D. (2001) *Free Market Environmentalism*, Basingstoke: Palgrave.

42-3   Criticisms of equal opportunities are contained in: Cavanagh, M. (2002) *Against Equality of Opportunity*, Oxford: Clarendon. For a virulent attack on egalitarianism, see: Rothbard, M. (2000) *Egalitarianism as a Revolt Against Nature and Other Essays* (2nd edn), Auburn, AL.: Ludwig Von Mises Institute.

43   Trickle-down economics is the idea that if you pour greater wealth into affluent households it will percolate down to everyone else eventually.

44   Friedman defended the view that markets are non-discriminatory and so promote non-discrimination in general.

45-7   For the view that the state should have little role to play in education, see: Tooley, J. (1999) *Reclaiming Education*, London: Continuum International Publishing Group Ltd.

Marxist Socialism and Communism (Chapters Five–Six)

Marxism, socialism and communism offered a considerable challenge to liberal and conservative ideas for over a century, though their influence has declined sharply since the 1980s. There are many different, often overlapping strands of each. On pages 54–8 I have drawn from the classical Marxist account of historical and social development. I have also been influenced by the 'utopian socialism' which flourished in the nineteenth century and which the Finland Estate is intended to embody. Marx and Engels criticised this movement for incorrectly imagining that socialism could emerge by constructing experimental communities in pre-revolutionary circumstances. They obviously supported the decent healthcare, housing, amenities, employee rights and all the other innovations that flourished briefly in those communities, but believed that a general social revolution in class relations was necessary if such rights were to be fully realised in a post-capitalist society.

Yet the question of what a true communist society would actually look like has always been a difficult one to address. Marx never specified. Of course, communism came to be widely associated with the one-party centralised state of the USSR and post-1949 China, but if we assume that these were largely a debasement rather than a realisation of radical Left principles and aims, and if communism could have taken a number of alternative roads, then I like to think that communists would have been influenced by the experimental communes envisaged by the early utopian socialists. Such, at least, was the assumption of many in the New Left's attempt in the 1960s to combine Marxist critiques with a more libertarian and less dogmatic set of aspirations.

Yet Marx and Engels were not wrong. We are all free to club together and live according to cooperative, egalitarian and collectivist principles. However, without wider changes in social institutions, economic circumstances and property regimes such experiments tend either to disband or are forced to accommodate themselves so much to capitalistic practices that they lose their original rationale. But the utopian socialists and other critics of revolutionary socialism were not wrong either. Whatever its strengths as a philosophical, sociological and economic critique of capitalism, attempts to translate Marxist communism into social realities have ended almost entirely in disaster. Like its free market opponents on the Right, the radical Left has also possessed its version of the ideal society and the ideal person. Given that such ideals cannot materialise without giving history a push, so the reasoning goes, we must re-engineer human environments until they do.

Whether a reformist but still radical socialism can re-emerge in the changing circumstances of the twenty-first century is yet to be seen.

Key reading

Bellamy, E. (1996 [1888]) *Looking Backward*, New York: Dover.
Engels, F. (2006 [1880]) *Socialism: Utopian and Scientific*, New York: Mondial.
Hayek, F. (1988) *The Fatal Conceit*, Chicago: University of Chicago Press.
Kolakowski, L. (2005) *Main Currents of Marxism*, New York: W.W. Norton & Co.
Marx, K. (1977) *Selected Writings*, edited by David McLellan, Oxford: Oxford University Press. (See especially: 'On the Jewish Question', 'Economic and Philosophical Manuscripts', 'Theses on Feuerbach', 'The German Ideology', 'The Communist Manifesto', 'Critique of the Gotha Programme'.)
Morris, W. (1986 [1890]) *News from Nowhere*, Harmondsworth: Penguin.
Owen, R. (1991 [1813]) *A New View of Society*, Harmondsworth: Penguin.
Popper, K. (2002 [1945]) *The Open Society and its Enemies: Volume 2*, London: Routledge.
Sassoon, D. (1995) *One Hundred Years of Socialism*, London: I. B. Tauris.

Text notes

54–8   For a defence of the Marxist interpretation of human nature, as an historical construct immersed in struggles of and for power, see: Sayer, S. (1998) *Marxism and Human Nature*, London: Routledge. A critique of freedom can be found in Tucker, D. (1982) *Marxism and Individualism*, London: St. Martin's Press; for a socialist but non-Marxist alternative, see: Tawney, R. H. (1964 [1951]) *Equality*, London: Allen & Unwin.

62–7   The Finland Estate's internal organisation was inspired by the utopian socialists (especially Bellamy); see also: Devine, P. (1988)

Democracy and Economic Planning, Cambridge: Polity. The classic statement of the need for garden cities is: Howard, E. (1965 [1902]) *Garden Cities of Tomorrow*, Massachusetts: MIT Press.

63   For one of the earliest and best arguments that social justice must involve women's liberation, see Fourier, C. (1996 [1808]) *The Theory of the Four Movements*, Cambridge: Cambridge University Press.

63   Gorz defends the idea that work is only truly free and fulfilling when it is accompanied by creativity, social interaction and the liberation of time: Gorz, A. (1989) *Critique of Economic Reason*, London: Verso.

64   Cohen argues that social justice ultimately cannot appeal to monetary incentives and unequal rewards in his essay, 'Justice, Incentives and Selfishness'. See: Cohen, G.A. (2000) *If You're an Egalitarian, How Come You're So Rich?*, Harvard: Harvard University Press.

68–9   The first speaker perhaps has something resembling market socialism in mind. See: Roemer, J. (1996) *Equal Shares*, edited by Wright, E.O., London: Verso.

69–70   The second speaker voices a position similar to that of MacIntyre, A. (1995 [1953]) *Marxism and Christianity* (2nd edn), London: Duckworth.

Conservatism (Chapters Seven–Ten)

Conservatives are often thought of as either (1) combining a defence of free markets and private property with a strong emphasis upon family, nation, traditional authority and so on, or (2) non-ideological pragmatists. In fact, conservative philosophies are richer than this and revolve around an ambivalence towards modernity. Some reject the individualism, egalitarianism and what they see as the dangerous relativism of modern 'mass society' (Spengler, Ortega y Gasset); others welcome them while also warning about the dangers inherent in modern sociocultural developments (Tocqueville, Santayana). For the most part, conservatives are ambivalent towards modern society and the best conservative philosophy (Gehlen, Oakeshott) and literature (T.S. Eliot, Yeats) derives from an articulation of that ambivalence.

Conservatives prefer a society in which freedom and self-interest are constrained, and where government and state have to be strong and disciplinarian. They believe the sources of morality and community lie within the family, national history, the locality, the church.

These are thought, in turn, to reflect the natural order of things. Living a good life involves respecting and submitting to the authorities which govern traditional customs, values, symbols, social habits and practices, i.e. their cultures. What conservatives fear is social anarchy and instability. Therefore, interactions between individuals should be governed by firm, top-down and hierarchical political, religious, economic, cultural and legal systems. For conservatives, human nature is driven by emotion, selfishness and appetites. Individuals largely have to be told what to believe and how to behave.

Modern conservatism dates to the eighteenth century, a period when old certainties had died – rule by monarchical, aristocratic and spiritual authorities – and some saw a need to counter the rising influence of liberalism, individualism, Romanticism, scientific rationalism and revolutionary radicalism. I have tried to depict how a conservative 'counter-modernity' might look if it tried to reverse the tide of free markets, social equality and socialism. In both its paternalistic and more authoritarian guises, 'the poor' are seen as being culturally distinct from those who, morally and economically, occupy 'normal' society.

Critics allege that conservatism is out of step with the modern world, invoking old certainties in an era when coping with rapid change and insecurity requires a constant process of rethinking and reinvention that conservative totems and taboos cannot provide. 'How does tradition require me to live?' has become a less relevant question than 'why should I act in this rather than that way?' Furthermore, in its pursuit of stability, order and socio-historical continuity, conservatives typically recommend that established political, economic and cultural authorities be allowed to rule, and are less concerned with the injustices and discriminations this might involve.

Key reading

Burke, E. (1968 [1790]) *Reflections on the Revolution in France*, Harmondsworth: Penguin.

Gehlin, A. (1980 [1957]) *Man in the Age of Technology*, New York: Columbia University Press.

Kekes, J. (1998) *A Case for Conservatism*, New York: Cornell University Press.

Kirk, R. (1985) *The Conservative Mind* (7th edn), Washington: Regnery Publishing Inc.

Kristol, I. (1995) *Neoconservatism*, New York: Free Press.

McAllister, T. (1997) *Revolt Against Modernity*, Kansas: University of Kansas Press.

Oakeshott, M. (1962) *Rationalism in Politics*, London/New York: Methuen & Co.

Oakeshott, M. (1975) *On Human Conduct*, Oxford: Clarendon.

Scruton, R. (2007) *Political Philosophy: Arguments for Conservatism*, London: Continuum.

Strauss, L. (1953) *Natural Right and History*, Chicago: University of Chicago Press.

Strauss, L. (1968) *Liberalism, Ancient and Modern*, New York: Basic Books.

Vedlitz, A. (1988) *Conservative Mythology and Public Policy in America*, New York: Praeger.

Vierek, P. (2004) *Conservatism Revisited: The Revolt Against Ideology*, New York: Transaction.

Voeglin, E. (2000) *Modernity without Restraint*, Columbia and London: University of Missouri Press.

Text notes

87	For the view that citizenship should be earned, rather than considered an automatic status that grants certain basic rights, see: Mead, L. (1997) *The New Paternalism*, Washington: Brookings Institute.
88	The view that more, and more enforceable, obligations are owed by the poor than the non-poor is defended by Schwartz and Mead in: Mead, L. and Beem, C. (eds) (2005) *Welfare Reform and Political Theory*, New York: Russell Sage.
88-9	A distinction is drawn between the deserving (or what he calls the 'innocent') and the undeserving poor in Chapter 17 of Niskanen, W. (1998) *Policy Analysis and Public Choice*, Aldershot: Edward Elgar.
89	Some conservatives are indeed as hostile to the 'cash nexus' (such as Thomas Carlyle, who coined the phrase) as some on the Left.
89-90	We sometimes refer to people as conservatives when they are predominantly right-wing liberals. Conservatives are sceptical towards unregulated, laissez faire capitalism, though tend to support a capitalism whose roots are strongly embedded in family values, charitable assistance, private property, church and neighbourhood associations. Free markets, they believe, should only be permitted if they are shored up by such strong social institutions.

Egalitarianism (Chapter Eleven)

The egalitarianism contained here describes the theories of social and distributive justice that have dominated thinking on the Left over the last 40 years. Of course, these ideas have their roots in the last two centuries of socialist and communist thought, with most on the Left believing it is unfair for people to be either advantaged or disadvantaged due to factors beyond their control. If some are fortunate due to the natural or social circumstances of their birth, such as being born into a wealthy family, then such 'accidents' should not be allowed to determine the pattern of social relationships or the distribution of social goods, for example, income and wealth. Egalitarians attack conservatives and free market liberals for believing that inequalities are natural, inevitable or desirable, and so advocate radical political and economic reforms. Some would like to see capitalism overthrown; some combine their egalitarianism with other principles, for example, liberalism or feminism, (typically rejecting Marxism, although sometimes continuing to be heavily influenced by it); while others accommodate their egalitarian instincts to existing social priorities and developments, for example, social democrats. Some believe that inequalities are justified if, and only if, a fair equality of opportunity prevails. This means ensuring that people truly merit and deserve their offices, success and possessions. Others believe that egalitarianism is essentially incompatible with any system of privilege or unequal status.

Within political philosophy the key figures have been John Rawls, Ronald Dworkin, Richard Arneson, Michael Walzer and David Miller. Those who concentrate upon questions of just distribution have often been referred to, somewhat misleadingly, as 'luck egalitarians'.

Critics suggest that luck egalitarianism is too concerned with concepts of autonomy, choice and desert and that, instead, egalitarianism should be based more strongly upon notions of care, empathy and benevolence. The idea that we can isolate individual agency from social background, making people responsible for the former but not necessarily for the latter, is one with which many advocates of social justice are uncomfortable. If individuals are only responsible for what they freely will, then presumably we must make a determination of what is and is not 'free will'. This is an ontological debate that some egalitarians prefer to avoid; though, personally, I suspect the difference between luck and non-luck egalitarians to be one of emphasis. Critics on the Right, of course, propose that social egalitarianism is an unrealistic goal which fails to understand the real motivations and drives of people. On the Left, Marxists allege that such egalitarian ideas have cut themselves adrift from a radical (anti-capitalist) reading of history and political economy.

Key reading

Barry, B. (2005) *Why Social Justice Matters*, Cambridge: Polity.

Cohen, G. (2000) *If You're an Egalitarian, How Come You're So Rich?*, Cambridge, Mass.: Harvard University Press.

Cohen, G. (2008) *Rescuing Justice and Equality*, Cambridge, Mass.: Harvard University Press.

Dworkin, R. (2000) *Sovereign Virtue*, Harvard: Harvard University Press.

Miller, D. (1999) *Principles of Social Justice*, Harvard: Harvard University Press.

Nagel, T. (1991) *Equality and Partiality*, Oxford: Oxford University Press.

Nussbaum, M. (2006) *Frontiers of Justice*, Harvard: Balknap Press.

Phillips, A. (1999) *Which Equalities Matter?*, Cambridge: Polity.

Rawls, J. (1972) *A Theory of Justice*, Oxford: Oxford University Press.

Tawney, R. H. (1964 [1952]) *Equality* (4th edn), New Jersey: Barnes & Noble.

Temkin, L. (1993) *Inequality*, Oxford: Oxford University Press.

Walzer, M. (1983) *Spheres of Justice*, Oxford: Blackwell.

Text notes

110–13 For an even more sinister version of this machine see Kurt Vonnegut's story 'Harrison Bergeron' in his book *Welcome to the Monkey House*.

112–13 Heisenberg's Uncertainty Principle says the following: (1) the position and momentum of a sub-atomic particle cannot be known simultaneously (this is not a question of 'altering particles through observation', as the uncertainty occurs at theoretical and mathematical levels too) but can only be estimated in terms of probability since the more you know of one the less you know of the other; (2) particles do not have a definite position or momentum *until* they are observed.

116–17 Myllan expresses the view that inequality in and of itself is unjust. Luck egalitarianism, he seems to imply, does not overturn social relations based upon competition and self-interest.

117-18   It seems Anders is more of a social democrat.

118   Aon raises a challenge to the egalitarian project. See also Chapters Fourteen–Fifteen. In mentioning values such as care she raises concerns about recent theories of social justice that echo those of others; see Scheffler, S. (2003) 'What is Egalitarianism?', *Philosophy and Public Affairs*, 31(1): 5-39; Anderson, E. (1999) 'What is the Point of Equality?', *Ethics*, 109: 287-337. The subsequent intervention by Zadie allows the debate to be aired.

Culturalism and Identity Politics (Chapters Fourteen–Fifteen)

This describes a confluence of ideas that have developed and cross-fertilised over recent decades. 'Identity politics' dates to the 1960s and refers to campaigns made by the 'new social movements' (NSMs) for social status and against both overt and covert forms of discrimination and disadvantage. The NSMs stressed difference rather than sameness, diversity in addition to equality, and insisted that cultural representations were as vital as economic and material distributions. These developments found an academic counterpart in the theories of postmodernism and post-structuralism which had become highly popular by the 1980s. Such ideas challenged centuries old assumptions about philosophy and society. They resisted the attempt to find secure, immutable, uncontestable foundations for knowledge. Instead they proposed that objects, events and living beings do not possess an essential nature because the social world is thoroughly 'discursive', i.e. things have meaning and 'presence' only in so far as they are named, where naming is a dynamic, intertextual, communal process of perpetual reinterpretation. They also alleged that so-called universalism principles and frameworks, e.g. 'The Rights of Man', are not universal but, instead, allow one set of interests (masculine ones, in this example) to speak for all of us. Universalism is a mask of, and so serves, power.

By the 1990s many of these ideas had crystallized around the 'politics of recognition'. This is the demand that we be receptive and sensitive to multifaceted cultural differences and group identities. Multiculturalism, for instance, advocates that we conceive of a social culture as heterogeneous rather than homogeneously uniform. Though the pioneers (Young, Taylor, Honneth, Fraser) worked within differing intellectual traditions they agreed that we commit symbolic violence towards others when we traduce their self-understandings, self-images and self-descriptions. Respect, esteem and value and important moral and political principles. A progressive politics demands that we recognise and appreciate diversity.

Critics worry, though, that (1) excessive respect means that thin-skinned sensitivities get to dictate social interaction, representation and speech; (2) we actually risk 'freezing' group identities, treating them as homogenised entities rather than as contingent, temporary relations that possess their own 'internal' dynamics and conflicts, (3) we end up allowing groups priority over individual rights, (4) a rejection of – or at excessive scepticism towards – universalism risks surrendering many of the welcome advances of the modern period.

Key reading

Appiah, K. (2005) *The Ethics of Identity*, Princeton University Press.

Barry, B. (2001) *Culture and Equality*, Polity Press.

Benhabib, S. (2002) *The Claims of Culture*, Princeton University Press.

Butler, J. (1997) *The Psychic Life of Power*, Stanford University Press.

Fraser, N. (1997) *Justice Interruptus*, Routledge.

Fraser, N. (2008) *Adding Insult to Injury*, Verso.

Fraser, N. and Honneth, A. (2003) *Redistribution or Recognition?*, Verso.

Gutmann, A. (ed.) (1993) *Multiculturalism and the Politics of Recognition*, Princeton University Press.

Honneth, A. (2007) *Disrespect*, Polity Press.

Kymlicka, W. (1995) *Multicultural Citizenship*, Clarendon.

Parekh, B. (2008) *A New Politics of Identity*, Palgrave Macmillan.

Taylor, C. (1994) *The Ethics of Authenticity*, Harvard University Press.

Young, I.M. (1990) *Justice and the Politics of Difference*, Princeton University Press.

Text notes

141–3   Feminism, the politics of identity, recognition theorists, etc. tend to focus upon aspects of the everyday that political and social theories have traditionally ignored.

143–4   For further exploration of the possible relationship between identity, cultural recognition, social distribution and poverty see: Lister, R. (2004) *Poverty*, Polity Press.

145–9   See the recommended book by Brian Barry (above) for a considered rejection of the philosophies and politics of difference, such as multiculturalism. One argument is that not all differences are equally valuable and some are not worth valuing at all.

145-9 For a useful discussion of equality and difference see: Cooper, D. (2004) *Challenging Diversity*, Cambridge University Press.

151-3 Of course, feminism has a long and rich history which it would be misguided to interpret solely through the lens of recognition and similar debates. Nevertheless, theorising in recent decades has weaved in and out of those debates to a considerable extent, exemplified in the work of Butler, Fraser and Young.

152 The photo is of the 1888 Match Girl Strike Committee led by Annie Besant.

153-5 Arguments over the progressiveness, long-term value and contemporary salience of the Enlightenment (roughly, the eighteenth and nineteenth centuries when science, reason and liberalism were widely championed) raged in the 1980s, largely due to the influence of post-structuralists. See: Foucault, M. (1984) *The Foucault Reader*, edited by Paul Rabinow, Penguin; for a defence of the Enlightenment see: Habermas, J. (1987) *The Philosophical Discourse of Modernity*, Polity Press.

158 A good short introduction to multiculturalism is: Modood, T. (2007) *Multiculturalism*, Polity Press.

Environmentalism (Chapters Sixteen–Seventeen)

Environmental philosophy objects to what it sees as the 'anthropocentrism' of all other philosophies, whether moral or political. To be anthropocentric is to be human-centred; that is, to regard humans as superior to non-human life-forms and thus as the source and locus of value. Liberals, for instance, regard individual freedom as the highest value but, for an environmentalist, this involves an artificial and damaging separation of ecology into the human and the non-human since, as socio-natural beings, we are immersed in our natural environments. Therefore, freedom may be one value but, especially to the extent it reflects that division, has to be contextualised by others, e.g. a recognition of our dependency on biological diversity. Environmentalists are committed to an ethic of sustainability, in that the job of politics and philosophy is to show how we may live in greater harmony with nature, preserve the resources upon which we depend and pay due attention to other species and to future generations.

However, there are significant differences of opinion within the environmental movement over what this implies. Some take an uncompromising stance, insisting that environmentalism represents a radical alternative to all existing forms of moral theory, political theory and political and social organisation. Here, nature is regarded as having an intrinsic value that humans despoil. Others believe that we can only achieve sustainability by working according to existing assumptions and principles, and trying to change them gradually and pragmatically. Our job should be to avoid the catastrophes resulting from global warming but not to assume that doing so requires a major 'Green' revolution in our beliefs and practices. Many advocate a synergy between environmentalism and existing theories and ideologies; it is possible to discern free market, conservative, liberal, Marxist, social democratic and feminist versions of the environmental position.

Environmentalism has been challenged, of course. Apart from those who deny that global warming is real, or that it is real but is not caused by humans, some argue that the case for environmentalism has been overstated. Existing social institutions and political-economic systems are capable of adapting without the need for wholescale change. For instance, the costs of pollution, resource use and other externalities can be factored into prices and the development of green technologies can be financially encouraged. Growth and affluence can be accommodated within a low carbon economy.

Key reading

Benton, T. (1993) *Natural Relations*, Verso.

Bookchin, M. (1980) *Toward an Ecological Society*, Black Rose Books.

Callicott, J. B. (1989) *In Defense of the Land Ethic*, State University of New York Press.

Dobson, A. (ed.) (1999) *Fairness and Futurity*, Oxford University Press.

Dobson, A. (2007) *Green Political Thought*, 4th ed., Routledge.

Dryzek, J. (1997) *The Politics of the Earth*, Oxford University Press.

Eckersley, R. (1992) *Environmentalism and Political Theory*, UCL Press.

Fox, W. (1995) *Toward a Transpersonal Ecology*, State University of New York Press.

Jamieson, D. (2001) *A Companion to Environmental Philosophy*, Blackwell.

Leopold, A. (1949) *A Sand County Almanac*, Oxford University Press.

Light, A. and Katz, E. (1996) *Environmental Pragmatism*, Routledge.

Næss, A. (1989) *Ecology, Community, Lifestyle*, Cambridge University Press.

Plumwood, V. (1993) *Feminism and the Mastery of Nature*, Routledge.

Regan, T. (1983) *The Case for Animal Rights*, Routledge & Kegan Paul.

Singer, P. (1975) *Animal Liberation*, Random House.

Text notes

169-70   There are many 'isms' within environmental philosophy, as the literature recommended above demonstrates. Here, biocentrism refers to the most non-anthropocentric position it is possible to hold; a 'deep ecology' view which insists that humans must radically alter how they see themselves in relation to the rest of nature.

170-1   There is a school of environmental thought which insists that only small-scale, fully self-governing communities living close to nature can realise the sustainability ethic. (Of course, direct democracy was also a feature of the communist society in Chapter Three.) Such anarchism has always had a Left-Right split. Anarcho-communists think that actually existing communism failed because it relied too heavily upon the state; for those on the Right free markets are indispensable to self-organisation.

172   'Callenville' is named in honour of Ernest Callenbach's 1975 depiction of a 'steady-state', green utopia in *Ecotopia*, Bantam Books.

172-3   The social system defended by Hughes is more centralised and seems to depend upon regulated markets. The later discussion between Hughes and Williams looks at the various merits of centralisation and decentralisation.

177-9   For the classic defence of mutualism and mutual aid see: Kropotkin, P. (2006 [1902]) *Mutual Aid*, Dover Books.

177-9   The case for environmentalism is usually associated with the dangers of global warming, etc., but the arguments for an environmental philosophy and politics do not stand or fall simply on that basis.

178   The notion of localising production and consumption is a common one in environmental thought. For an introduction to 'local economies', including local currencies, see: North, P. (2006) *Alternative Currency Movements as a Challenge to Globalization?*, Ashgate.

178   Effecting reductions in employment-time and taking the emphasis away from materialism and consumption is also popular with environmentalists. See Chapter 7 of: Paehlke, R. (2004) *Democracy's Dilemma*, MIT Press.

Republicanism, Communitarianism and Deliberative Politics (Chapters Eighteen–Nineteen)

In the 1980s some philosophers challenged the predominance of liberal ideas in political thought, criticising both the excessive individualism of free market liberalism and libertarianism, and what they saw as the asocial, mechanical approach to distributive justice of the Rawlsians.

Within political philosophy republicanism is a notion that the best society is one which governs itself by reference to what it reasonably judges to be in the best interests of all, i.e. the 'public good'. We are not just private individuals. We are citizens with public responsibilities towards fellow members of the same polity ('political body'). A republican society is not an aggregation of individuals' self-interest but an arena of common membership and participation in which people act and deliberate together for the good of each other. Pettit has further argued that republicanism implies 'non-domination' such that no individual should be capable of being made subject to the whim of another – what makes someone free is not merely the absence of coercion but the *power* to resist coercive interventions by others. This implies an egalitarian distribution not only of income and wealth but also of property and basic assets. (That said, there are also non-egalitarian and indeed non-democratic strands within the republican tradition.)

Communitarianism overlaps with republicanism but they are not identical. The latter is concerned with political participation in a public endeavour, the former with membership of particular communities. Such communities may provide the basis for public citizenship, but not necessarily. Communal belonging is a good in itself even if this does not involve participation in government. Communitarians insist that obligations are more important than rights, communal membership is more important than personal interests (because individuals derive their identities, relationships and goals from their communal contexts), and thus realising 'the good life for man' should take precedence over individual choice. Liberalism is charged with treating individuals as self-creating, insular, asocial 'atoms'. People should therefore be guided and, if necessary forced, to make the correct decisions about how to live and what to believe. As with republicanism, there are alternative versions of communitarianism (left and right, democratic and authoritarian).

'Deliberativeness' bears similarities to both of the above. For instance, 'deliberative democrats' recommend that we integrate collective decision-making, discourse and reflection more closely and effectively into our political and social institutions and procedures. This could involve more referenda, activism beyond political parties, internet petitions and debates, citizens' juries and parliaments, 'deliberation days' and greater interaction between experts and laypeople. The idea is that whereas representative democracy largely confines itself to counting preferences, its public debates being dominated by relatively few voices, a deliberative democracy allows preferences to be aired and transformed through discursive interaction with others.

Note that the distinction between liberalism and each of the above is often a matter of degree. Liberals can acknowledge the importance of public participation and citizenship, communal membership and deliberativeness, but still insist that individual liberties ought to constitute the framework for deciding which interventions such notions can and cannot legitimate. Community may be important to your sense of wellbeing but you should still possess rights against that community if it proves to be oppressive or unjust.

Key reading

Dagger, R. (1997) *Civic Virtues*, Oxford University Press.

Dryzek, J. (2000) *Deliberative Democracy and Beyond*, Oxford University Press.

Fishkin, J. and Laslett, P. (eds) (2003) *Debating Deliberative Democracy*, Blackwell.

Gutmann, A. and Thompson, D. (2004) *Why Deliberative Democracy?*, Princeton University Press.

MacIntyre, A. (1981) *After Virtue*, Duckworth.

Miller, D. (2000) *Citizenship and National Identity*, Polity Press.

Oldfield, A. (1990) *Citizenship and Community*, Routledge.

Pettit, P. (1999) *Republicanism*, Oxford University Press.

Rousseau, J.-J. (1973 [1762]) *The Social Contract and Discourses*, J. M. Dent & Sons.

Sandel, M. (1982) *Liberalism and the Limits of Justice*, Cambridge University Press.

Sandel, M. (2009) *Justice*, Allen Lane.

Taylor, C. (1989) *Sources of the Self*, Cambridge University Press.
Young, I. M. (2000) *Inclusion and Democracy*, Oxford University Press.

Text notes

185   An 'Agora' literally means an open-air or public space. In the Ancient world it denoted a political space outside of formal institutions (parliament, senate, etc.) where people could discuss important matters of state and public affairs.

187-90   For a discussion of conditionality that draws from communitarian and republican ideas see: White, S. (2003) *The Civic Minimum*, Oxford University Press; the proposal to provide certain basic resources unconditionally is discussed in: Fitzpatrick, T. (1999) *Freedom and Security*, Macmillan.

189   Whereas the first speaker is a republican the second is more of a communitarian.

194-5   The concept of the general will was formulated by Rousseau. To some extent it corresponds to the idea of a common good which serves, but is more than, the sum of individual goods. Critics, though, allege that it is a vague term which having inspired the French Revolution is also responsible for its effects, i.e. the Terror. Many architects of the American Revolution were also republicans (which is commonly taken to mean rule by an elected head of state) but were more down-to-earth than Rousseau; see Madison, J., Hamilton, A. and Jay, J. (1987) *The Federalist Papers*, Penguin.

197   For the funeral oration of Pericles see pp 144-51 of: Thucydides (1954) *History of the Peloponnesian War*, Penguin (its exact date of composition is unknown).

And finally...

Chapter Thirteen borrows loosely from the 'relative state' (often called the 'many worlds') interpretation of quantum physics, formulated by Hugh Everett in 1957. This had actually been anticipated 20 years earlier by Murray Leinster's 'Sideways in Time', Jack Williamson's *The Legion of Time*, Jorge Luis Borge's 'The Garden of Forking Paths' and, in the best SF novel ever, Olaf Stapledon's *Star Maker*. For good introductions see David Deutsch's *The Fabric of Reality*, Michael Lockwood's *The Labyrinth of Time* (pp 304-30) and John Gribbin's *In Search of the Multiverse* (Chapter 3). Central to the prospects for quantum computing is the Decoherence interpretation of quantum physics, a cousin to Everett's but one that throws sober water on its more fanciful claims and/or interpretations; see Murray Gell-Mann's *The Quark and the Jaguar* (Chapter 11) and Roland Omnès' *Quantum Philosophy* (Chapters 9-11). In *The Fabric of the Cosmos* (Chapter 7) Brian Greene highlights some of Decoherence theory's difficulties (also Chapter 5 and pp 448-58). In *Physics of the Impossible* Michio Kaku highlights the links between quantum computing and quantum transportation, such that the one may make the other possible too. A good introduction to quantum computing is George Johnson's *A Shortcut through Time*.

Alternative histories, time travel and many-world multiverses are familiar themes within SF. In addition to Stapledon, the best examples include: H.G. Wells's *The Time Machine*, Ray Bradbury's 'A Sound of Thunder', Philip K. Dick's *The Man in the High Castle*, Isaac Asimov's *The End of Eternity*, Kurt Vonnegut's *Slaughterhouse Five*, Ward Moore's *Bring the Jubilee*, Poul Anderson's *Tau Zero*, Keith Roberts's *Pavane*, Michael Moorcock's *Behold the Man*, Madge Piercy's *Woman on the Edge of Time*, Norman Spinrad's *The Iron Dream*, David Gerrold's *The Man Who Folded Himself*, Gregory Benford's *Timescape*, Greg Bear's *Eon*, William Gibson and Bruce Sterling's *The Difference Engine*, Connie Willis' *Doomsday Book*, Harry Turtledove's *The Guns of the South*, Stephen Baxter's *The Time Ships* and Robert Wilson's *The Chronoliths*. Non-genre examples include Vladimir Nabakov's *Ada or Ardor*, Audrey Niffenegger's *The Time Traveller's Wife*, Philip Roth's *The Plot against America* and Christopher Priest's *The Separation*.